Studia Fennica
Litteraria 9

The Finnish Literature Society (SKS) was founded in 1831 and has, from the very beginning, engaged in publishing operations. It nowadays publishes literature in the fields of ethnology and folkloristics, linguistics, literary research and cultural history.

The first volume of the Studia Fennica series appeared in 1933. Since 1992, the series has been divided into three thematic subseries: Ethnologica, Folkloristica and Linguistica. Two additional subseries were formed in 2002, Historica and Litteraria. The subseries Anthropologica was formed in 2007.

In addition to its publishing activities, the Finnish Literature Society maintains research activities and infrastructures, an archive containing folklore and literary collections, a research library and promotes Finnish literature abroad.

Studia Fennica Editorial board
Editors-in-chief
Pasi Ihalainen, Professor, University of Jyväskylä, Finland
Timo Kaartinen, Title of Docent, University Lecturer, University of Helsinki, Finland
Taru Nordlund, Professor, University of Helsinki, Finland
Riikka Rossi, Title of Docent, University Researcher, University of Helsinki, Finland
Katriina Siivonen, Title of Docent, University Teacher, University of Turku, Finland
Lotte Tarkka, Professor, University of Helsinki, Finland

Deputy editors-in-chief
Eeva Berglund, Title of Docent, University of Helsinki, Finland
Anne Heimo, Title of Docent, University of Turku, Finland
Saija Isomaa, Professor, University of Tampere, Finland
Sari Katajala-Peltomaa, Title of Docent, Researcher, University of Tampere, Finland
Eerika Koskinen-Koivisto, Postdoctoral Researcher, Dr. Phil., University of Helsinki, Finland
Laura Visapää, Title of Docent, University Lecturer, University of Helsinki, Finland

Tuomas M. S. Lehtonen, Secretary General, Dr. Phil., Finnish Literature Society, Finland
Tero Norkola, Publishing Director, Finnish Literature Society
Kati Romppanen, Secretary of the Board, Finnish Literature Society, Finland

Editorial Office
SKS
P.O. Box 259
FI-00171 Helsinki
www.finlit.fi

Contents

Foreword 7

KRISTINA MALMIO AND MIA ÖSTERLUND
Introduction 8

I Transforming Traditions

LENA KÅRELAND
Re-Imagining Girlhood
The Revision of Girls' Books in Monika Fagerholm's DIVA *and* The American Girl 25

KAISA KURIKKA
Becoming-Girl of Writing
Monika Fagerholm's DIVA *as Minor Literature* 38

HANNA LAHDENPERÄ
Reading Fiction as/and Theory
Monika Fagerholm's DIVA *as a Barthesian Text and Feminist Theory* 53

KRISTINA MALMIO
A Portrait of the Technological Sublime
DIVA *and the History of the Digital Revolution* 66

II New Forms of Pleasure, Anxiety and Writing

ANNA HELLE
When Love and Death Embrace
Monika Fagerholm's The American Girl *and* The Glitter Scene *as Postmodern Melodrama* 83

MARIA MARGARETA ÖSTERHOLM
The Song of the Marsh Queen
Gurlesque and Queer Desire in Monika Fagerholm's novels The American Girl *and* The Glitter Scene 99

III Transformations and Forms of Reading

Ann-Sofie Lönngren
Oppression and Liberation
Traditional Nordic Literary Themes of Female Human-Animal Transformations in Monika Fagerholm's Early Work 119

Mia Österlund
'A Work You Cannot Explain, Only Experience'
The Struggle with Readability in the Reception of Monika Fagerholm's Novel Lola uppochner 134

List of Authors 155
Abstract 157
Index 158

Foreword

Novel Districts is the first major volume in which Finland-Swedish author Monika Fagerholm is studied in a Nordic and international context. The study grew out of the special seminar arranged by the Society of Swedish Literature in Finland, where the Council for Literature dedicated a whole meeting to the work of Fagerholm on the 19th of April 2013. Here Nordic scholars presented readings of Fagerholm's work from different theoretical perspectives.

Scholars and critics have repeatedly argued that Fagerholm's works demand new ways of reading. In this volume the perspectives offered by current literary theories open up new approaches and interpretations. The insights and concepts of gender, feminist and girlhood studies as well as narratology, poststructuralism, posthumanism and reception studies are tested in close readings of Fagerholm's works between 1990 and 2012. The ideas of transition, transformation and transgression connect the articles in the volume.

We are grateful to the Society of Swedish Literature in Finland and especially the Council for Literature for assisting us in arranging the seminar in 2013. We also wish to thank the researchers for their contributions to this volume. We are grateful to Dr. Maria Lassén-Seger, Åbo Akademi University and Dr. Marlene Broemer, University of Helsinki for help with proofreading the English and for great comments on the content. We are especially thankful to the Department of Finnish, Finno-Ugrian and Scandinavian Studies at the University of Helsinki for funding the proofreading. In addition, we would like to express our gratitude to our two anonymous peer reviewers whose sound and constructive comments on our manuscript helped us greatly in the final revision. We are especially grateful to the Finnish Literature Society for including our book in this international publication series. Last but not least, we want to thank Monika Fagerholm for her vivid participation at the seminar in 2013 and for providing us with such extensive thought-provoking material that surely will be interpreted again and again in future research. We hope that the scope of this volume is as intriguing as the literature it represents.

Helsinki and Turku, Finland May 2016
Kristina Malmio and Mia Österlund

Kristina Malmio and Mia Österlund

Introduction

An Aesthetics of Her Own

In April 2010 Finland-Swedish[1] writer Monika Fagerholm's novel *The American Girl* was featured on American media mogul Oprah Winfrey's talk show as the first Nordic novel to gain attention for the broad public in USA. The odds of a Nordic author, who writes within the domain of a small minority literature in a faraway country, to appear so visibly in American media, are indeed small. There are, however, many reasons why this is not all that surprising in the case of the writer in question.

Monika Fagerholm's witty play with literary traditions coupled with visionary and wild descriptions of girlhood, in a suggestive, provocative, repetitive and transgressive form has long had an impact on the Nordic literary landscape, with many literary followers of both her mainstream and young adult fiction. Her experimental, puzzling and daring novels *Underbara kvinnor vid vatten* (1994), *DIVA* (1998), *Den amerikanska flickan* (2004), *Glitterscenen* (2009) and *Lola uppochner* (2012) have attracted much critical attention; she has won several literary awards[2] and her works have travelled across national and cultural borders as they have now been translated into

---

1   There is a population of approximately 300 000 people (ca 5 % of the whole population) in Finland who speak Swedish as their mother tongue. By Finland-Swedish literature is meant the literature written by Finnish authors who write in Swedish.
2   *Underbara kvinnor vid vatten* (Wonderful Women by the Sea) was nominated for the Finlandia prize in 1994, the August prize in Sweden in 1995, the European Union's Aristeion prize in 1996 and the International IMPAC Dublin Literary Award in 1998. It was awarded the Runeberg prize in 1995 and a *Tack för boken* (Thank You for the Book) medal in 1995. *DIVA* was nominated for the Nordic Council's Literature Prize and received Nyland Art Council's prize in 1999 and the Swedish Längmanska stiftelsen's prize in 2003 for creating modern classics with immense impact on the younger generation of authors. Fagerholm's international breakthrough *Den amerikanska flickan* (The American Girl) was nominated for the Nordic Council's Literature Prize in 2004. It won the Swedish August prize in 2005 and received the Aniara prize for daring experimental prose from the Swedish Library organization in 2005. This book was also recognized by the Swedish Books Society in Finland and by *Göteborgsposten* in 2005. In 2010 Fagerholm received the prestigious Pro Finlandia medal and in 2013 *Glitterscenen* (The Glitter Scene) was nominated for the Nordic Council's Literature Prize. In 2016 she won the Nordic Prize from the Swedish Academy.

several languages.[3] The English translations of her central novels, *Wonderful Women by the Water* (transl. 1997 by Joan Tate, *Wonderful Women by the Sea* in the US a year later by Joan Tate), *The American Girl* (transl. 2009 by Katarina E. Tucker) and *The Glitter Scene* (transl. 2010 by Katarina E. Tucker) enhance the international attention on her authorship. The current interest in Nordic authors due to the popularity of Nordic noir fiction similarly paves the way for the visibility of other interesting Nordic contemporary authors like Fagerholm.[4] In literary histories her ability to unite entertainment and experimentation has been repeatedly emphasized as she combines features typical of reader friendly realism – suspense, interesting characters and living depictions of milieus – with daring renewal of the narrative conventions of prose (Ingström 2014; Ekman 2014; Korsström 2013). However, there are only a few scholarly works that deal with Fagerholm's texts and no work that fully grasps her authorship.

This is precisely where the book you read comes in. *Novel Districts. Critical Readings of Monika Fagerholm* is the first volume in which the central themes and features of the works of Monika Fagerholm, by far one of today's most important and appealing contemporary Nordic authors, are studied. We will first give an overall introduction to her life, letters and the minority literature context of her writing, before we briefly describe the scholarship on Fagerholm's works. After that, we will present the contributions in this book. Our overall aim is not only to enhance and deepen the understanding of Fagerholm's fiction, but also to suggest some important trends that take place in contemporary Nordic literature. The common point of departure of this volume is the recognizable Fagerholmian idiom: a unique form of language use and its complex relation to the topics and themes depicted in the novels such as love and death, identity, sexuality, corporeality, girlhood and small town social life.

Fagerholm and the Conditions of a Minority Literature

Monika Fagerholm's (b. 1961) career as an author began in 1987 when her first book, *Sham*, a collection of short stories, was published. Before that

---

3   The list is long: *Wonderful Women by the Sea* has been translated into Danish, Finnish, French, Lithuanian, Dutch, Norwegian, English and German. *DIVA* has only been translated into Finnish, Dutch and Norwegian, probably because it is the most experimental novel and therefore a great challenge for translators. *The American Girl* has been translated into Albanian, Danish, Finnish, French, Lithuanian, Dutch, Norwegian, Russian, German, Hungarian and English while *The Glitter Scene* has been translated into Albanian, Danish, Finnish, French, Dutch, Norwegian and English.
4   *The American Girl* also featured on the net pages of Oprah Winfrey's *O. The Oprah Magazine* under the heading 'A Helsinki Whodunit. A Masterful, Thoughtful Thriller about a Girl *without* a Dragon Tattoo'. Thus, a reference to the tattooed protagonist Lisbeth Salander in Swedish author Stieg Larsson's famous thriller series, The Millennium Trilogy, was used in order to introduce Fagerholm to a new reading audience, already intoxicated with the lure of Nordic crime fiction.

she had studied psychology and literature at the University of Helsinki. She had also worked as a journalist and was one of the founding members and driving forces behind the most important cultural journal of her generation: *KLO* (1985–1987). The debut was soon followed by another collection of short stories, *Patricia* (1990). In these early collections, she depicted the individualism and depressive tendencies of complex girl characters in the middle of metamorphosis and boundary breaking.

Fagerholm's breakthrough as an author occurred with *Underbara kvinnor vid vatten* (1994), a postmodern novel describing a couple of summers in the countryside, mostly told from the perspective of a young boy. Depicting women's liberation and a growing consumer culture through a nostalgic portrayal of the late 1960s, the novel was soon adapted for the screen. In 1998 Fagerholm continued her postmodern depictions of childhood in the novel *DIVA*, a witty, ironic and metafictional story about an extraordinarily mature and strong school girl in a suburb in the 1970s. After a break of six years, she published *Den amerikanska flickan* in 2004, and its sequel, *Glitterscenen* was available in 2009. If *DIVA*, which has the curious subheading *En uppväxts egna alfabet med docklaboratorium (en bonusberättelse ur framtiden)* [The Alphabet of Adolescence with a Laboratory of Dolls (A Bonus Tale from the Future)], was mostly humorous and cheerful, the two following novels form a tragedy which also flirts with thriller conventions, as the story begins with the mysterious death of a young American girl in a small rural place in Finland at the end of 1960s. Fagerholm's latest publications include *Havet* [The Sea], a collection of essays written with Martin Johnson, and the novel *Lola uppochner* [Lola Upsidedown]; both appeared in 2012. *Lola uppochner* continues the depiction of young women and focuses on a murder in a small, rural town. The novel has currently been adapted for television by Finland-Swedish film director Ulrika Bengts.

Fagerholm writes in Swedish in Finland and belongs to the small but vital Finland-Swedish minority literature, which has managed to survive in a milieu dominated by the overall presence of Finnish language and literature. In addition to Finnish, Swedish is an official language in Finland as it was not until the late 19th century that Finnish became the most predominant language. For centuries before that, Swedish was the language of administration, education and culture in Finland because Finland was part of the Swedish territories from 12th to 1809, when it became a Grand Duchy of Russia. Gradually, however, towards the end of the 19th century, the use of Finnish increased in all areas of society and Swedish authors writing in Finland became increasingly aware of their position as minority authors. Written in Swedish, but published in Finland is the core condition of the Finland-Swedish literature and book market. Therefore, the development of Swedish literature in Finland has at times been highly independent, at times more or less similar to Swedish or Finnish literature. The Swedish spoken and written in Finland differs slightly from the Swedish used in Sweden, which has at times been a trouble, at times an advantage for the Finland-Swedish authors (Ekman 1995; Tidigs 2014). For example, it has been suggested that compared to Finnish, Swedish in Sweden, and other Nordic literatures, the early, modernist breakthrough in Finland-Swedish poetry in the 1920s was at least partly due to the linguistic circumstances among the Swedes in Finland. Surrounded by Finnish, a language with no common features whatsoever with Swedish, the Finland-Swedish minority authors were already from the beginning positioned in a milieu in which the language they used was 'strange' and unstable. This condition might also have made them especially open to different kinds of experiments with language and literary conventions.

Obviously, even Fagerholm belongs to the category of authors who creatively make use of the special features and resources of the Swedish language written in Finland. It has been argued that her literary language is highly characterised by its use of precisely those Finland-Swedish special language features (to be found in vocabulary and phrases) not found in the Swedish spoken and written in Sweden, due to the influences from Finland-Swedish dialects, and the physical proximity to both the Finnish and Russian languages.

Finland-Swedish literature has had an important task in the production and reproduction of the cultural identity of a linguistic minority. When compared to some other minority literatures, the Finland-Swedish literature has been a privileged one, due to its sound economic resources and own publishing houses. When successful, a novel written in Swedish in Finland will soon be translated to Finnish and published in Finland and then distributed even to Sweden, meaning that a Finland-Swedish author can occasionally become a participant in three different publishing systems. This has also been the case for Fagerholm, whose writings have managed to overcome the limited conditions and small audiences of Finland-Swedish minority literature. Due to the power and originality of Fagerholm's writing, her novels are considered modern classics and she has become a trendsetter and a cult author among young female authors in Sweden and Finland, creating a literary school with many followers. For example, Swedish authors like Sara Stridsberg, Sanne Näsling, Elisabeth Berchold, Sara Shamloo, Matilda Roos, Mara Lee and Sara Tuss Elfvik have been seen as followers of Fagerholm (Österholm 2012: 307). The Finland-Swedish literary reviewer Tuva Korsström even names her literary history *Från Lexå till Glitterscenen* [From Lexå to the Glitter Scene] with a reference to Fagerholm as the most important point of departure for a new generation of Finland-Swedish female authors such as Hannele Mikaela Taivassalo, Sanna Tahvanainen, Malin Kivelä, Emma Juslin, and Johanna Holmström (Korsström 2013: 480–517).

Transformations of Traditions, 'High' and 'Low'

Fagerholm's stories are set in sometimes realistically, sometimes metaphorically depicted Nordic milieus from the 1960s, 1990s and 2000s, where remarkable characters experience odd events. Her novels depict the lives of young, maturing girls and women in the middle of processes of becoming and both the composition and the language are multisequential, repetitive and highly intertextual. At the core of her prose lies the power of fiction and language to change people, lives and stories. Characters are formed and transformed by the endless stories they tell each other and language in the form of citations, songs, allusions and phrases steer the fate of the protagonists. Not only does Fagerholm in *The American Girl* describe a place called the District, the storytelling that takes place also creates odd, novel spaces and places.

'DivaLucia', 'Babywonder': in this fashion Monika Fagerholm introduced her iconic character, the thirteen-year-old schoolgirl Diva in 1998.[5] The novel *DIVA* set the mode for numerous novels to follow, all reconceptualising the girl character as new and different. Fagerholm's Diva exceeds both girlhood and the discourses and paradigms around the literary girl. In both form and content, the novel is highly transformative, visionary yet recognisable. Fagerholm is a postmodern author par excellence whose works blur the boundaries between genres, high and low, trivial and poetic. She often uses popular culture in transforming the novel genre and the affinity of her works with those of the American director David Lynch's TV series *Twin Peaks* has been emphasized. Her highly self-reflexive prose also transforms one of the central features of the Nordic noir, the conventions of the thriller story.

The dense intertextual and intermedial relations of Fagerholm's prose show how 'worldly' contemporary Finland-Swedish literature is: it is open to influences from contemporary international fiction, art and popular culture. This literature is part of a global culture, but also very local and in this sense Fagerholm belongs to the neo-avant-garde of globalized late modernity. Late modern traits such as postmodern and posthumanist tensions, de- and reterritorializations, affective and emotional investments are all markers for the paradigm shift Monika Fagerholm's authorship constitutes in a Nordic context.

Fagerholm's language is in constant fluctuation and the novels are characterized by movement. Not only are the protagonists in phases of transition, the works transform and transgress literary tradition and conventional ways of writing. By the performative power of language Fagerholm creates novel districts, charts new territories of being, creates feminine, linguistic and fictive worlds that have not been experienced before and demonstrates an ongoing politics of transformation. Furthermore, the title of this volume, *Novel Districts* was chosen because of the many scholarly comments and other responses to Fagerholm's prose emphasising the novelty of the worlds created in her prose and its demands for new ways of reading. The innovative way Fagerholm positions herself in relation to tradition and renewal creates new territories of being, especially in her prose where girls form new and wonderful ways of being, just as her protagonist's mother repeatedly tells her daughter Diva: 'I want you to be in another way. **New. Fantastic. Different**' (*DIVA* 1998: 33).

---

5   The festival of Lucia is celebrated annually on the 13th of December when a young, often blonde, girl dressed in a long, white dress with candles in a crown in her hair, appears in public as Saint Lucia, a martyr who died in Italy in the 13th century. The Italian tradition has been adopted in Sweden and other Nordic countries.

Earlier Scholarship on Fagerholm's Prose

Although Finnish and Swedish scholars began to study Monika Fagerholm's prose already in the 1990s when her breakthrough took place, there have been surprisingly few scholarly attempts to capture the originality of this important writer. No monograph has yet been written on the works of Monika Fagerholm; only separate articles have been published in diverse volumes, written mostly in Finnish and Swedish and only at times in English.

We will here briefly introduce the most significant contributions in the studies of Fagerholm's works, studies with which many of the authors in this volume also enter a dialogue. The aim is to enable non-Swedish or non-Finnish readers to apprehend what has been written on Fagerholm's works in other languages than English. The presentation shows the wide range of topics discussed so far as well as the growing interest in Fagerholm's works among scholars.

Finland-Swedish literary scholar and reviewer Åsa Stenwall is one of the first scholars to contextualize Fagerholm's prose in a tradition of Nordic women writers. In her collection of essays dealing with women and modernity in the late modern Finland-Swedish literature volume *Portföljen i skogen* [Briefcase in the Woods] (2001) her chapter on Fagerholm is called 'Oförvägen jungfru i ny tappning' [Daring Maid in a New Version]. Stenwall's sharp insight into Fagerholm's postmodern construction of her literary works has been influential for later research. She compiles a wide range of comments on Fagerholm's writing and discusses postmodernist traits, depictions of girlhood, narrative techniques and raises the question of new ways of reading as essential to comprehend Fagerholm's novels. Many of Stenwall's remarks have proven to be fruitful and useful in the emergence of a Fagerholm scholarship.

Literary critic Pia Ingström has commented on Fagerholm's oeuvre in a range of essays in a literary historical context. In *Nordisk kvinnolitteraturhistoria* [Nordic Women's Literary History] (2014), the article ('Leken och det fruktansvärda allvaret hos Monika Fagerholm' [Play and Dreadful Seriousness in Monika Fagerholm]) updates her earlier entry on Fagerholm called 'Att hålla saknaden från livet' [To Keep the Longing from Your Life], where she had summarized Fagerholm's authorship as a combination of reader-friendly realism with a bold renewal of narrative conventions in prose. Since her debut in 1987 with a collection of short stories, *Sham*, and with *Patricia* in 1990, Fagerholm has written herself out of a conventional realism, Ingström claims. In both thematics and language, she has broken norms. As Ingström notes, metafictive playfulness has helped the reader to recognize dimensions far from a realistic realm and a chronologically driven reading. Ingström stresses that one way of doing this is hyperbolic and excessive use of surface in the form of the glamorous props in *Wonderful Women by the Sea*. Thus, both girlhood and womanhood are written out of limiting concepts and are presented geographically while marginal places such as suburbs and small towns get larger narratives. In Fagerholm's writing, girls and women play with the insignia of femininity; they live on the edge of tragedy and rage. Pia Ingström points out that intense allusions constitute a new literary mode. In an earlier essay 'Jag, mitt livs tappra hjältinna' [Me, My Life's Brave Heroine] (1995), Ingström discusses the creation of a literary heroine and observes the net of metafictive comments in the novels where Fagerholm makes overt statements on how to read her stories.

According to literary scholar Michel Ekman in *Finlands svenska litteratur 1900–2012* [Finland's Swedish Literature 1900–2012] (2014), Fagerholm's depictions of girlhood and womanhood are about the right to speak and to claim space and this is done very convincingly by inventing and introducing renewed, avant-garde genre conventions with girls and women as collective protagonists. In her essay 'Flickbokens nya kläder. Om Monika Fagerholms *Diva*' [The New Clothes of Girls' Books] (2004), Lena Kåreland has contextualised Fagerholm in a tradition of girls' books, something she elaborates on further in this volume.

Kaisa Kurikka in her essay 'Tytöksi-tulemisen tilat. Monika Fagerholmin *Diva* utopistisena tekstinä' [The Spaces of Becoming-Girl. Monika Fagerholm's *Diva* as a Utopian Text] (2005) focuses on girlhood and utopia in her analysis, while Anna Helle in her article 'Kuoleman lumous nuorella iällä'. Tytöt ja kuolema Monika Fagerholmin *Amerikkalaisessa tytössä* ['Death's Spell at a Young Age'. Girls and Death in Monika Fagerholm's *The American Girl*] (2008) elaborates on the motifs of girlhood and death.

As literary scholar Kristina Malmio suggests in her essay on popular culture and comic strip heroines in *DIVA*, 'Phoenix-Marvel Girl in the Age of *fin-de siècle*. Popular Culture as a Vehicle to Postmodernism in *Diva* by Finland-Swedish Author, Monika Fagerholm' (2012), the novel constitutes a turning point for Finland-Swedish literature since it breaks so intensely with every aspect of earlier literary tradition. According to Malmio, the novel stages a struggle between modernism and postmodernism and by its use of popular culture it shatters the tradition of the 'narrow room' in Finland-Swedish literary tradition. The 'narrow room' is a concept literary scholar Merete Mazzarella has coined in her book *Det trånga rummet* [The Narrow Room] (1989) to capture the theme of a masochistic, limited horizon in combination with closed spatiality containing individualistic self-mirroring and loneliness that is typical of Finland-Swedish prose fiction.[6] Fagerholm is true to this revisionist technique in all her writing; she chooses popular genres such as the melodrama or the crime story and twists all genre expectations until the narration becomes new. One of her devices is the use of playing and *gurlesque* as literary scholar Maria Margareta Österholm has shown in her thesis *Ett flicklaboratorium i valda bitar. Skeva flickor i svenskspråkig prosa från 1980 till 2005* [A Girl Laboratory in Chosen Parts. Queer Girls in Swedish and Finland-Swedish Literature from 1980 to 2005] (2012). The concept of the *gurlesque* is an aesthetic mixing of feminism, femininity, cuteness and disgust (grotesque and cruel) and a gurlesque aesthetics combines feminism and queer theory with depictions of sweetness

---

6   According to Mazzarella, the narrations of the narrow room have been frequent since the beginning of the 20th century in Finland-Swedish minority literature due to the linguistic situation in Finland.

and disgust on both a narrative level and in the queer ideas on doing gender that the novels encapsulate.

Sexuality is also a theme in Pauliina Haasjoki's thesis *Häilyvyyden liittolaiset. Kerronnan ja seksuaalisuuden ambivalenssit* [Allies in Wavering. The Ambivalences of Narrative and Sexuality] (2012) where she considers narrative formations, sexuality and norm breaking. Haasjoki shows that Fagerholm is a pioneer in writing beyond a normalised heterosexualization, since she writes in a queer mode that questions normative structures, relations and romances. Fagerholm thus deterritorializes literary places while writing about typical Finland-Swedish locations such as the coast line and small towns and dark swamps, as if they were new Moominvalleys[7], shivering with poetic playfulness and gurlesque poetics. Haasjoki has also elaborated on the theme in her article 'Mitä tiedät kertomuksestani? Biseksuaalinen ambivalenssi ja queer-lukeminen' [What Do You Know about My Story? Bisexual Ambivalence and Queer Reading] (2005).

Ann-Sofie Lönngren, who in her article 'Mellan metafor och litterär materialisering: heteronormer och djurblivande i Monika Fagerholms novell Patricia Kanin' [Between Metaphor and Literary Materialization – Heteronormativity and Becoming Animal in Monika Fagerholm's Short Story 'Patricia Rabbit' (1990)] (2011) deals with the process of becoming animal. Based on animal studies she reads Fagerholm's short story 'Patricia Kanin' as breaking with heteronormativity. Lönngren is interested in the negotiations of becoming and of the borders between human and animal life.

From the earlier scholarship on Fagerholm, it is evident that the material has attracted a wide range of readings oriented towards postmodernism, post-humanism and queer studies; these all share an interest in non-normative narratives. Amanda Doxtater in her essay 'Women Readers, Food and the Consumption of Text' (2004) exemplifies this while she writes about Diva's unrestrained consumption of text and food and the constant mixing of high culture and popular culture in the novel. In Doxtater's mind a depiction of a feminist consumption strategy that challenges norms and dichotomies such as the one between consumption and creativity is therefore created.

Another doctoral thesis that deals with Fagerholm's prose is Alva Dahl's study *I skriftens gränstrakter. Interpunktionens funktioner i tre samtida svenska romaner* [In the Border Land of Writing. The Function of Interpunctuation in Three Contemporary Swedish Novels] (2015). Dahl studies Fagerholm's novel *DIVA* via the Bakhtinian concept of 'dialogism' in a study of *languaging* as an interactive, situated process. Dahl's focus on linguistic details shows that punctuation is an integrated element of style and characterization and important also for the thematic aspects of the work. Shifts in voice and tone in Fagerholm's novel depend on punctuation. The broken chronology and the contested grammatical rules all function as

---

7   The Moominvalley is the creation of the Finland-Swedish author Tove Jansson (1914–2001), who in her books for children portrayed a valley inhabited by Moomin Trolls, fantasy creatures which are very human in their behaviour and emotions.

a way to use a queer aesthetics according to Dahl.[8] Dahl also comments on how Fagerholm addresses a double readership and creates double implicit reading positions, one Finland-Swedish and one Sweden Swedish, since the language supposedly passes without notice for a Finland-Swedish reader while a reader in Sweden might find Fagerholm's style more original and inventive (Dahl 2015: 95).

Bo G. Jansson's collection of essays *Ljuga vitt och brett utan att ljuga. Den svenska prosaberättelsen i den postmoderna skärmkulturens tidevarv* [Lies without a Limit. Swedish Prose in a Postmodern Digital Age] (2013) has pointed out that DIVA is a strong monologue (Jansson 2013: 1). He and many other scholars remark on how the omnipotent, unreliable narrator is central for the interpretation of the novel as a whole.

While many feminist literary scholars have emphasised the utopian dimensions of Fagerholm's novels, Jussi Ojajärvi reads them in a more critical manner when he studies the function of brand names in, among others, Fagerholm's first novel *Underbara kvinnor vid vatten* and, briefly, in *DIVA*. In his article '"Benson & Hedges-sytyttimellä." Kulutustavaroiden ja tavaramerkkikerronnan ulottuvuuksia vuosituhannen vaihteen suomalaisessa romaanissa' ['With a Benson & Hedges Lighter.' Perspectives on Consumerism and Consumer Goods in the Turn of the Century Finnish Novels] Ojajärvi (2012: 70) posits that while consumer goods are used to outline a historical period, they also reveal the capitalist context of the time of writing. In Fagerholm's novels specifically, Ojajärvi relates consumer choice to a performative subjectivity: 'In a way [the protagonist of *Wonderful Women by the Water*] is absorbed into a representation of consumer culture. It seems to restrict her identity, and she then repeats this position "performatively" – she fits herself into the position more individually, tries to repeat it "differently"' (Ojajärvi 2012: 61).

Ojajärvi is not the only one who contributes interesting analyses of Fagerholm's works. The development of literary studies becomes visible when one scrutinizes what has been written about them. Perspectives offered by feminist studies now reside together with girlhood studies and queer studies and narratological approaches exist side by side with both perspectives offered by consumerism and digitalisation and with Deleuzian and posthumanist frameworks. That Fagerholm's novels can fruitfully embrace such a variety of theoretical approaches, testifies to their special innovativeness and vigour as literary artefacts.

---

8   For example, Dahl discusses the enigmatic dog figure which is a vignette in *DIVA*. The reader is puzzled by its diffuse role on the limit between text and paratext (Dahl 2015: 90). Texye, the terrier, is in Dahl's eyes a queer dog, whose dogginess is compromised since it is always carried around. Both in the text and as vignette this dog also functions as a decorative element pointing to a queer reading. Followers of Fagerholm such as Sanne Näsling use a similar device, but choose butterflies as vignettes instead of dogs.

The Essays

Novel Districts. Critical readings of Monika Fagerholm enhances and deepens the understanding of Fagerholm's fiction brought forward by earlier scholarship and contributes to the growing interest and attention of literary scholars to her works. The articles enlighten the ways in which literary and cultural conventions can be innovatively re-employed within 20th and 21th century literature. As a Finland-Swedish minority writer, Fagerholm offers insight into the conditions of small minority literature in the late modern era. By exploring the development of Fagerholm's writing, the book also opens up new and multiple perspectives on contemporary Nordic literature and ongoing cultural and social developments.

Our anthology is the first major study of Fagerholm's works in a Nordic and international context. In this edited volume, literary scholars explore the central themes and features that run through Fagerholm's works and introduce novel ways to understand and interpret her writings. In essays written by eight Finnish and Swedish scholars the oeuvre of Fagerholm is scrutinized from perspectives of contemporary scholarly interest: queer, narratology, late modernity, gurlesque, digitalisation and reading strategies. The essays demonstrate that Fagerholm's literary prose, rich with local mannerisms, literary allusions and repetitions in a fugue style is able to challenge and transform many literary and theoretical forms of writing and thinking. Taking their starting point in the theme of transformation, the articles represent an urge for new forms of reading and understanding. The articles also show that Fagerholm's novels promote and inspire various, even opposite interpretations and stimulate an intense dialogue among readers and scholars. The use of gender studies, feminist studies, girlhood studies, narratology, poststructuralism, posthumanism and reception studies enhances the value of this volume in education, introducing up-to-date discussions on both theory and literature.

The book contains three parts. Part One, 'Transforming Traditions' offers four articles of which three focus on Fagerholm's probably most experimental girlhood depiction, *DIVA. En uppväxts egna alfabet med docklaboratorium (en bonusberättelse ur framtiden)* [The Alphabet of Adolescence with a Laboratory of Dolls (A Bonus Tale from the Future)] (1998).

The book opens with Lena Kåreland's article, 'Re-imagining Girlhood. The Revision of Girls' Books in Monika Fagerholm's *DIVA* and *The American Girl*', which offers an overall introduction to Monika Fagerholm through the topic of genre. Kåreland discusses the sabotage Fagerholm carries out on genre conventions and scrutinizes the ways in which especially girls' books are transformed in her works. The relation between women and language, central to Fagerholm, is studied using the ideas of Julia Kristeva.

Kaisa Kurikka's chapter 'Becoming-Girl of Writing. Monika Fagerholm's *DIVA* as Minor Literature' examines the 'inhuman territories of girlhood' in the novel. Kurikka studies the politics of minorization through the materiality of Fagerholm's language and approaches her writing as an inherently political act, in which not only the thematic, but also the style is important. By using the views of Gilles Deleuze and Félix Guattari on minor literature, Kurikka shows how the composition of the novel deterritorializes conventional ways of writing and reading.

Hanna Lahdenperä's chapter 'Reading Fiction as/and Theory. Monika Fagerholm's *DIVA* as a Barthesian text and Feminist Theory' argues that Fagerholm deconstructs generally accepted knowledge about gender, the body and subjectivity, and produces new explanations and definitions. Lahdenperä's points of departure are the works of literary scholar Roland Barthes and feminist scholar Teresa de Lauretis, including their views on fiction and theory. In order not to recreate a hierarchy between theory and fiction, she reads the novel *DIVA* as a contribution to theoretical discourse. By foregrounding the narrators' attitudes towards philosophy and theory, Lahdenperä scrutinizes how the novel 'does' feminist theory.

Kristina Malmio's chapter 'A Portrait of the Technological Sublime. *DIVA* and the History of the Digital Revolution' analyses the narrative structures in *DIVA* using literary scholar Fredric Jameson's concept of the 'technological sublime'; she relates the novel to the digitalization of the Nordic society that took place in the 1990s. The overall, exhaustive and enigmatic diversity of the novel and its 13-year-old schoolgirl protagonist are interpreted as an allegory of the internet and its development in the 1970s and 1990s, showing the possibilities offered by the worldwide web for a minority literature. The transformations of time, place and identity in the novel are related to the development of new media.

In Part Two entitled 'New Forms of Pleasure, Anxiety and Writing', central topics and themes in Fagerholm's later novels are studied in relation to both the tradition of melodrama and a new global style called the *gurlesque*. The authors also emphasize the ability of Fagerholm's prose to arouse affects and emotions in readers.

Anna Helle in her chapter 'When Love and Death Embrace – Monika Fagerholm's *The American Girl* and *The Glitter Scene* as Postmodern Melodrama' studies the themes of love and death that are central to both novels. She traces the intertextual relations of Fagerholm's themes, discusses the centrality of a young dead girl by the water in the Western imagination and finally shows how Fagerholm employs melodramatic traits such as excess, over-sentimentality and a polarized vision between good and evil in order to tackle the question of importing melodrama into the postmodernist context.

In the chapter 'The Song of the Marsh Queen' Maria Margareta Österholm uses the term *gurlesque* coined by Arielle Greenberg and Lara Glenum to analyse an aesthetic mixing of feminism, femininity, cuteness and disgust, a form of feminine grotesque in *The American Girl* and *The Glitter Scene*. The relation between the gurlesque aesthetics and queer desires is also studied. Österholm shows the effects of the text on readers becoming involved in the fights, sexuality, pleasure and anxiety of Fagerholm's girl characters.

Part Three, 'Transformations and Forms of Reading' introduces analyses of a couple of Fagerholm's early texts as well as her latest published novel, *Lola uppochner*. Here the relation of Fagerholm's works to an ancient Nordic tradition is scrutinized. The last chapter finally turns from the works to their reception. Ann-Sofie Lönngren's chapter 'Oppression and

Liberation. Traditional Nordic Literary Themes of Female Human-Animal Transformations in Monika Fagerholm's Early Work' discusses two early works of Fagerholm, *Patricia* (1990) and *Wonderful Women by the Water* (1994). In her article Fagerholm's use of mythological and folklorist motifs is discussed in relation to gender and sexuality. Lönngren shows how the intertextual relation between folklore and literature can manifest itself in the 20th century and discusses the significance of norms regarding gender and sexuality in the discursive construction of the human literary character in Finland-Swedish authorship.

The topic of Mia Österlund's chapter '"A Work You Cannot Explain, Only Experience." The Struggle with Readability in the Reception of Monika Fagerholm's Novel *Lola uppochner*' is the reception of Fagerholm's latest novel from 2012, seen both as a failure and a challenge. Since her first publication, Fagerholm has frequently had to face questions about the readability of her works and many reviewers have argued that her experimental fiction demands specific reading skills. Österlund scrutinizes the reading strategies of reviewers in Finland and Sweden as they try to comprehend the novel and shows that the novel demands a collaboration of traditional and oppositional reading strategies.

The breadth of the perspectives offered in this volume testifies to the vigour of Fagerholm's prose; her texts inspire new readings and continue to puzzle and disturb. The articles in the book not only introduce Fagerholm's works and suggest innovative readings of her novels in light of up-to-date literary theory, but also they enter into a fruitful dialogue with each other. They confirm that theoretical approaches can be turned into productive readings. As the scholars in this volume discuss the same novels from different perspectives, the articles will necessarily include a certain amount of repetition. However, each article can be read separately, if desired. We hope that the scope of this volume is as intriguing as the literature that it presents.

References

Dahl, Alva 2015: *I skriftens gränstrakter. Interpunktionens funktioner i tre samtida svenska romaner.* [In the Border Land of Writing. The Function of Interpunctuation in Three Contemporary Swedish Novels] Skrifter utgivna vid institutionen för nordiska språk vid Uppsala universitet 91, Uppsala.

Doxtater, Amanda 2004: Women Readers, Food and the Consumption of Text. Karin Boye's *Kris* and Monika Fagerholm's *Diva*. In *Gender, Power, Text. Nordic Culture in the Twentieth Century*. Ed. Helena Forsås-Scott. Norvik Press, Norwich, 125–137.

Ekman, Michel 1995: 'I novembers tröstlösa nätter.' Om Helsingforsskildringen hos några yngre finlandssvenska prosaister. [Depictions of Helsinki by Young, Finland-Swedish Authors of Prose Fiction] In *Rudan, vanten och gangstern. Essäer om samtida finlandssvensk litteratur.* [Essays on Contemporary Finland-Swedish Literature] Eds. Michel Ekman and Peter Mickwitz. Söderströms, Helsingfors, 209–231.

Ekman, Michel 2014: Prosa. Bred epik och nyanserad novellkonst. [Prose. Broad Novels and Nuanced Short Stories] In *Finlands svenska litteratur 1900–2012*. [Finland's Swedish Literature 1900–2012] Ed. Michel Ekman. Svenska litteratursällskapet i Finland, Helsingfors.

Haasjoki, Pauliina 2012: *Häilyvyyden liittolaiset. Kerronnan ja seksuaalisuuden ambivalenssit.* [Allies in Wavering. The Ambivalences of Narrative and Sexuality] Turun yliopiston julkaisuja, Annales Universitatis Turkuensis *Sarja – Ser. C Osa – Tom. 343*, Scripta lingua Fennica edita. Turun yliopisto, Turku. (http://www.doria.fi/handle/10024/78758) (Accessed 29.2.2016)

Haasjoki, Pauliina 2005: Mitä tiedät kertomuksestani? Biseksuaalinen ambivalenssi ja queer-lukeminen. [What Do You Know About My Story? Bisexual Ambivalence and Queer Reading] – *Naistutkimus* 18 (2) 2005, 29–39.

Helle, Anna 2008: 'Kuoleman lumous nuorella iällä'. Tytöt ja kuolema Monika Fagerholmin *Amerikkalaisessa tytössä*. ['Death's Spell at a Young Age'. Girls and Death in Monika Fagerholm's *The American Girl*] – *Kirjallisuudentutkimuksen aikakausilehti Avain* 2/2008, 59–64.

Ingström, Pia 2014: Leken och det fruktansvärda allvaret hos Monika Fagerholm. [Play and Dreadful Seriousness in Monika Fagerholm] In *Nordisk kvinnolitteraturhistoria.* [Nordic Women's Literary History] Ed. Elisabeth Møller Jensen et al. Bra Böcker, Höganäs. (http://nordicwomensliterature.net/article/play-and-dreadful-seriousness-writings-monika-fagerholm#article) (Accessed 29.2.2016)

Ingström, Pia 1995: Jag, mitt livs tappra hjältinna. [Me, My Life's Brave Heroine] In *Rudan, vanten och gangstern. Essäer om samtida finlandssvensk litteratur.* [Essays on Contemporary Finland-Swedish Literature] Eds. Michel Ekman and Peter Mickwitz. Söderströms, Helsingfors, 180–208.

Jansson, Bo G. 2013: *Ljuga vitt och brett utan att ljuga. Den svenska prosaberättelsen i den postmoderna skärmkulturens tidevarv. Filosofisk grund, innehåll och form.* [Lies without a Limit. Swedish Prose in a Postmodern Digital Age] Rapport 2013: 1. Högskolan Dalarna, Falun.

Korsström, Tuva 2013: *Från Lexå till Glitterscenen. Finlandssvenska tidsbilder, läsningar, författarporträtt 1960–2013* [From Lexå to the Glitter Scene. Finland-Swedish Pictures of the Age, Readings and Portraits of Authors] Schildts & Söderströms, Helsingfors.

Kurikka, Kaisa 2005: Tytöksi-tulemisen tilat. Monika Fagerholmin *Diva* utopistisena tekstinä. [The Spaces of Becoming-Girl. Monika Fagerholm's *Diva* as a Utopian Text] In *PoMon tila. Kirjoituksia kirjallisuuden postmodernismista.* [The Space of PoMo. Texts on Postmodern Literature] Eds. Anna Helle and Katriina Kajannes. Jyväskylän ylioppilaskunnan julkaisusarja numero 74. Kampus Kustannus, Jyväskylä, 56–72.

Kåreland, Lena 2004: Flickbokens nya kläder. Om Monika Fagerholms *Diva*. [The New Clothes of Girls' Books] In *Omklädningsrum. Könsöverskridanden och rollbyten från Tintomara till Tant Blomma.* [Changing Rooms. Gender Transgressions and Changes of Roles from Tintomara to Tant Blomma] Eds. Eva Heggestad and Anna Williams. Studentlitteratur, Lund, 121–137.

Lönngren, Ann-Sofie 2011: Mellan metafor och litterär materialisering: heteronormer och djurblivande i Monika Fagerholms novell Patricia Kanin. [Between Metaphor and Literary Materialization – Heteronormativity and Becoming Animal in Monika Fagerholm's Short Story 'Patricia Rabbit' (1990)] – *lambda nordica* 16 (4) 2011, 53–84.

Malmio, Kristina 2012: Phoenix-Marvel Girl in the Age of *fin de siècle*. Popular Culture as a Vehicle to Postmodernism in *Diva* by Finland-Swedish Author, Monika Fagerholm. In *Nodes of Contemporary Finnish Literature*. Ed. Leena Kirstinä. Studia Fennica Litteraria 6. Finnish Literature Society, Helsinki, 72–95.

Mazzarella, Merete 1989: *Det trånga rummet. En finlandssvensk romantradition.* [The

Narrow Room. A Finland-Swedish Prose Tradition] Söderströms, Helsingfors.
Ojajärvi, Jussi 2012: 'Benson & Hedges -sytyttimellä.' Kulutustavaroiden ja tavaramerkkikerronnan ulottuvuuksia vuosituhannen vaihteen suomalaisessa romaanissa. ['With a Benson & Hedges Lighter.' Perspectives on Consumerism and Consumer Goods in the Turn of the Century Finnish Novels] – *Kirjallisuudentutkimuksen aikakausilehti Avain* 2/2012, 52–75.
Stenwall, Åsa 2001: *Portföljen i skogen. Kvinnor och modernitet i det sena 1900-talets finlandssvenska litteratur.* [Briefcase in the Woods. Women and Modernity in Late 20th Century Finland-Swedish Literature] Schildts, Helsingfors.
Tidigs, Julia 2014: *Att skriva sig över språkgränserna. Flerspråkighet i Jac. Ahrenbergs och Elmer Diktonius prosa.* [Crossing Linguistic Borders in Writing. Multilingualism in the Prose of Jac. Ahrenberg and Elmer Diktonius] Åbo Akademis förlag, Åbo.
Österholm, Maria Margareta 2012: *Ett flicklaboratorium i valda bitar. Skeva flickor i svenskspråkig prosa från 1980 till 2005.* [A Girl Laboratory in Chosen Parts. Queer Girls in Swedish and Finland-Swedish Literature from 1980 to 2005] Rosenlarv förlag, Stockholm.

Transforming Traditions I

Lena Kåreland

Re-Imagining Girlhood
The Revision of Girls' Books in Monika Fagerholm's *DIVA* and *The American Girl*

Monika Fagerholm states in an interview in 2005, 'The traditional critic of literature wants at any cost to decide which genre a novel represents, and to separate between form and content' (Peterson 2005).[1] This statement indicates that Fagerholm is not interested in dividing literature into competing categories and genres. Although I respect her opinion, my aim in this article is to study the play with genres that is typical of Fagerholm's authorship, by focusing on how she rewrites one particular genre: the girls' books. I also briefly touch upon how the use of intertextuality and allusions to other works connect to the playing with genres in her works since these literary devices reveal which genre the novel revisions. However, an intertextual approach differs radically from traditional comparativism. Instead, it follows a Bakhtinian view of the text as dialogic and embraces Julia Kristeva's way of describing intertextuality as an interplay between texts that goes beyond situatedness in historical and social contexts (Bakhtin 1981; Kristeva 1986: 34). Kjell Espmark defines this intertextual link between texts as different voices that roar behind the text (Espmark 1985: 23). Fagerholm's novels are rich with echoes from earlier texts and they invite intertextual and generic analysis. Therefore, the main subject of this article is Fagerholm's use of girls' books and young adult novels in the light of intertextuality as a means to re-imagine girlhood.

During the 19th century to the middle of the 1960s, the genre label *girls' books* commonly served as a marker for depictions of normative girlhood with traces of rebellion, whereas gender separated genres were later questioned and the genre label young adult novel was used as an umbrella concept for these stories that depicted young protagonists and adolescence. In line with the feminist movement, it was no longer appropriate to separate books for girls and books for boys because of the cementing of stereotypical patterns (Theander 2006: 10). Nevertheless, in my following discussion of the different images of girls presented in Fagerholm's novels, girls are the main protagonists and I take my examples from *DIVA* and *The American Girl* where a complex girl comes into being.

---

1 Translation from Swedish into English is mine.

A study of the influence of literature for girls in Fagerholm's writing inevitably links to the development of feminism. Fagerholm's starting point is feminist, as she admits herself (Sandin 1991: 4). The odd and the marginal fascinate her, especially human beings – often girls and women – and events that are unimportant and superficial in the eyes of mainstream culture. She shows her readers that great things can occur in banal surroundings, even the grey suburbs. Fagerholm is influenced by French theorists such as Julia Kristeva and Hélène Cixous, and in particular Kristeva's theories of language are important to her (Sandin 1991: 4). As a poststructuralist feminist, Kristeva underlines women's way of expression as a threat to the established male order. Women's writing is in this light a border phenomenon, disrupting the borderline between subject and object. Kristeva's discussion of the semiotic and symbolic phase in children's development has influenced Fagerholm. The semiotic phase is a preverbal phase that later becomes the symbolic order of verbal language and is crucial in developing an alternative way of writing. The semiotic breaks when Logos enters the reason with its fixed laws. In the semiotic phase, poetry and revolt also have their domicile. Thus, language is emotional and sensual, far from the codified signification of the words. Therefore, semiotic writing is characterized by components such as rhythm, melody and intonation (Kristeva 1990). The girl Diva, the protagonist in Fagerholm's novel of the same name, creates such a language. Fagerholm's prose is often trivial, but also poetic. The everyday language mixed with poetic passages sometimes turn her novels into comedies but more often to tragedies.

Besides Kristeva, Hélène Cixous is one of the mothers of poststructuralist feminist theory. Her most influential article, 'The Laugh of the Medusa', investigates the relationship between sexuality and language (Cixous 1976). Influenced by the French philosopher Jacques Derrida, in particular his theory of the hierarchical system of language that in Western culture values the written language more than the spoken, she explores women's writing. An important concept for both Derrida and Cixous is the *phallogocentrism* according to which the phallic language, that is men's language, is privileged while women's writing is defined by a lack of language. Cixous stresses the importance for women to find a kind of language that allows them to express themselves not only in words, but also by their bodies by writing the body into the text (Cixous 1976). Fagerholm's novels circle around women's potential to write and their right to take possession of the language. Her tendency to break boundaries of various kinds appears strongly in her language and particularly in her ambition to give girls and women voices.

Fagerholm is conscious of the fact that women writers are rooted in a literary tradition where women in earlier ages were subordinated and expected to remain silent. It is, she states in an interview, impossible to leave out of an account of the condition of girls and women, either in life or fiction (Sandin 1991: 4). In Western culture and fiction, girls are largely related only to their sexuality and biology. In opposition to this silencing and oppression of girls, the main subjects in Fagerholm's novels are girls in a small town setting, a theme that has contributed to give her a special position in contemporary Nordic prose where girlhood has slowly entered the surface as one of the main motifs that occupy female writers as well as their male counterparts. This succeeds partly by the play with and the rewriting of genres such as the girls' books. In the following, I discuss how Fagerholm's rewrites the genre of girls' books in the light of the tradition of women's writing. First, here are a few words about intermedial patterns in her novels.

Genre Revisions

To study Fagerholm's authorship from an intertextual perspective gives some indications of genre and reveals the larger patterns in which the authorship is situated. Nevertheless, the numerous references are perhaps both overwhelming and maybe even misleading, as they also function as false threads. Intermedial transformations, that is the relationship and interaction between structures and devices from different art fields such as visual art, film and music, are typical of Fagerholm's authorship. Her writing is influenced by films, as she has declared in the interview mentioned above (Sandin 1991), where she states that she wants to write in a way that can be compared to John Cassavetes's films. Cassavetes's films are, according to her, both open and improvised and at the same time very strictly bridled. There has been no study of this relationship between the cinematographic genres and Fagerholm's way of writing and it is not possible to treat it in this article.

However, the links between literature and music in Fagerholm's writing will be discussed. She transforms literature into music and the importance of music is prominent in her writing as an underlying structure. She writes like a composer, using a broken prose, where the sentences sometimes are unfinished and intertwined. In her texts, as in music, one theme attaches to another and the chords are repeated. Circles and repetitions of phrases and words go in and out of each other as themes in a piece of music. This pattern is very far from the genre of girls' books and thus Fagerholm's use of girlhood and topical moments in girls' books are revised via intermedial transformation of the narrative form through musical structure and references.

For Fagerholm, music is a form of art that transgresses borders; therefore, it can reach areas at the limits of perception. There is a musical rhythm to her prose. In *The Glitter Scene* there are overt references to Gustav Mahler and one might explore how and if his work is essential to the narrative structure. One answer to this question is that musical aspects are visible in multiple ways in Fagerholm's musical, poetical and sensual prose. Her prose is in this aspect very close to the semiotic phase that Kristeva discusses as mentioned above. Fagerholm's constant repetitions give associations to the leitmotifs of music. The subtitle of *Glitterscenen*, 'och flickan hon går i dansen med röda gullband' [And the girl she moves in the dance with red, golden ribbons] which is lost in the English translation, *The Glitter Scene. A Novel,* is a phrase taken from a folksong and the construction of a folksong with many stanzas and refrains provides a structure for Fagerholm's composition of her text.

The Girl at the Centre of Fiction

Fagerholm's novels are rich with associations to girls' books and young adult fiction: stories that deal with the theme of how a girl becomes a woman. This is a standard pattern of girls' books, observed and studied by many scholars both in Sweden and abroad (see e.g., Toijer-Nilsson and Westin 1994; Österlund 2005; Franck 2009; Trites 2000). Historically, literature for girls has been overlooked, neglected and criticized. Earlier girls' books usually provided reoccurring topoi of the girl's ordinary life, her relation to family, school, boys and men, future marriage and family. Thus, the girl's personal development has been at the centre and the genre considered more conservative than radical. Contemporary studies, however, show that there are also subversive levels in earlier books for girls. In Fagerholm's novel *DIVA*, as the subtitle of *DIVA* indicates, becoming girl is to vegetate in a doll laboratory, where different attitudes to girlhood can be tested and investigated and the foundations of being a girl can be reshaped.

Thus, with her doll laboratory images, Fagerholm recycles the traditional ingredients of girls' books into new contexts and rewrites patterns as will be shown in the following. *DIVA* is described in a literary history of Finland-Swedish literature both as a young adult novel and as an act of sabotage against the young adult novel as a genre (Ingström 2000: 326). In that sense, Fagerholm has created a sort of work that is an anti-girls' book or anti-young adult fiction, while reimagining these genre patterns especially in relation to girlhood. The perspective is turned upside down, and the girl, so often marginalised in literature, becomes powerful and grandiose in Fagerholm's literary universe. The girl is no less than a bearer of important existential questions.

When writing *DIVA* Fagerholm had one of her favourite books, *The Catcher in the Rye* by J.D. Salinger, in mind (Fagerholm 1999: 66). The main character in Salinger's novel, Holden Caulfield, has his place in a long literary tradition of young boys as exponents of Western culture and mediators of knowledge. As a classic example of young adult fiction, this novel is also in vivid opposition to the genre of girls' books. What Fagerholm does then is to insert a girl protagonist in a similar narrative structure; thus, she interrupts the gender script of the young adult novel. Consequently, she also states that a girl can mediate knowledge and experiences and the main purpose when writing *DIVA* was to show how this is possible by creating a totally new and fantastic girl hero. Holden Caulfield is, according to Fagerholm, a literary character who 'takes the liberty of being in the world on his own conditions, looking upon the world, with his own language and with his own voice' (Fagerholm 1999: 66). Diva has the same attitude to life as Holden and the same ironic way of expressing her thoughts. Holden presents himself as twelve years old: 'But exceptionally big for my age'. Diva is, as Holden, to some extent omnipotent, full of desire for everything in the world and described as physically big. When Fagerholm links Diva to Salinger's male hero, she underlines Diva's preference for mimicking a male position in the gender system.

In Fagerholm's literary universe girls play a prominent role and young women transform and free themselves from the limits of their gender. They interpret and form the world and decide how the world can be comprehended. Diva's mother teaches her daughter that there are hundreds of possible ways to act and behave (*DIVA* 1998: 33). She instructs Diva that she has to surprise people, and not be fixed in any given position or accept what others have thought before her or be satisfied with a life consisting of ready-made 'quotations', that is repetition and copying (*DIVA* 1998: 34). As an answer to this imperative the girl character becomes a representation of a human being, an incarnation of the best of humankind and is in this respect a sort of superhero (Malmio 2012). However, the girl is also exposed and threatened. Fagerholm's fictional girls are not easy to grasp and do not fit easily into given patterns. In contrast, women who are ready to do everything in order to follow gender norms are included to make the girls' revolt against normativity even more distinct. In *DIVA* women do not always know who they are, because they are so occupied with performing a gender norm.

Girls and women in Fagerholm's oeuvre are complex and full of contradictions. Her novels are well suited to be studied in line with girlhood studies, which focus on how a girl is described in fiction and how she is modelled upon different feminist theories and contributes to comment on feminist ideas (e.g., Frih and Söderberg 2010). Since the 1990s, the development of girlhood studies has emphasized the powerful girl, challenging earlier limits for a girl's behaviour known as the core paradigm of girls' books. Girlhood studies have since then become an important field of research, and many scholars illustrate how the fictional girl is on a large scale moving from adjustment to norms towards protest and revolt. Girls in fiction come across as having to confront contradictory demands. 'Doing girlhood' in fiction is therefore always a question of balancing between social and cultural structures of power and norms in society. As girlhood is relational and experimental in Fagerholm's novels the theme from girls' books, that is how girls experiment with their girlhood in different ways in relation to norms, is brought forward both as a comment on tradition and as a renewal.

Girlhood studies discuss the girl in the light of theories of monstrosity and queer, and she is considered as strange and twisted, simultaneously grotesque and gurlesque. One scholar who has developed this way of considering girlhood is Maria Margareta Österholm who explores queer girls in Fagerholm's novels as well as in other Swedish novels published during the period 1980–2005 (2012). Österholm's concepts allude to the subtitle of Fagerholm's *DIVA* where the term 'Doll Laboratory' is used: 'The Alphabet of Adolescence with a Laboratory of Dolls (A Bonus Tale from the Future)' underlines the central poetics of late modernity as a laboratory of gender; thus, this text points to how central Fagerholm's remodelling of girls' books is for the literary field as a whole. The concept of queer is a useful tool to discover how girls in Fagerholm's novels occupy different positions on the curve of normality, which is what is at stake in the girls' books. It is important to remember that the concept of queer does not signify a sexual identity, but a critical attitude to what is seen as normative

(Rosenberg 2001). In this context, I would like to add that both *DIVA* and *The American Girl* can be read as disguised girls' books. A discussion of girlhood, its transformation and potential is the main heritage from the girls' books, while the transformations of the genre appear on the level of style and form.

Writing Feminist Fiction

Fagerholm's feminist project resembles playing with dolls in a doll laboratory, during which genres such as girls' books and literary characters are disguised, reinvented and altered. In *DIVA*, the protagonist Diva wants to be in control of both her life and its representation in narration and places herself in the role as seducer in an active traditionally male position. Like Tintomara, the Swedish author Carl Jonas Love Almqvist's protagonist in the novel *The Queens Tiara* (*Drottningens juvelsmycke* 1834), she appeals to both men and women. Tintomara is an androgyne, a double creature, always slipping away and difficult to grasp. Like Diva, she moves between different ways of being and challenges society's expectations of how women ought to be.

Diva, the character, can also be compared to world-famous Swedish author Astrid Lindgren's girl character Pippi Longstocking. Lindgren's books about Pippi are not girls' books since Pippi is only nine years old and the format is a children's book. Nevertheless, Diva, at thirteen years old is an intellectual Pippi Longstocking, a 'girlwoman', who is living outside the normative gender structure. Diva is as straightforward and outspoken as Pippi when she frankly declares: 'I do not suffer from ANY illness. I am healthier than all people in the world' (*DIVA* 1998: 184).[2] Diva has the vitality and vigour of Pippi Longstocking. They are both androgynous and enjoy testing different roles. Diva and Pippi also share a tendency to make up stories and play with the truth. The border between truth and lies is in flux for both Diva and Pippi. Diva's mother often tells her daughter that she lies so that her ears flutter (*DIVA* 1998: 88). Diva wants to make a spectacle of life. Like Pippi she exaggerates and uses hyperbolic narration. Nevertheless, Diva's strength and cocksureness, illustrated above, has some weak spots: 'I am only a little girl in the world, a little girl who goes to school', Diva says (*DIVA* 1998: 266).[3] Pippi Longstocking too bears loneliness in her heart. However, in spite of her feelings of solitude, Diva is a powerful contrast to stereotypes of weak girls; therefore, she is also in alignment with the strong girl in the girls' books (see Kåreland 2004: 128–138).

Being Diva is being full of contradictions; her character is in many ways ambiguous. She is not only a breaker of norms, someone who sticks out, she is sometimes traditional and conventional in her desire to accept prevalent ideals of beauty. She cares about her appearance, and wants to be

---

2   Jag lider inte av NÅGON sjukdom. Jag är friskare än samtliga människor i världen (*DIVA* 1998: 184). All translations from *DIVA* are mine.
3   Jag är bara en liten flicka i världen trots allt, en liten flicka som går i skolan (*DIVA* 1998: 266).

Lucia. Accordingly, Pippi wants to be a nice lady wearing an elegant hat. Nevertheless, Pippi also protests against common concepts of beauty. When she sees a poster in a shop aimed at those suffering from freckles, she enters the shop declaring with emphasis: 'I am not suffering from freckles'. The sales clerk looks astonished at Pippi saying: 'But your whole face is full of freckles'. Moreover, Pippi finds her answer: 'But I am not suffering from them', she states. 'I like them' (Lindgren 1946:18).

Similarly, Diva's self-confidence is considerable. She is the most beautiful person imaginable, at least if Diva's description of herself is to be believed. She is a teenager who is great and all embracing, with an intellectual capacity that borders on the brilliant; she is called both 'BabyWonder' and a typical 'Lucia', queen of the light. The girl and her life serve as an ideal existence in Fagerholm's novels. However, this existence is fragile, even though many of Fagerholm's girls give proof of power and strength. Nevertheless, adulthood seems frightening to them and madness is a constant threat to their norm breaking (*DIVA* 1998: 271). To become an adult woman not only concerns the biological development where sexuality is at the core; it is not only about menstruation, sex and the possibility of pregnancy as in ordinary young adult fiction. The becoming is more rich and complex than that, as Diva says:

> **I am not by definition my sexuality, which is wild and unlimited.** I am not a sexual way of being. **The world can be RED and YELLOW and GREEN and BLUE**, says my friend Franses. There are one million ways of being, thousands of not investigated possibilities. (*DIVA* 1998: 84 f)[4]

Girlhood in Diva's mind is unfixed, following no special pattern. Girls may take several positions and test sexual roles. It is an example of a queer sexuality, as Österholm states (Österholm 2012).

One trait that Fagerholm plays upon in the genre of girls' books is the theme of friendship between girls. This is predominant in her novels especially in *The American Girl*. The girls' friendship in Fagerholm's novel is much more complicated and more serious than in the girls' books in general. It has symbolic dimensions, stands for security and protection and gives the girls a place, which is a safe haven from the threat of the adult world. The description of the friends Sandra and Doris is intense and strong. Like magnets, the girls are drawn to each other and become friends: '[they were] the best of playmates, in their very own little world' (*The American Girl* 2009: 108).[5]

The encounter between these neglected girls, disregarded by the adults, exploited and removed, makes it possible for them to create a world of their own. When Sandra meets Doris, she finds a soul mate, which is a strong

---

4 **Jag är inte per definition min sexualitet, som per definition är vild och obegränsad.** Jag ÄR ingen sexuell inriktning, **världen kan vara RÖD och GUL och GRÖN och BLÅ**, säger min väninna Franses. Det finns miljoner sätt att vara, tusen outforskade (*DIVA* 1998: 84 f).

5 Bästa lekkamrater dessutom, i en alldeles egen liten värld (*Den amerikanska flickan* 2005: 109).

and important experience for her. Their community means something quite new for Sandra, something that she '[...] would never, for the rest of her entire life, experience so intensely. It could certainly be imitated but never recreated' (*The American Girl* 2009: 104).[6]

Doris and Sandra are both abused girls, but they embody different facets of mistreatment, one is physical, the other is emotional. Doris Flinkenberg, described as the 'mistreated child', is a figure well known from girls' books, and has visible scars on her body caused by maltreatment (*The American Girl* 2009: 100). In addition, Sandra whose parents do not manage to deal with their parenthood is also modelled on the figure of the maltreated child known from girls' books. The scene, which relates Sandra's feelings as she witnesses her mother flying away in a helicopter together with her German lover leaving her daughter – as it seems forever – is a strong portrayal of the abandonment of a child.

> And then the moment was over. Lorelei [the mother] climbed up into the helicopter and before disappearing inside completely, she turned around – of course, the classical – one last time and looked at the rock by the edge of the woods and then, in that microscopically short moment, it was only the two of them in the entire world. [...] And then, when everything was over and it was too late, Sandra lifted her hand – it was heavy like lead – to wave to Lorelei Lindberg one last time.
> And the helicopter rose and was gone. Just a few seconds and the great silence and paralysis and the heat had settled, quivering and quiet over the house in the darker part again. (*The American Girl* 2009: 113)[7]

As I have shown, Fagerholm uses themes such as friendship from the traditional girls' books. Nevertheless, she breaks up the story of a girl's development and process of maturity and makes it fragmentary. By using intertexts such as Tintomara and Pippi Longstocking she demonstrates the complexity of the girl, her strength and her weakness as well as the ambiguity in her attitude to femininity. She does not tell her story following a chronological line, but instead follows a queer timeline (Halberstam 2005). Thus, she refuses to write traditional novels of development and does not consider human life or the development of human beings as a continuous and ordered path or timeline from childhood infantilism to adult competence and understanding. Instead, an existence that is always

---

6   Detta var mötet med en tvillingsjäl och det var en känsla som Sandra aldrig någonsin efter det här i hela livet skulle vara med om lika starkt, det skulle kunna härmas nog men aldrig återskapas (*Den amerikanska flickan* 2005: 106).
7   Och så var ögonblicket över. Lorelei klättrade upp i helikoptern och innan hon försvann helt och hållet in i den vände hon – förstås, det klassiska – sig om en sista gång och såg på stenen vid skogsbrynet och då, i den mikroskopiskt korta stunden, var det bara de två i hela vida världen. [...] Och först då, när allt var för sent och förbi hade Sandra lyft sin hand – den var blytung – för att vinka till Lorelei Lindberg en allra sista gång. Och helikoptern hade lyft och varit försvunnen. Några sekunder bara och den stora tystnaden och förstelningen och hettan hade lagt sig dallrande och stum över huset i den dyigare delen igen (*Den amerikanska flickan* 2005: 114).

changing and never finished is a positive path according to her novels. In line with a postmodern approach, she looks positively at everything that is in movement. Maturity and normality are for her, as well as for her female protagonists, not worth attaining. Puberty is instead a state worth pursuing, corresponding to the view on girlhood in girlhood studies.

Reshaping and Mocking Girls' Books

As I have pointed out *DIVA* and *The American Girl* are variations of traditional girls' books. In some ways, the novels show similarities to the genre; in other ways, they take an ironical stance to them. The titles of the chapters in *Diva* associate to girls' books: 'The Diary' [*Dagboken*], 'Me and My friends' [*Jag och mina vänner*], 'The Dog-Girl' [*Hundflickan*] and 'Me and My day' [*Jag och min dag*]. Other titles refer to well-known authors or to other novels: 'Everything My Mother Knows about Henry Miller' [*Allt min mamma vet om Henry Miller*], 'My Uncle the Wizard [*Min morbror trollkarlen*] and 'The Bell Jar (a book for everyone)' [*Glaskupan (en bok för alla)*].[8] The scope of literary references is great, but the allusions to young adult fiction are continuously present as an undertone. When Diva describes her conversation with one of her teachers, she says: 'It would be as in a novel for young adults, where suddenly and when you least imagine, bridges appear between the world of adults and that of young people' (*DIVA* 1998: 267).[9] Diva has an ironic attitude to young adult novels, in particular to the way language is used in them: 'I am, as a teenager would say, lost in reading comics' (*DIVA* 1998: 12).[10]

In particular, *DIVA* is a parodic play on the genre of girls' books. An earlier ideal of the genre distinguishes Diva from traditional characters. She is not a victim of oppression in a society ruled by men. She is not sweet and self-sacrificing, nor is she maladjusted and dissatisfied with herself. Instead, she is very self-assured, as some of the more radiant girls in traditional girls' books also were. Diva has discovered 'her dimensions', she declares with a reference to the famous Finland-Swedish avant-garde poet Edith Södergran.

Diva's relationship to her mother also echoes the pattern of girls' books, although in this case, Diva has a positive relationship to her mother. She often quotes and refers to her mother and her mother is quite different compared to Sandra's and Doris's mothers in *The American Girl*. In the description of Diva's mother, the gender system is criticized. The mother is a feminist and she attacks women's tendencies to deny themselves. Furthermore, she recommends an authentic life that also is Diva's ideal. When authentic life is emphasized in this manner it also indirectly expresses a critique of other girls, the so called 'kisses-and-hugs birds' (*pussochkramfåglarna*) who live

---

8   'Glaskupan' might be an allusion to the Swedish translation (1974) of Sylvia Plath's famous novel *The Bell Jar*, 1963.
9   Det skulle vara som i en ungdomsbok, där det plötsligt och när man minst anar det slås upp bryggor mellan vuxenvärld och ungdomsvärld (*DIVA* 1998: 267).
10 Jag är, som det heter på tonårssätt, fördjupad i ett seriemagasin (*DIVA* 1998: 12).

their lives according to a strict pattern and follow the conventions. Their dreams for the future are to find nice husbands and have nice children (*DIVA* 1998: 40). By ironic use of intertextuality and by exaggerating and mocking, rewriting and revisioning the genre of girl's books, Fagerholm actively reshapes fictional girlhood. The cornerstones for this revision are familiar from the girls' book: play and friendship.

How Playing Enriches Girlhood

Girls playing, which in many ways connects to the theme of friendship, is a central activity in Fagerholm's novels as well as in girl's books. Play has an important role in the fictional girls' development and is also a therapeutic function for them. For Doris and Sandra in *The American Girl*, playing is a preoccupation that helps them to overcome their fear. Their games as well as their discussions about their activities are to some extent based on their own life-stories. Their common interest in what has happened to the mysterious American girl also provides a link between them. They enact her tragic history as one of their favourite games. She has been dead for some years and was probably murdered. The two girls give an accurate account of their play:

> The games would not be played at the same time, but in turn. The first game would be the Lorelei Lindberg and Heintz-Gurt [Sandra's mother and her lover] game, the other would be called the Mystery with the American Girl.
> And everything would to be based on reality. Everything had to be true. (*The American Girl* 2009: 108)[11]

Sandra and Doris like to keep company in the empty swimming pool in Sandra's house. The pool is a good place for Loneliness and Fear, the feelings that join the two children and these words are painted on their sweaters. Sister Night and Sister Day are other names they give each other. When the girls play, they deal with existential questions of life and death, conflict and reconciliation.

From an intertextual perspective a parallel can be seen between Fagerholm's story about Sandra and Doris and the Swedish author Peter Pohl's young adult novels, in which he describes children who are left without any support from adults (Österlund 2007). Sandra and Doris, the two maltreated and abandoned girls, are examples of children forced to become adults. Due to lack of care and security, they become hard and cold. Such children also occupy a predominant role in other Fagerholm's stories and they frequently occur in Pohl's writing during the 1990s and the first decade of the 21th century. These maltreated children can, in both Pohl's

---

11 Lekarna skulle inte lekas samtidigt, men i tur och ordning. Den första leken skulle vara Lorelei Lindberg och Heintz-Gurtleken, den andra leken skulle heta Mysteriet med den amerikanska flickan, [hon som fått ge boken dess titel]./Och allt skulle ha verklighetsbakgrund. Allt skulle vara sant (*Den amerikanska flickan* 2005: 110).

and Fagerholm's novels, help each other and share the extreme experiences they have in common.

'You and I, Sandra', as Doris states, 'We've certainly been treated badly enough. Me with my scars and you with your tragic family background' (*The American Girl* 2009: 139).[12] Both girls know what it is to suffer. Peter Pohl's books deal with neglected children, sudden death, deceit and violence. One example is his debut novel *Johnny, My Friend*. Themes and motifs from this first book are repeated and varied in Pohl's later works, in a reparative method that resembles Fagerholm's use of repetition within certain frames. As in Fagerholm's novels, friendship is a frequent theme in Pohl's books. When Fagerholm emphasizes how girls play this can be a therapeutic method of healing, in a similar way to how Pohl emphasizes understanding and helping maltreated children.

Refusing Adulthood

One of the major variations of the girls' books that Fagerholm employs is adding sexual desire more overtly: 'I am good at seducing girls and boys and I enjoy it', Diva says (*DIVA* 1998: 89).[13] A lesbian desire expressed in both *DIVA* and *The American Girl* and the heterosexual standard called into question points to a revision of girlhood in the direction of a lesbian continuum, that is, according to Adrienne Rich, a fluidity in femininity considering the amount of desire between women (Rich 1980). An erotic and lesbian desire, noticed between Sandra and Doris is crucial for the rewriting of the girls' books. Once, when the girls embrace, have a tussle together and kiss on the grass, a sudden seriousness enters their game: 'The seriousness spread between the girls, so proud and, yes, so serious./Sandra felt a real sensation and it was both true and interesting and important, but decidedly not amusing, not at all' (*The American Girl* 2009: 155).[14] Have the girls taken a step into adulthood? No, not really; they will not accept adulthood and they are not ready to change into something that already is decided and thus limited. This is their understanding of adulthood. They want to preserve an existence, which is open to all possibilities like the twining way they now follow. Therefore, they refuse adulthood.

This tension between adulthood and childhood, or rather girlhood, is constant in Fagerholm's novels. It is present in *DIVA* where the protagonist transgresses borders as Sandra and Doris do in *The American Girl*. Otherwise, there are not many resemblances between Diva and Sandra and Doris. Diva is different from Sandra and Doris, as she is omnipotent and

---

12 'Du och jag, Sandra', som Doris säger. 'Man har farit alldeles tillräckligt illa med oss. Jag med mina ärr och du med din tragiska familjebakgrund' (*Den amerikanska flickan* 2005: 140).
13 Jag är bra på att förföra flickor och pojkar och jag njuter av det (*DIVA* 1998: 89).
14 Allvaret bredde ut sig mellan flickorna, så stolt och ja, så – allvarligt. /Sandra kände en riktig känsla och den var både sann och intressant och viktig, men avgjort inte lustig, inte alls (*Den amerikanska flickan* 2005: 153).

arbitrary, convinced of her undisputable value. She wants to create a place for herself in the middle of the world. '[...] there are no borders, except for those that one decides oneself', she says (*DIVA*: 47).[15]

There is a strong pathos of emancipation in Fagerholm's novels. The underlying and challenging question in her texts is where to find a place in the world, which would give self-confidence to young girls. Fagerholm mixes element from girls' books, such as first love and relations to friends, teachers and family members. What makes her oeuvre special is its advanced narrative technique, including the play with genres and allusions to other authors and works that have previously commented on girlhood.

Girls' books, novels for young adults, fairy tales, thrillers. With components from all these genres, Fagerholm creates stories written with such power and expressive language that she sometimes makes readers lose their breath. When riding her merry-go-round the question of genre in some way loses its importance.

References

Primary Sources

Fagerholm, Monika 1998: *DIVA. En uppväxts egna alfabet med docklaboratorium (en bonusberättelse ur framtiden)*. [DIVA. The Alphabet of Adolescence with a Laboratory of Dolls (A Bonus Tale from the Future)] Söderströms, Helsingfors.
Fagerholm, Monika 2005: *Den amerikanska flickan*. Bonniers, Stockholm.
Fagerholm, Monika 2009: *The American Girl*. Translated by Katarina E. Tucker. Other Press, New York.
Fagerholm, Monika 2010: *The Glitter Scene*. Translated by Katarina E. Tucker. Other Press, New York.

Secondary Sources

Bakhtin, Mikhail 1981: *The Dialogic Imagination. Four Essays*. Edited by Michael Holquist, translated by Caryl Emerson and Michael Holquist. Texas University Press, Austin.
Cixous, Hélène 1976: The Laugh of the Medusa. – *Signs* 4/1976, 875–893.
Espmark, Kjell 1985: *Dialoger*. [Dialogues] Norstedts, Stockholm.
Fagerholm, Monika 1999: Att bli till. [To Become] *Bang* 1/1999.
Franck, Mia 2009: *Frigjord oskuld. Sexuellt mognadsimperativ i svensk ungdomsroman*. [Liberated Virginity. Sexual Maturation Imperative in Swedish Young Adult Fiction] Åbo Akademis förlag, Åbo.
Frih, Anna-Karin and Söderberg, Eva (Eds.) 2010: *En bok om flickor och flickforskning*. [A Book on Girls and Girlhood Studies] Studentlitteratur, Lund.
Halberstam, Judith 2005: *In a Queer Time and Place. Transgender Bodies, Subcultural Lives*. New York University Press, New York.

---

15 [...] där inga gränser finns utom dem man själv bestämmer (*DIVA* 1998: 47).

Ingström, Pia 2000: Den nyaste prosan. [New Prose] In *Finlands svenska litteraturhistoria 2*. [Finland's Swedish Literary History 2] Publ. by Clas Zilliacus, ed. Michel Ekman. Svenska litteratursällskapet i Finland, Helsingfors.

Kristeva, Julia 1986: *The Kristeva Reader*. Ed. Toril Moi. Colombia University Press, New York.

Kristeva, Julia 1990: *Stabat Mater*. Ed. and transl. by Ebba Witt-Brattström. Natur och Kultur, Stockholm.

Kåreland, Lena 2004: Flickbokens nya kläder. Om Monika Fagerholms *Diva*. [The New Clothes of Girls' Books] In *Omklädningsrum. Könsöverskridanden och rollbyten från Tintomara till Tant Blomma*. [Changing Rooms. Gender Transgressions and Role Changes from Tintomara to Tant Blomma] Eds. Eva Heggestad and Anna Williams. Studentlitteratur, Lund, 121–138.

Lindgren, Astrid 1946: *Pippi Långstrump går ombord*. [Pippi Longstocking on Board] Rabén & Sjögren, Stockholm.

Malmio, Kristina 2012: Phoenix-Marvel Girl in the Age of *fin-de siècle*. Popular Culture as a Vehicle to Postmodernism in *Diva* by Finland-Swedish author Monika Fagerholm. In *Nodes of Contemporary Finnish Literature*. Ed. Leena Kirstinä. Studia Fennica Litteraria 6. Finnish Literature Society, Helsinki, 72–95.

Peterson, Marie 2005: Monika Fagerholm. Flickornas försvarare. [Monika Fagerholm. Defender of Girls] – *Dagens Nyheter* 3.1.2005.

Rich, Adrienne 1980: Compulsory Heterosexuality and Lesbian Existence. – *Signs* 5/1980, 631–660.

Rosenberg, Tiina 2001: *Queerfeministisk agenda*. [A Queer Feminist Agenda] Atlas, Stockholm.

Sandin, Maria 1991: Det ofärdiga jagets förvandlingar. Samtal med Monika Fagerholm. [Transformations of the Uncompleted Self. Conversation with Monika Fagerholm] – *Horisont* 5–6/1991, 2–10.

Theander, Birgitta 2006: *Älskad och förnekad. Flickboken i Sverige 1945–65*. [Loved and Denied. Girls' Books in Sweden 1945–65] Makadam, Göteborg.

Toijer-Nilsson, Ying and Westin, Boel (Eds.) 1994: *Om flickor för flickor. Den svenska flickboken*. [About Girls for Girls. The Swedish Girl's Books] Rabén & Sjögren, Stockholm.

Trites, Roberta Seelinger 2000: *Disturbing the Universe. Power and Repression in Young Adult Literature*. Iowa University Press, Iowa.

Österholm, Maria Margareta 2012: *Ett flicklaboratorium i valda bitar. Skeva flickor i svenskspråkig prosa från 1980 till 2005*. [A Girl Laboratory in Chosen Parts. Queer Girls in Swedish and Finland-Swedish Literature from 1980 to 2005] Rosenlarv förlag, Stockholm.

Österlund, Maria 2005: *Förklädda flickor. Könsöverskridning i 1980-talets svenska ungdomsroman*. [Girls in Disguise. Gender Transgression in Swedish Young Adult Fiction from the 1980s] Åbo Akademis förlag, Åbo.

Österlund, Mia 2007: Den förträngda flickkroppen i Peter Pohls ungdomsroman *Janne, min vän*. [The Suppressed Girl Body in Peter Pohl's Young Adult Novel Johnny, My Friend] In *Kvinnor, kropp och hälsa*. [Women, Body and Health.] Eds. Elina Oinas and Jutta Ahlbäck-Rehn. Studentlitteratur, Lund, 239–251.

Kaisa Kurikka

Becoming-Girl of Writing
Monika Fagerholm's *DIVA* as Minor Literature

Monika Fagerholm's second novel *DIVA* (1998) makes constant use of repetitions (words, sentences, paragraphs) to the extent that it appears to follow a paradoxical logic: the repetitions pile up into a series of details, which allows them to seem familiar, yet also unknown and strange. The novel itself takes up the question of repetitious details with a self-conscious twist:

> In every person's life there are details that are repeated in different situations and are guaranteed not to mean anything however hard one tries to come up with a meaning, or tries to force one onto them. If such a relation does not exist, one can create it by repeating the detail again and again in a given situation. **Any author**, for example, knows this. (*DIVA* 1998: 235)[1]

According to this citation tiny details become meaningful only through repetition. In this article I deal with some details of Fagerholm's novel, but do not broadly attempt to find deeper meaning lurking within. Instead, I concentrate on connecting these details with each other and on finding the operational logic of this connectedness called the style.

As a textual variation the use of repetition typical of *DIVA* can be linked to postmodern literature. Claire Colebrook (2000: 103) has distinguished two forms of postmodernism. These forms can also be defined as having a different attitude towards repetition. The first, according to Colebrook, would be to regard postmodernism as a movement that quotes, mentions and repeats styles without a sense of a proper or privileged style (aka 'language games'). The other form appears as an emergence or birth of sense, even a monstrous birth, since it would consist of the (sometimes chaotic) production of sounds and voices. This other form of postmodernism is a movement towards a particular style of writing. It indicates an emerging

---

1   Det finns i alla mänskors liv detaljer som upprepat framträder i olika situationer och garanterat inte betyder något hur man än anstränger sig att få fram en sådan betydelse, eller då tvinga fram den. Finns det inte en sådan där förbindelse kan man få den att uppstå genom att om och om igen upprepa detaljen i ett given sammanhang. Det vet till exempel **författare som författare** (*DIVA* 1998: 235). Translations from Swedish into English are mine. Italics and bold letters of the quotes are original unless stated otherwise.

force that disrupts any generality of concepts and thinking by putting forth questions concerning the basic processes of signification and sense making. I argue that *DIVA*[2] (1998) does precisely this: it takes language to its limits by exceeding signifying processes. As a novel *DIVA* operates by a set of laws of signification and representation required for literature as the cornerstone of human actions – to make sense to the reader – but simultaneously *DIVA* is in the presence of something else, something beyond sense making.

This paradoxical appearance of *DIVA* manifests itself in the oscillation between signification and a signifying process; it has been categorised in various ways. The novel has been characterized as experimental (Haasjoki 2012: 106), postmodernist (Kurikka 2005), metafictive fiction (Kurikka 2008) and gurlesque aesthetics (Österholm 2012), to name but a few examples. These definitions share at least one trait: they all deal with writing, which seems to function through complex and often contradictory layers of expression whether in terms of themes, narration, characterization, or the relationship with the real. All these overlapping explications apply to Fagerholm's novel, which indeed appears as a celebration of stratified elements.

The processes of stratification include my reading of the novel. Ten years ago, while discussing the textual strategies of *DIVA*, I described it as a novel that tends to move along as an indefinitely displaced middle (Kurikka 2005). With the help of *Reading Narrative* (1998) by J. Hillis Miller, I argued that *DIVA*'s excessive repeated phrases, words, scenes and prologues do not follow the logic of beginnings, endings and middles of a narrative line usually reserved for reading stories in a (more) conventional manner. I wrote, that if it were possible to draw the narrative line of Fagerholm's novel, it would inevitably turn out to be a zig-zagging web with various turning-points, returns and detours without a beginning or end. The only line possible with *DIVA* is to trace a *line of flight* (*ligne de fuite*, Deleuze and Parnet 1987: 54), since the novel seems to escape the constraints of traditional depictions of young girls while simultaneously fabricating a new kind of texture of writing on and about girls. The difficulty of reading *DIVA* as a conventional text is thus embedded in its fabric and texture.

This idea of describing Fagerholm's novel as 'writing-the-middle' still holds true today. In this article I want to explore, or even experiment with, this process of 'writing the in-betweenness' by taking it a bit further than before. This conception refers not only to story lines, but also to characters and themes. *Diva. En uppväxts egna alfabet med docklaboratorium (en bonusberättelse ur framtiden)* [DIVA. The Alphabet of Adolescence with a Laboratory of Dolls (A Bonus Tale from the Future)] tells the story of its central character, a 13-year-old girl named Diva. Because of her age, Diva herself is placed somewhere in the middle of childhood and young adult life, and womanhood in particular. Diva and other teenage girls in the novel, in fact the whole novel, can be situated in the midst of the entire Western tradition of describing girls: *DIVA* is writing itself into this tradition and at

---

2 When referring to the novel, I use capital letters (*DIVA*); 'Diva' refers to the central character of the novel.

the same time out of it following a two-fold movement, since conventional ways of depiction and narration are constantly juxtaposed with new ways of literary expression.

I use concepts created by two French philosophers, Gilles Deleuze and Félix Guattari. Thinking about and reading *DIVA* with their 'materialist epistemology', 'process philosophy' and 'ontology of becoming' points to the potential of literature and its ability to bring about new ways of writing. My way of reading follows a cartographic conception of literature; it is about drawing a map and tracing connecting lines between various elements of the novel. Gilles Deleuze (1997: 63) has described this cartographic conception of thinking in the following way: '[…] from one map to the next, it is not a matter of searching for an origin, but of evaluating *displacements*. Every map is a redistribution of impasses and breakthroughs, of thresholds and enclosures […]'. With Deleuze and Guattari it is impossible to think of *DIVA* as a *representation* of girlhood. *DIVA* is not so much about re-presenting girls. Rather, it is an *expression* of what it might mean to become a girl: *DIVA* gives expression to the event of becoming-girl. I am going to elaborate on the concept of 'becoming-girl' in connection to *DIVA*, and link the novel with yet another tradition of writing, namely *minor literature* (*une littérateur mineure*) as proposed by Deleuze and Guattari. When discussing various elements of *DIVA*, I also suggest something that could be called the singular *style* of Monika Fagerholm.

I began this article by introducing the two separate forms of postmodernism as described by Claire Colebrook. I place *DIVA* in the latter form of postmodernism, a way of writing which questions various signifying elements and literary conventions by either making excessive use of them or by turning them upside down. Yet, I want to take Colebrook's formulation even further by suggesting a combination of the two forms. Could there be postmodern writing that both uses and abuses intertextual references and citations by repeating them in multiple contexts, yet simultaneously succeeds in becoming a singular style? This is the idea I experiment with in this text. Instead of attempting to make sense of *DIVA*'s complexities by trying to interpret them through the laws of signification, or to find a meaning for them, I wish to focus on the flows of operation at work in the novel. Rather than posing the question 'What does *DIVA* mean?' my problematic appears as 'What does *DIVA* do?' and 'How does the novel work?' The reason for these queries comes from my reading of *DIVA* as a novel in a state of constant transformation. To give meaning – even momentarily – to transformation is an oxymoron, a violent way of capturing something that flees being defined. The assumption here is that it makes sense to try to stop making sense, especially if the making requires stopping the sense.

The Becoming-Other of the Girls Kari and Diva

I begin in the middle, since there is nowhere else to begin with *DIVA*. Let us enter a scene, in which Diva talks about her mother's opinions concerning the nature of good literature. In this scene Diva's mother insists that especially good literature is connected to reality or to something seemingly real, such as dreams about reality. According to Diva, her mother, however, is wrong; Diva declares: 'Literature is not a semblance. [...] Art is about constructing worlds, **about figuring out**' (*DIVA* 1998: 86).[3] Indeed, imagination plays a huge role in the novel, where both Divas-as-narrators build their worlds in such ways that it is difficult, if not impossible to decide whether the depicted events are actually taking place in the reality of the novel or whether they are fantasies. This quotation can be linked to two elements of *DIVA*: firstly to the concept of semblance, 'likelihood' and secondly to the question of writing. Telling stories is a constant topic in the novel. There are at least three layers in which this story-telling function operates: Diva denies that she will ever write fiction, but she keeps a diary as a teenager; the narrator of the future talks about a 'photo model novel' she is supposed to have written and Diva's mother is a poet and a translator. Furthermore, Diva refers to several authors and philosophers in her narration.

The narrators are literally telling stories. They in particular tell the story of a marginalized girl, Kari, repeatedly adding new bits of information and perspectives. The importance of this 'bonus story', which is referred to in the subtitle of the novel, is enormous and the narrator of the future even addresses her words to Kari by naming *her* as the narratee. In the course of the novel, the different Divas become convinced that Kari's story needs to be told; however, each singular Diva finds it difficult to decide how it *should* be done. Kari, a sister of Diva's friend, lies on the bed in her room listening to the tape recorder never uttering a word aloud, but later she speaks the most perfect Swedish learnt from listening to others.

Kari's sister has defined Kari's room as 'The Doll-Laboratory', which is yet another, updated version of the traditional Nordic doll-house, by sticking a nametag on its door. Kari's room is filled with dolls in various colours, shapes and sizes. Kari herself belongs to this doll collection as a living but mute human doll, a toy girl with which others can play. Kari is not depicted so much *as* a doll through resemblance or imitation, but in the actuality of her story she becomes a doll. Becoming is not 'a resemblance, an imitation, or, at the limit, an identification', as Deleuze and Guattari (1988: 237) write. Becoming is the series of events taking place between heterogenetic bodies that enables something else to emerge. These becomings are a matter of perception on behalf of the reader. In becomings it is possible to perceive traits or characteristics of both 'bodies' (the one to depart from and the one to reach for) and through their coming together a new way of being begins to take shape. In the becoming-doll of Kari she is placed motionless between immobile dolls; a reciprocal juxtaposition is affirmed with this placement.

The becoming-doll of Kari opens a passage to the inhuman territories of girlhood. This feature of connecting girls to dolls is varied in other writings of Fagerholm as well, especially in her latest novel *Lola uppochner* [2012, Lola Upsidedown] in which the name Lola is reserved for a big rag-doll. In *DIVA* the mixture of human and inhuman aspects of girlhood is enhanced not only by the collection of dolls but also by Kari's story. One version of

3   Litteratur är inte likhet. [...] Konsten är att bygga världen, **att tänka sig** (*DIVA* 1998: 86).

Kari's story – as told by Diva – makes an explicit intertextual reference to the Rapunzel fairy tale of the Brothers Grimm and its line 'Rapunzel, Rapunzel, let down your hair'. Diva talks about how during the night Kari's hair begins to grow and grow, falling through the window and making solid golden steps for boys to climb up to Kari's room. According to Diva, 'This is how Kari's room becomes **an open room**' (*DIVA* 1998: 49).[4] It is open for boys to enter; thus, Kari's room evidently makes her a (sexual) toy to play with.

Kari's character is filled with incorporeal transformations, becomings-other. The laboratory tag on her room's door also transforms her into a guinea pig for the boys entering her room. Her sister SannaMaria, with the help of her friends, turns Kari into a kind of a laboratory rat; they lock Kari into another 'alternative' laboratory, a dark closet at their school, where she is supposed to undergo a metamorphosis into a beautiful butterfly. Yet another incorporeal transformation takes place verbally when Diva juxtaposes Kari to Saint Lucia. These transformations emphasize Kari as a passive creature, almost as an object without a will of her own.

Nevertheless, one particular transformation depicts Kari as an active agent. Although her story is told in many versions, Kari eventually meets the same tragic end. Diva describes how Kari leaves her room, steps inside a telephone booth on the street and sets herself on fire. This image of Kari burning in flames in a phone booth builds another transformative shift bringing her together with Saint Lucia. According to the legend, before she became a Saint, Lucia was also burnt in a bonfire although without success. Kari turns into a burning doll, which Diva's mother talks about when Diva tells her about the events in Kari's room. Her mom says: 'Inside every woman there lives a burning doll, a Coppelia. A ballet-performance' (*DIVA* 1998: 31).[5]

Diva's mother is referring to *Coppelia*, the traditional classical ballet performed for the first time in Paris in 1870. It is an adaptation of *Der Sandmann* (1815) by E.T.A. Hoffman. In the ballet version of the story, Coppelia is a mechanical doll built by Dr Coppelius. Everybody takes the doll to be a real woman, since it is built with magnificent craftsmanship. A young man called Franz flirts with the doll just one day prior to his wedding with Swanilda. Swanilda then takes the part of the doll pretending to be 'her', so in the ballet the combination of a young woman and a mechanical doll is taken to the extreme when Swanilda plays Coppelia. The fact that Diva's mother mentions the ballet version of Hoffman's *Sandmann* is interesting also in the sense, that in the art of ballet dancing, ballerinas appear as inhuman dancing dolls in their technical prowess and perfection, aiming at overcoming the laws of gravity, which keeps humans on the ground. Kari's burning is a manifestation of the burning Coppelia: human, mechanical and inhuman at the same time. The collection of dolls is also set on fire; they are 'dolls which mean nothing at all' (*DIVA* 1998: 369).[6]

4 Så blir Karis rum **ett öppet rum** (*Diva* 1998: 49).
5 I varje kvinna bor en brinnande docka, en Coppelia. En balettföreställning (*DIVA* 1998: 31).
6 Dockorna som inte betyder något alls (*DIVA* 1998: 369).

DIVA does not reserve the expression of the becoming-doll only for Kari. Diva herself is equated with Kari several times during the novel and explicitly when Diva says: 'I see, now I see. Kari in the darkness. I believe that she is I. She looks precisely as I do [...]' (*DIVA* 1998: 428).⁷ Both girls change as characters and the way they are depicted is constantly modified. Diva, at the age of thirteen, appears as a perfect girl, something extraordinary, almost divine; she is inhuman, or rather, an imaginative element enters her character without references to the girls of the actual world. Thus, Diva becomes a figure that belongs to the world of fantasy; she is a superhero, 'Phoenix-Marvel Girl' as she calls herself referring to the famous Marvel comics series (see Malmio 2012). Her statement concerning literature as belonging to the category of 'ways of world making' comes true in her own character.

Diva describes herself as a 'Girlwoman' at the very beginning of the novel: 'Girlwoman. DivaLucia. Thirteen years, soon fourteen. BabyWonder. She nobody believed existed' (*DIVA* 1998: 11).⁸ In other words, Diva is the stuff of dreams, something to imagine, and something to tell stories about. All in all, the novel sets forth the workings of *fabulation* functioning transversally on different narrative layers. Fabulation means literally inventing stories, letting the creative forces flow towards the future. As a way of thinking, fabulation does not follow the rules of tracing the past through memories or re-telling something already experienced or lived. Rather, fabulation invests in transforming lived experiences. Deleuze writes: '[...] fabulation – the fabulating function – does not consist of imagining or projecting an ego. Rather, it attains these visions, it raises itself to these becomings and powers' (1997: 3). As a Deleuzean concept fabulation is linked with becomings and with *powers of the false* (*puissance du faux*). Instead of thinking that One Truth exists, the powers of the false celebrate the existence of 'false', fictive, untrue and unreal things, characters and stories and through this celebration the creative forces give birth to something new.

The basic nature of the false is in becomings, in metamorphoses (Flaxman 2012: xviii). Kari-Diva-Lucia-Coppelia-Phoenix Marvel Girl-Rapunzel (together with all the other intertextual references) generate a multiplicity, a series of becomings to the point that there is no more One Truth or 'one I' in the characterization of Diva nor Kari; there are only becomings-other. Deleuze writes about the powers of the false: '[...] contrary to the form of the true which is unifying and tends to the identification of a character [...], the power of the false cannot be separated from an irreducible multiplicity. "I is another [*Je est un autre*]" has replaced Ego=Ego' (1985: 133).

On the other hand, Deleuze and Guattari emphasize the imaginative forces at work in fabulation. Simultaneously Deleuze insists that fabulation always has a political dimension. Ronald Bogue (2007: 3–4; 2010: 18–20) links the concept to the invention and creation of a new social collective,

---

7   Jag ser, nu ser jag. Kari i mörkret. Jag tror att hon är jag. Hon ser precis ut som jag [...] (*DIVA* 1998: 428).
8   Flickkvinnan. DivaLucia. Tretton år, strax fjorton. BabyWonder. Hon man trodde att inte fanns (*DIVA* 1998: 11).

a yet non-existent community, which Deleuze calls 'people-to-come'. Deleuze writes: 'To catch someone in the act of telling tales is to catch the movement of constitution of a people. A people isn't something already there. A people, in a way, is what's missing [...]' (1995: 125–126). In *DIVA* Monika Fagerholm evokes a-people-who-is-missing by imagining the ways in which this 'people' might consist of girls: a fabulation of a *girl*-people-to-come.

Politics of Minor Literature

Monika Fagerholm (Kurikka 2009: 38) herself has said that as a feminist it is extremely important for her to bring forth the cultural narratives concerning women and girls, since they are so often neglected. Placing women, and especially teenage girls, at the centre of writing is in itself a political act. Even more political are the ways in which these stories are being told: it is politics of the aesthetic realm when writing takes a stand against more traditional ways of depicting and telling stories about girls. Correspondingly, *DIVA* is about the politics of age. As teenagers Diva and Kari do not belong to the category of children; neither are they yet women; they are moving along the line between childhood and womanhood and on this line the politics of becoming-girl is actualized.

With the constant transformations and becomings-other of the main characters Diva and Kari, *DIVA* argues for the emergence of sexual politics that simultaneously points towards a way out of the dichotomies of heterosexual and patriarchal rule. As Pauliina Haasjoki (2012) has convincingly shown, *DIVA* opens itself to a queer and sexually ambivalent reading not only because of Diva's allegedly sexual relationships with both females and males, but also because of the ambivalent narrative structure. Instead of arguing that gender and sexual differences are categories of rigid organization, *DIVA* blurs these boundaries and lines by combining traditional traits of femininity, masculinity and sexualities. Diva's omnipotence – extremely beautiful, excessively clever, ex-tremendously superb – is described as taken for granted by just naming these characteristics in a way traditionally reserved for male protagonists. At the same time Diva is utterly feminine, but her femininity consists of the potential of becoming-woman, the positive forces of a womanhood-to-come: Diva belongs to the sphere of fabulation.

In other words, *DIVA* deals with a multiplicity of minorities and marginal phenomena and this deal is political. As such the novel can be defined as belonging to minor literature as discussed by Deleuze and Guattari. The connotation of a 'minority' in the concept does not refer much to subjectivities (such as race, gender, class) or circumstances (developed or developing societies) and the minor does not belong to a socio-political or ethnic minority. Instead, the minor designates a process of becoming, a minorization (Flaxman 2012: 228–229). Minor literature cannot be considered as a simply representative category (Lambert 2012: 74). The politics of minorization in *DIVA* appear to celebrate the difference between girls and their situatedness in-between. The *minor* in the concept of Deleuze and Guattari refers to a quality or ability to change rather than to a quantity.

Deleuze and Guattari (1986: 16–17) have named three different components in relation to minor literature. Firstly, they say that everything in minor literature is political. Individual concerns are immediately connected with politics, since they are always linked with wider social milieus. The social milieu does not serve as a mere background to the individualization of a character. Thus, conceptually minor literature calls for taking the material spatialisation of character-setting into account. Time-frames, social environments and actual places and spaces are always part of characterization, but in the manner of linking the individual with wider perspectives. For example, Diva is situated sitting at the kitchen table in her family's home; Diva is placed in various rooms of a school-building; Diva walks in the street near the telephone booth in which Kari sets herself on fire. Although these scenes concentrate on Diva, they situate her in the midst of familial, social, cultural and sexual concerns, which always go beyond her as an individual.

As Deleuze and Guattari explain: 'The individual concern thus becomes all the more necessary, indispensable, magnified, because a whole other story is vibrating within it' (1986: 17). In the individuality of Kari's story there are vibrations regarding the tragic destiny of Saint Lucia and the Rapunzel fairy tale that can be linked to many cultural stories reserved for women. The stories of Kari's fellow students, however, also vibrate within her: 'Kari with her memories, with her forgetfulness, among the memories of the Eastern Secondary School, among the forgetfulness of the Eastern Secondary School' (*DIVA* 1998: 332).[9] Although Diva actualizes her individuality according to her mother's wishes of being 'new, fantastic, different' (*DIVA* 1998: 33), she is depicted in connection to other girls, Kari, SannaMaria and Franses in such a way that her individualization always takes place in relation to others. Diva is different, but she also differs from another group of girls, which she calls 'kisses-and-hugs birds' (*pussochkramfåglarna*). These girls are depicted as typical girls of their age: they are regarded as 'appearing to be modest', they want to light a candle to love, they dream of having a child with 312 nice men and they dream of Superman. Although Diva is an exceptional girl-figure, she is also restricted by the laws of her gender. This becomes clear, when the narrator talks about Diva's brother: 'In reality all doors are open for him. He knows that' (*DIVA* 1998: 107).[10] With this remark the narrator makes an explicit political stand in terms of gender. In another context Diva talks about her mother's admiration for a bright young man appearing as a cultural renovator, which 'girls cannot be' (*DIVA* 1998: 92).

Another component of minor literature is closely related to its political nature. Deleuze and Guattari (1986: 17) write that in it everything takes on a *collective* value, and that 'the political domain has contaminated every statement': becoming-minor is produced by a collective assemblage of enunciation. The answer to the question 'Who is speaking in *DIVA*?' appears to be manifold. As my article has mentioned, or rather hinted at before, there are different versions of Diva functioning as narrators in the novel: one

9   Kari med sina minnen, sin glömska, bland Östra läroverkets minnen, Östra läroverkets glömska (*DIVA* 1998: 332).
10 I verkligheten står alla dörrar öppna för honom. Han vet det (*DIVA* 1998: 107).

appears as the Diva of the present and the other as the Diva of the future. This system of narrators is complex and confusing. I differentiate between two character-narrators: Diva as the 'experiencing I' of the events and a Diva of the 'times-to-come', even though these two narrators cannot be separated from each other fully and at all points. Other literary critics such as Kristina Malmio (2012) and Pauliina Haasjoki (2012) have named yet another narrator, namely an 'author-narrator' or an authoritative instance responsible for the overall *mise-en-scène* of the novel with its possible parodic impulses, intertextual layers and miscellaneous authorial manoeuvres. Thus, the system of narrators also emphasizes movement between different points and perspectives. In other words, the form of *DIVA* is transformation, a constant process of re- and de-forming action.

The difference between these two narrators, Divas as subjects of enunciation, cannot be explained by pointing out changes in temporal patterns, since both Divas mainly use the present tense and sometimes even the future tense (Kurikka 2005). For example, Diva of the present talks about her emotions for her brother, whom she calls 'Middlebear' (*Mellanbjörn*) referring to the *Goldilocks* fairytale: 'I hate Middlebear NOW, but it will settle down. I am not so much going to love Middlebear but I will feel some affinity for him, which is going to gush vividly in me at least for some months' (*DIVA* 1998: 239).[11] Talking about the feelings of the future Diva (wilfully) makes it even more difficult to separate the two narrators: it often appears as if they both tell stories with a collective voice.

The collective nature of the narrators is enhanced by the third narrating agent. Kristina Malmio (2012: 78) names the third narrating instance 'a narrator' responsible for all the paratexts and intertextual allusions. However, Malmio states that 'this distinction between the narrators and the two Divas, narrating the story, is arbitrary and used only for the analysis'. Pauliina Haasjoki (2012: 112, 127) divides the narrative levels of the novel into three categories that are inhabited by different narrators. Diva experiencing the events and Diva talking about these experiences are closely linked to a third fictional personality, that of 'author-abstraction' stemming from the relation between the two other Divas. Haasjoki also links this 'abstraction of the author' with an intentionality responsible for all the narrative solutions in depicting the fictional world of *DIVA*.

Even though Haasjoki sees these narrators as separate from, they can still be identified with each other. It is very difficult and even unnecessary to separate these narrators. They speak through each other's voices, as an assemblage, a collective in a passage from the first person to the third: the I of Diva becomes she-Diva by travelling between the present and future tenses, and also through reminiscing about the past. This becoming-third of Diva can be read in the following sentences, where the past is brought to the present and the earlier Diva becomes equal with the later one: 'And if I try really hard, I remember my footprint in the sand, traces of my hands.

---

11 Jag hatar Mellanbjörn NU, men det kommer att utjämnas. Jag kommer att om inte älska Mellanbjörn igen så känna en affinitet för honom som kommer att bubbla upp handfast i mig om inte alltför många månader (*DIVA* 1998: 239).

[...] **Sand**. I roll around in it. Study my footprints, traces of hands' (*DIVA* 1998: 93).[12] This kind of collective assemblage of enunciation and the use of the present tense bring about an intense atmosphere of presence, instantaneity and expression into which the reader is not just allowed but also welcomed as a member of a-people-to-come.

Towards a Singular Style

The third component of minor literature is related to language. Minor literature does not need to be written in a minor language. More so, the language of minor literature is written with a dominant language constantly deterritorializing itself. This has nothing to do with language games or playing with language (Deleuze 1997: 5), the first form of postmodernism to which Colebrook refers, but it has everything to do with a minorization of the major language by way of making it strange and unknown; it is a kind of a bastard use of a major language (Deleuze and Guattari 1988: 105). In order to clarify this kind of minorization of language, the concept of *style* becomes useful.

'Art begins not with flesh but with the house', Deleuze and Guattari (2009: 186) write in *What is Philosophy?* By naming the house as the beginning of a creative process, Deleuze and Guattari emphasize acts of designing, making, constructing and doing. The compilation of an artwork, its composition and the construction of its intensive relations are emphasized. The artist with her material being affects these different materials of art and the materiality of art affects the artist. What kind of a house is being built in this creative process is a matter of style.[13] With the concept of style it is also possible to finally return to the beginning of this article and specifically to my suggestion that Monika Fagerholm is an author who *combines* the two different forms of postmodernism that Claire Colebrook has named.

For Gilles Deleuze style has nothing to do with linguistics or formalism. Style is not an ornament with which we decorate our thought. Rather, style is productive in the very form of our thought (Colebrook 2000: 51). Thinking does not exist somewhere merely waiting for our representation with a certain style; style is already in thinking itself. When style is understood this way, as thinking, everything I have written in this article about *DIVA* belongs to the sphere of the becoming-style of Monika Fagerholm. To depict girls as always being in connection with other girls – whether through intertextual references or juxtaposing girl-characters of the novel – and to depict them as continuously transforming into something else; to use a complex structure

12 Om jag tänker efter minns jag mina fotspår i sanden, avtrycken av händer. [...] **Sand**. Jag rullar runt i den. Studerar mina fotspår, handavtryck (*DIVA* 1998: 93).
13 The concept of style has been largely ignored in literary studies for some decades because of its dubious and unclear nature. 'Literary style' has been understood as referring to a formalistic reading. Lately, new approaches, such as feminist rhetoric and cognitive poetics, have led style free of previous cages of linguistics and formalism.

of narrators whose voices slide into each other, into a collective, and to take a political stand by placing individual characters in larger milieus is to create a Fagerholmian style. I insist that authors are not the creators of style but vice versa: style creates authors in the process of thinking with/about language, with/about words. The materiality of language, the matter of compiling a novel – syntax, sentences, chapters – affect the author in a reciprocal manner to the extent that it is not possible to name the author as either the origin or the beginning of a literary style.

When writing about style Deleuze is mostly concerned with literature. He defines style by referring to Marcel Proust:[14] '"Great literature is written in a sort of foreign language". That is the definition of style' (Deleuze and Parnet 1987: 5). This definition comes very close to the above-mentioned third component of a minor literature, the deterritorialisation of language. Literary style means both entering the social order of language and laws of signification (territorialisation) and breaking them (deterritorialisation) by tracing a line of flight. These concepts can also be understood as a means of identification: through the processes of territorialisation a body (inhuman or human body) fixes itself a kind of 'identity', a stable structure in relation to other bodies. Reterritorialisation occurs when this identifiable body occupies another territory while maintaining the properties achieved in the earlier surroundings. Colebrook takes up citations, quotes and repetition as belonging to so-called language games; all these features can be named as belonging to the phenomenon of reterritorialisation. To draw a line of flight is a way out of fixed identities and meanings, an escape into new territories of being; deterritorialisation marks repetition born out of difference.

In a television-film called *L'Abécédaire de Gilles Deleuze* (*Gilles Deleuze from A to Z*, Boutang 2012), Deleuze defines literary style with two distinct elements. First, he stresses how language is treated in a certain way, where not only elements of syntax are put into motion, but also the desires, wishes, needs and necessities of the author move to such an extreme that language begins to stutter. Second, Deleuze emphasizes the way in which in this system of breaking down of the syntax language is pushed towards a limit that sides with music. If an author succeeds with these two elements, a style 'as music of language' is born. In other words, the style of literature emerges from deterritorialisation.

This relationship between literary style and music is very interesting when thinking about Fagerholm's novels. Not only do her novels make frequent references or allusions to music (e.g., *Lola uppochner* with *Bolero* (1928, Maurice Ravel); *The Glitter Scene* 2009 with a traditional Finland-Swedish folk song), but their language and structure can also be linked to musical terms. Especially *DIVA* makes use of constant repetitions by repeating phrases and whole paragraphs. For example, the phrase 'the cradle

---

14 Marcel Proust, *By Way of Saint-Beuve*. Transl. Sylvia Townsend Warner. Chatto and Windus, London, 1958: 194–195: 'Great literature is written in a sort of foreign language. To each sentence we attach a meaning, or at any rate a mental image, which is often a mistranslation. But in great literature all our mistranslations result in beauty'.

of Western culture'[15] is repeated three times in four consecutive pages. Its first appearance takes place in a scene, where Diva's teacher and lover Daniel is lecturing about Western literature and the world and nature while they are out together camping. Daniel baptizes their sleeping bag as 'the cradle of Western culture' (*DIVA* 1998: 14). With this name a territorialisation of the phrase takes place: the sleeping bag is situated in a territory, a concrete 'terrain', but it also signifies a romantic encounter between Diva and Daniel. A sleeping bag where two people are making love in one sense is the beginning of a great culture, but not in the eyes of official cultural history.

Two pages later, when the phrase is mentioned again, it sustains this ironic tuning in a somewhat altered state. This time the phrase appears in a more natural way when Diva merely states that Daniel sleeps in the cradle of Western culture: the phrase is a place name. This instance functions as a reterritorialisation of the phrase. The last time this phrase comes up it is linked with the expression of Diva '**fluffing in the cradle of Western culture**' (*DIVA* 1998: 17)[16] meaning that Diva is not thinking with concepts or words but she is following her sensations by touching Daniel inside the sleeping-bag: 'Against thoughts only skin can help' (*DIVA* 1998: 17).[17] The last context of 'the cradle of Western culture' is a total counter-point to the whole conception of (normative) culture. Diva contradicts the wisdom of the skin, touching and making love with the Great Culture of the Thinking Mind. The phrase is, in other words, a form of deterritorialisation.

Each time the phrase 'the cradle of Western culture' is used, its meaning is changed, while still maintaining the previous uses; thus, it becomes the source of a series of *differences* and repetitions. The only element that remains the same is the act of repetition. These repetitions can be conceptualized as *ritornellos*, refrains that bring about the rhythm and melodies of writing and simultaneously assemble various territories (Deleuze and Guattari 1988: 317–318). In the processes of repetition, in the making of a refrain, a singular style as the event of individualization is achieved as the poetics and politics of rhythm. In *DIVA* the rhythmic force of language is also actualized in the typographical layout of the text, since most of these repetitious phrases are printed in bold and sometimes in capital letters.

This bolding of letters functions on the level of accentuations, brings about a special stress and speed to these words and phrases and differentiates them from sentences printed in normal font. For example, the phrase 'Believe this: **the world can be RED, YELLOW, GREEN and BLUE**' (*DIVA* 1998: 19, 58, 71, 85, 87, 238, 243, 244, 246, 248, 389, 407, 440)[18] occurs in the novel almost twenty times. The first time it appears as an identifying phrase, a description of Franses Fagerström, the girl with whom Diva is in love. Mostly this statement is repeated in a similar form with a reterritorialising

---

15 [...] den västerländska kulturens vagga.
16 [...] alltså **mufflar** där, högtidligen, **i den västerländska kulturens vagga** (*DIVA* 1998: 17).
17 Det ända som hjälper mot tankar är hud (*DIVA* 1998: 17).
18 Tror: **att världen kan vara RÖD, GUL, GRÖN och BLÅ** (*DIVA* 1998: 19, 58, 71, 85, 87, 238, 243, 244, 246, 248, 389, 407, 440).

effect bringing not only Frances to the story line repeatedly, but also Diva's affection for her. Closer to the end of the novel, the phrase is deterritorialised by mixing its connotations into a new version: **'Franses RED YELLOW BLUE AND GREEN'** (*DIVA* 1998: 301).[19] In this rephrasing not only the world, but also Franses is regarded as a multi-coloured entity. A bit later in the novel, the phrase is transformed to be even shorter: **'YELLOW RED GREEN and BLUE'** (*DIVA* 1998: 391)[20] as if to denote that anything can become anything.

Fagerholm alludes to music in most of her novels and also in *DIVA* there are many references to music and pop songs. One of Diva's friends, Sebbe Nsson refers to 'Helpless' by Neil Young (1970) saying that 'the only song in the world one cannot live without is: HELPLESS HELPLESS HELPLESS HELPLESS' (*DIVA* 1998: 48). Another scene depicts Diva's brother, who is smoking a cigarette, and after smoking '[…] he runs. A song in his head, like a nursery rhyme. **Born to run away**' (*DIVA* 1998: 50).[21] In this 'Born to run' by Bruce Springsteen (1975) and in Neil Young's song the repetition of title phrases appears in a territorialising way although mostly *DIVA* makes use of *ritornello* as a means of deterritorialisation.

In the totality of *DIVA* the refrains are closer to free-floating jazz than pop-music riffs. The novel itself links jazz with style when Diva describes her mathematics teacher: "**'Jazzloops'**, he says. "Long jazzloops. Listen. Isn't it stylish?"' (*DIVA* 1998: 424).[22] Repetition produces difference with deterritorialising forces and intensities, which go beyond sense making effectuating a potentiality of writing-in-the-middle, 'the becoming-girl' of writing.

According to Deleuze (2000: 48), style produces instability, in which something is constantly born in a process of metamorphosis. Style does not function as a guarantee of coherence and it has nothing to do with perspectives following each other. On the contrary, multiple perspectives work simultaneously in a clause, in a sentence, and in between them. Deleuze and Guattari (1988: 313–314) distinguish between rhythm and metre. The latter is formed with the logics of territorialisation, while the former, rhythm, takes place in a transmissional phase between space and times. Rhythm is the area of constant deterritorialisation. I argue that *DIVA's* novelistic composition deterritorialises the conventional ways of writing and reading according to plots or story lines, chronological order of scenes and so forth. This deterritorialisation takes place via rhythmic variations accomplished by taking repeated refrains to the utmost extreme, to excess. This operation typical of *DIVA* draws a line of flight, escaping conventional writing and stepping into the faculty of minor literature. The minorization of story telling marks the way to the singular style of Monika Fagerholm, the becoming-girl of literature.

19 **Franses RÖD GUL BLÅ OCH GRÖN** (*DIVA* 1998: 301).
20 **GULT RÖTT GRÖNT och BLÅTT** (*DIVA* 1998: 391).
21 […] springer han. En sång i huvudet, som en ramsa. **Född att springa bort** (*DIVA* 1998: 50).
22 '**Jazzslingor**', säger han. 'Långa jazzslingor. Lyssna. Är det inte stiligt?' (*DIVA* 1998: 424).

References

Primary Sources

Fagerholm, Monika 1998: *Diva. En uppväxts egna alfabet med docklaboratorium (en bonusberättelse ur framtiden)*. [DIVA. The Alphabet of Adolescence with a Laboratory of Dolls (A Bonus Tale from the Future)] Söderströms, Helsingfors.

Secondary Sources

Bogue, Ronald 2007: *Deleuze's Way. Essays in Transverse Ethics and Aesthetics*. Ashgate, Hampshire and Burlington.
Bogue, Ronald 2010: *Deleuzian Fabulation and the Scars of History*. Edinburgh University Press, Edinburgh.
Colebrook, Claire 2000: Inhuman Irony: The Event of the Postmodern. In *Deleuze and Literature*. Eds. Ian Buchanan and John Marks. Edinburgh University Press, Edinburgh, 100–134.
Deleuze, Gilles 1985: *Cinema 2. The Time-Image*. Transl. Hugh Tomlinson and Robert Galeta. The Athlone Press, London.
Deleuze, Gilles 1995: *Negotiations 1972–1990*. Transl. Martin Joughin. Columbia University Press, New York.
Deleuze, Gilles 1997: *Essays Critical and Clinical*. Transl. Daniel W. Smith and Michael A. Greco. University of Minnesota Press, Minneapolis.
Deleuze, Gilles and Guattari, Félix 1986: *Kafka. Toward a Minor Literature*. Transl. Dana Polan. University of Minnesota Press, Minneapolis.
Deleuze, Gilles and Guattari, Félix 1988: *A Thousand Plateaus. Capitalism & Schizophrenia*. Transl. Brian Massumi. University of Minnesota Press, Minneapolis.
Deleuze, Gilles and Parnet, Claire 1987: *Dialogues*. Trans. Hugh Tomlinson and Barbara Habberjam. Columbia University Press, New York.
Flaxman, Gregory 2012: *Gilles Deleuze and the Fabulation of Philosophy. Powers of the False, Volume I*. University of Minnesota Press, Minneapolis.
Haasjoki, Pauliina 2012: *Häilyvyyden liittolaiset. Kerronnan ja seksuaalisuuden ambivalenssit*. [Allies in Wavering.The Ambivalences of Narrative and Sexuality] Turun yliopiston julkaisuja, Annales Universitatis Turkuensis *Sarja – Ser. C Osa – Tom. 343, Scripta lingua Fennica edita*. Turun yliopisto, Turku.
Kurikka, Kaisa 2005: Tytöksi-tulemisen tilat. Monika Fagerholmin *Diva* utopistisena tekstinä. [The Spaces of Becoming-Girl. Monika Fagerholm's *Diva* as a Utopian Text] In *PoMon tila. Kirjoituksia kirjallisuuden postmodernismista*. [The Space of PoMo. Texts on Postmodern Literature] Eds. Anna Helle and Katriina Kajannes. Jyväskylän ylioppilaskunnan julkaisusarja numero 74. Kampus Kustannus, Jyväskylä, 56–72.
Kurikka, Kaisa 2008: To Use and Abuse, to Write and Rewrite: Metafictional Trends in Contemporary Finnish Prose. In *Metaliterary Layers in Finnish Literature*. Eds. Samuli Hägg, Erkki Sevänen, and Risto Turunen. Finnish Literature Society, Helsinki, 48–63.
Kurikka, Kaisa 2009: Kirjoittaminen on tarinassa liikkumista. [Writing is Walking Around the Story] – *Kulttuurihaitari* 4/2009, 36–38.
Lambert, Gregg 2012: *In Search of a New Image of Thought. Gilles Deleuze and Philosophical Expressionism*. University of Minnesota Press, Minneapolis.
Malmio, Kristina 2012: Phoenix-Marvel Girl in the Age of *fin de siècle*. Popular Culture as a Vehicle to Postmodernism in *Diva* by Finland-Swedish Author, Monika

Fagerholm. In *Nodes of Contemporary Finnish Literature*. Ed. Leena Kirstinä. Studia Fennica Litteraria 6. Finnish Literature Society, Helsinki, 72–95.

Miller, J. Hillis 1998: *Reading Narrative*. University of Oklahoma Press, Norman.

Österholm, Maria Margareta 2012: *Ett flicklaboratorium i valda bitar. Skeva flickor i svenskspråkig prosa från 1980 till 2005*. [A Girl Laboratory in Chosen Parts. Queer Girls in Swedish and Finland-Swedish Literature from 1980 to 2005] Rosenlarv förlag, Stockholm.

Audiovisual material

Boutang, Pierre-André 2012: *Gilles Deleuze from A to Z with Claire Parnet*. Translated by Charles J. Stivale. Semiotext(e) Foreign Series, Los Angeles.

Hanna Lahdenperä

Reading Fiction as/and Theory
Monika Fagerholm's *DIVA* as a Barthesian text and Feminist Theory

> How long should these philosophical passages be in a text about being wild at heart and making ideology out of it? (*DIVA* 1998: 419)[1]

Diva, the protagonist of Monika Fagerholm's novel *Diva. En uppväxts egna alfabet med docklaboratorium (en bonusberättelse ur framtiden)* (1998), asks her question from a place separate from the diegetic level, the now of the novel. She makes a retrospective narrator's note and states: 'I can evoke it [my childhood] now, years later, in another place' (*DIVA* 1998: 419).[2] Just as her childhood self, the retrospective narrator expresses doubt in meta-language, in discourse about narrative itself. She also clearly states what she is doing: showing different ways of being a girl or a woman and making ideology out of the non-normative ways of doing gender. This comment puts the presumptive scholar on the spot. What is there left to do? Should the reader distrust the narrator and attempt to prove what Diva *really* does or take pride in having one's ideas about the novel conveniently confirmed by its narrator?

In this article, I will take the narrator's explicitly stated purpose at face value and instead treat it and the novel as a contribution to a theoretical conversation. Having said that, the actual content of such a contribution is less relevant for the purposes of this article. Here I am interested in both the purpose and function of placing a work of fiction alongside traditionally theoretical texts and reading them in the same way and less in the results of such a reading. A reading of *DIVA* with Roland Barthes essay 'From Work to Text' from 1971 will illustrate how the novel, through its central themes, becomes part of a discursive node. However, first I will turn to feminist scholar Teresa de Lauretis for an approach to *DIVA* through feminist theory.

The claim I make is that *DIVA* both deconstructs generally accepted knowledge about gender, the body and subjectivity and simultaneously produces new knowledge of these categories. In the quote above the

---

[1] Hur långa ska såna här filosofiska passusar vara i en text som handlar om att vara vild i hjärtat och göra ideologi av det? (*DIVA* 1998: 419) All translations from *DIVA* by Hanna Lahdenperä.
[2] Jag kan framkalla det nu, åratal efteråt, på en annan plats (*DIVA* 1998: 419).

retrospective narrator uses the word *text* to describe her narrative endeavour as she asks herself – or possibly the reader – how much philosophy she has to include. This conjures an image of her as a conscious creator, not merely a narrator: She knows she is writing a book. What is more, the book she is writing explicitly discusses conventions and their subversion, 'being wild at heart' as she puts it in the opening quote, and makes ideology of it. In other words, the retrospective narrator lets a stylized teenage version of herself narrate a rather extraordinary life for the purpose of making it the blueprint of a systematic critique of ideas.

Introducing *DIVA* tends to begin with a certain amount of floundering, since there is no traditional, linear plot to describe. There are events – momentous ones – and there is a chronology of sorts, but the two are only loosely connected. Literary scholar Pauliina Haasjoki notes that it is more productive to ask what there is in Diva/*DIVA* rather than what happens to Diva, since plot lines and temporal levels are characterized by parallels and variations (Haasjoki 2012: 109). At its most basic, *DIVA* is a description of a thirteen-year-old girl and her life in a fictional suburb in the 1970s delivered as a first-person narration. She goes to school, she hangs out in a shopping centre and she goes to the cinema with her boyfriend. She also seduces her teacher, climbs up to visit the girl next door along her hair like the prince to Rapunzel in the Brothers Grimm fairy tale, and turns into a bear.

These events raise questions about Diva's reliability as a narrator and about how the novel 'should' be read. Do the events actually take place and what kind of a world and reality does the novel present if they do? Is Diva fantasizing or lying and what would it mean if she was doing either or both? Fagerholm has created a narrative in which a character is both child and adult, both human and fantastical figure, simultaneously and without regard to chronology. However, despite its fantastical elements, *DIVA* is essentially a realistic novel that is neither fantasy nor magical realism, as much as objective truth and realism can matter in a postmodern context where a character makes a point of emphasising her status as a narrative construction. Everything Diva tells you *is* true: her lack of respect for convention, social norms and the laws of nature have been seen as traits that make her a utopian feminist character rather than an outright fantasy (see e.g., Björk 1998; Solomin 1998; Stenwall 2001; Österholm 2011; Österlund 1999). In *DIVA*, transforming into different fictional characters as well as physical shapes is emphasised and Diva narrates some of the transformations repeatedly, as if to convince both herself and the reader of them; thus, she reminds the reader of her role as a narrator. If readers then choose to be loyal to Diva, they have to believe her when she says she becomes a superheroine, sleeps for a thousand years or tells the truth. In fact, when they believe a fictional character, fantasy elements become part of the character creating herself as a subject rather than plot components, even if the fantasy is read literally and not as metaphor. Fantasy thus becomes a method to examine different ways of being in the world; therefore, it can be read as a part of a theoretical project. This means that the character is very much aware of the fact that reality and realism only allow for so much excess, but that the assumptions and conventions of reality and realism still can be questioned.

Diva's statement about making ideology raises further questions concerning what kind of a worldview is being put forward and how. What kind of assumptions about reality and values does the novel make and which are rejected? Above all, *how* is this done? In an essay on fiction, theory and fiction as theory, Teresa de Lauretis describes using novels in a seminar on feminist theory in order to shift focus from theory as an object of study to theory as living practice, to find 'figures of resistance inscribed in certain texts' (de Lauretis 2007: 253). Her central question concerns the paradox of being both defined by discourse and being a speaking subject. She quotes Shoshana Felman and asks: Is women's writing in feminist theory speaking the language of men or the silence of women? How can an author speak outside of language when language is what defines and dictates the concepts? (de Lauretis 2007: 242). De Lauretis finds the answer in reading and reading as a practice of language: readers are forced to confront the non-referentiality and otherness in the author's language. Much like Fagerholm does in *DIVA*, de Lauretis emphasises transformation and transfiguration,[3] both as tropes in novels and as a means of productive readings and misreadings (de Lauretis 2007: 259):

> [*Nightwood* by Djuna Barnes, *The Female Man* by Joanna Russ, *Orlando* by Virginia Woolf, *The Lesbian Body* by Monique Wittig, *Written on the Body* by Jeanette Winterson, *The Well of Loneliness* by Radclyffe Hall and *Beloved* by Toni Morrison] do not simply portray characters or *images* of women that do not accord to established conceptions of gender, sexuality, and race, but, while doing so, they also construct *figures*, at once rhetorical and narrative, that in resisting the logic of those conceptions, point to another cognition, a reading *other-wise* of gender, sexuality and race. This is the sense in which these texts 'do' feminist theory and are not simply feminist fiction. (de Lauretis 2007: 259)[4]

De Lauretis (2007: 252, 259) defines feminist theory as 'a controlled reflection and self-reflection, not on women in general but rather on feminism itself as a historico-political formation' and theory in general as 'elaboration of conceptual figures in language'. *DIVA* in turn 'does theory' by discussing and explaining phenomena and ideas such as gender, gender stereotypes, writing and fiction and mapping out its and the protagonist's knowledge of these phenomena, which do not necessarily coincide with the reader's knowledge. Even if postmodern fiction challenges uniform ideological and/or theoretical frameworks, it does not require or even assume a renunciation of theory and ideology as themes. *DIVA* examines a number of explanations, definitions and values, mostly in order to twist or reject them. Does this mean that something new is generated or defined through negation? In the following I shall discuss the novel as a starting point for theory and then examine how theory is expressed in *DIVA*.

---

3   de Lauretis (2007: 259) defines the trope of transfiguration as 'transformation and transit to another place', with an image viewed in a mirror as an example.
4   For discussion on de Lauretis, fiction and theory, see also Österholm 2012.

DIVA as a Barthesian Text

Earlier I set out to discuss how and why one might read a novel as part of a conceptual grid rather than its object. While Teresa de Lauretis provides a feminist incentive to do this, I will now turn to literary theorist Roland Barthes in order to approach similar questions from a literary position.

Through metafiction and various and unstable representations of gender, love, life and literature, *DIVA* encourages deconstruction as a method, a metalanguage on a different diegetic level than the plot, such as it is. Conversely, one could imagine theory as a magnifying glass, prism or a matrix which the enterprising scholar can use to unearth the innermost message of the novel. A third alternative would be to treat the novel as a practice, that is as a way to analyse the (im)possibility of philosophy through a character. The novel tests a feminist discussion: can the protagonist practise what the novel preaches? Is she the kind of multifaceted, constantly changing subject the novel seems to advocate? *DIVA*'s focus on the body, gender and subjectivity foregrounds a theoretical discussion in which the novel participates rather than merely illustrates.

Roland Barthes drives a wedge between a work and a text in his classical essay 'From Work to Text' from 1971, where he discusses the positions of the author, reader and critic in relation to fiction. The developments in, among others, Marxism, psychoanalysis and structuralism have destabilised the borders between scientific disciplines and thus the contours of generally accepted categories have been blurred (Barthes 1977: 155–156). Here Barthes calls for a new epistemological object beyond the traditional work as something an author has created by establishing meaning and intention. According to Barthes, *the work* exists in a chain of works, and it is a complete and closed vessel with a clear creator, who owns the legal rights to it. Above all, the work is a concrete object (Barthes 1977: 160). Literary scholar Michael Moriarty notes that institutions such as the literary marketplace and higher education provide a work with a classification, an interpretation and an authority of meaning, be it the author or another, originating work (Moriarty 1991: 143).

Barthes contrasts the work with what he calls *text* and approaches the text through concepts such as method, genre, sign, plurality, filiation, reading and pleasure. The text should not be seen as an object one can borrow at the library, but as a 'methodological field': '[T]he work can be held in the hand, the text is held in language, only exists in the movement of a discourse'. Barthes clarifies this by noting that the text cannot be contained on a bookshelf, since this discursive movement cuts across several works (Barthes 1977: 157). In practice, concerning *DIVA*, this implies a discursive crossing where what I consider the core questions of the novel meet theory: gender, the body and subjectivity. The text, Barthes writes, '*is experienced only in an activity of production*' (Barthes 1977: 157, emphasis in original) and according to Moriarty, this is an opposition between open and closed processes of production of meaning, as well as between practices of reading. He asks: 'Is this a theory of reading or a theory of modernity? Is it the institutions that turn a potential text into a work or are Works simply texts that invite this treatment?' His answer is, simply, both; he finds Barthes less concerned with exact definitions of the concepts than with the distinction between them (Moriarty 1991: 143–144).

DIVA also supports Barthes' view on the relationship between text and genre. He notes that a text relates to genres in the same frivolous manner it relates to library shelves: 'What constitutes the Text is, on the contrary (or precisely), its subversive force in respect of the old classifications' (Barthes 1977: 157). Even though it is self-evident that *DIVA* is a novel and not a philosophic treatise in disguise, the *DIVA* text is neither one nor the other and it does not have to be either. On a very concrete level *DIVA* has a fairly open relationship to genres and both critics and scholars have attempted to define the novel: *DIVA* is Diva and vice versa;[5] *DIVA* is a girls' book, a diary about a diary, a Bildungsroman or popular fiction (Kåreland 2004: 121; Malmio 2012: 72; Kurikka 2005: 59–60; Stenwall 2001: 205; Österlund 2005: 53). All these classifications can be correct even though the protagonist likes to claim the opposite and speaks against the novel as a genre and against its possibilities. Diva argues that she 'has no writing', she 'is not a collection of quotes', her 'relationship with literature=non-existent' (*DIVA* 1998: 117, 436; 55, 117, 436). Thus, the protagonist limits herself since her strongest attribute is her narrating voice, and by not engaging in writing and literature she disciplines it. However, her protest is aimed at literary convention rather than at her own narrative activity. Therefore, doing something unconventional means liberation rather than discipline. *DIVA*'s non-adherence to genre-related frameworks is a way to both illuminate traditional literary boundaries and to remind readers about the arbitrariness of genres. The point is that *all definitions are true at the same time*; for one to call *DIVA* a girls' book and nothing else, for example, would be to oversimplify it.

According to Barthes, a text approaches the limits of the pronounced, of the rational and readable. *DIVA*, with its occasionally trying idiom and uncertainty concerning reality/truth, certainly reaches these limits, yet Barthes notes that plurality does not mean content-related ambiguity, but that textual plurality consists of intertextual connections. This intertextuality should not be confused with a search for origins or determining a genealogy through a chain of works (Barthes 1977: 160). In other words, the individual connections in the intertextual universe produced through a multitude of references and quotes is less interesting than the function of the universe itself in creating *DIVA* as a text. Individual references in the novel come from more or less easily identifiable sources, but the whole they form is unique as a site for production of meaning.

Barthes also mentions reading and pleasure as important components in the production of a text. A work is consumed, since it is separated from other works by its quality, not the process of reading. According to Barthes, there is no structural difference between reading literary fiction and popular fiction. The text, in turn, is not read but created and written during reading.

---

5   '[T]he novel is not a novel *about* Diva and her life and family; the novel and the protagonist are the same' (Malmio 2012: 72).

Thus, Barthes wants to broaden the role of the reader and considers reading as play with the text, a game that demands the active presence of the reader rather than passive consumption. This demand for a more active, creative and *writerly* reading explains the lack of understanding many readers experience regarding 'difficult', experimental contemporary texts, films and paintings as Barthes suggests: '[T]o be bored means that one cannot produce the text, open it out, *set it going*' (1977: 162). To read and reread a work – he mentions Proust, Flaubert and Balzac – can be rewarding, but it is a pleasure of consumption that does not lead anywhere since the reader cannot rewrite them. To *read-write* involves a pleasure which is not completed, but keeps playing out in a network of language.

While a network might indicate connection, Moriarty notes that the Barthesian text scrambles communication as it disturbs the relationship between signifier and signified. Thus, it is productive; the reader is confronted with language as a disturbance rather than simply as a vessel and forced to take an active part in the production of meaning (Moriarty 1991: 145). Similarly, de Lauretis articulates the idea of the text and language:

> For reading entails a confrontation with an otherness in the text that escapes my ability to grasp it, retain it, hold it in my head (as Roland Barthes said, 'the work can be held in the hand, the text is held in language'). The failure of the interpretive moment shakes up the ground of my hermeneutic self-confidence and the certainty of my position as a subject. (de Lauretis 2007: 255, quoting Barthes 1977: 157)

Moriarty calls this jumbled interpretive moment 'a threat to one's self, one's settled pattern of subjectivity' (1991: 148), and it is precisely this unsettling of patterns that de Lauretis has used in her theory seminar. Similarly, *DIVA* with its uncertainty concerning reality/truth, metafiction and wide-ranging intertextuality implodes narrative conventions and encourages the reader to consider what these alternative figurations mean. Thus, reading *DIVA* as a Barthesian text connects the novel to the ideas it echoes rather than subjects it to them; consequently, a discursive node is formed.

So far I have discussed *DIVA* as both a Barthesian text and a novel. The former is an attempt to find a theoretical context for the novel without creating a hierarchy where, as a worst-case scenario, the novel is reduced or misrepresented in order to fit a theoretical framework. The latter, the references to the novel and its content, is a starting point for reading the novel as a theoretical text, as something other than artistic expression. In the following I will examine where and how this theory is produced in *DIVA* and describe it by discussing the narrator's attitude towards philosophy and theory.

DIVA as a Site of Theory

Diva's world is populated by individual characters as well as by ideas in the form of groups of people, such as humanists and women. Minor characters are frequently outlined through brief intertextual references rather than outright character description. For example, the uncle who is described with a half-finished master's dissertation and a Peter, Paul and Mary album, is placed both socially and culturally with an ironic twist.[6] Diva uses intertextuality and brand names for a similarly brief but effective description of the girls at school, the 'pk-birds' (short for *pussochkramfåglar* [kisses-and-hugs birds]), whose distinctly mainstream taste in music and literature (Swedish pop singer Paul Paljett,[7] Hans-Ulrich Horster's *Suchkind 312*[8]) defines them. As do their consumer choices: 'pk' is short for a Swedish 1970s' jeans brand, 'Puss och kram', which they all wear; they all use a certain lip gloss and wear similar hats.[9] The 'humanists' too are described with an ironic distance, and the group constitutes a way to place Diva's lover and substitute teacher Daniel in a social and class-related context. Daniel and his wife play tennis in order to, as Diva puts it, 'get away from the daily grind with its sorrows and joys' (*DIVA* 1998: 143).[10] They take turns earning a living in order to let the other focus on personal projects and sometimes they throw parties at which people quote Heidegger and Nietzsche between sips of red wine. They do not buy food in bulk, except for kibble for the cat, which is, naturally, called Madame Bovary: "'**I joke with it**" Daniel has said to me, **in high spirits**, "tell it **that Flaubert could not help it if Emma Bovary had not read her Marx**"' (*DIVA* 1998: 69).[11]

Diva says that Daniel speaks 'in high spirits', and does not call him 'corny', yet by quoting him she emphasises how very corny it is to say that you tell your pet jokes about Karl Marx. The humanists are described as pretentious and rather silly; they belong to a completely separate category compared

---

6   A US folk trio active in the 1960s; see http://peterpaulandmary.com. They mixed entertainment with a political message and their hits include *Leaving on a Jet Plane*, *If I Had a Hammer* and *Puff, the Magic Dragon*.

7   Paul Sahlin, popular mainly in Sweden during the 1970s. His hits include *Flyg min fjäril flyg* (Fly, my butterfly, fly), *Jag vill ge dig ett äventyr* (I want to give you an adventure) and *Guenerina*. *Paljett* is Swedish for sequin.

8   A melodramatic novel about lost love and a mother separated from her daughter during WWII. Popular fiction.

9   See Ojajärvi 2012 on the function of brand names in, among others, Fagerholm's first novel *Wonderful Women by the Water* (1997, *Wonderful Women by the Sea* in the US a year later) and, briefly, in *DIVA*. Ojajärvi (2012: 70) posits that while consumer goods are used to outline a historical period, they also reveal the capitalist context of the time of writing. In order for consumer goods and brand names to form a critique of capitalism, a text has to reflect other aspects of society besides consumer culture. In Fagerholm's novels specifically, Ojajärvi relates consumer choice to a performative subjectivity: 'In a way [the protagonist of *Wonderful Women by the Water*] is absorbed into a representation of consumer culture. It seems to restrict her identity, and she then repeats this position "performatively" – she fits herself into the position more individually, tries to repeat it "differently"' (Ojajärvi 2012: 61).

10 [K]oppla av från vardagen med dess sorger och dess glädjeämnen (*DIVA* 1998: 143).

11 '**Jag brukar skämta med den**' har Daniel sagt till mig, **spralligt**, 'säga till den, **att inte kunde Flaubert rå för att Emma Bovary inte hade läst sin Marx**' (*DIVA* 1998: 69). Bold type and capital letters according to the original unless otherwise noted.

to those in the ice hockey-centred world around school, where mothers, fathers, hockey-playing boys and admiring 'pk-birds' have strict roles and very little patience with intellectual endeavours. Diva herself continually comments on the world, yet she returns to the humanists' predilection for description and formulation:

> The definition of a humanist: it always has to figure out a clever wording. (*DIVA* 1998: 144)[12]

> Furthermore, it is characteristic for a humanist, **according to my mother**, that **it does not have its concepts in order**. It talks and talks and talks everything into bits and pieces, this is especially true for a humanist trying to give itself over to love. (*DIVA* 1998: 38; see also 183, 186, 271)[13]

Presumably humanists love too, but Diva accuses them of being distracted by their endlessly complicated concept of love and by speaking about it; she seems to say that it is only when they find themselves in silence, manage to stop the flurry of explanations, that they can really meet. That is why it is revealing that Daniel, who makes Diva experience both desire and love, is always lecturing: when he and Diva trudge through a forest, she is the one who is tormented by heat and insects, while he pontificates them all the way into a sleeping bag he jocularly has named 'the cradle of Western culture' (*DIVA* 1998: 12). Where the humanists in *DIVA* represent academically sanctioned and thus traditional knowledge, women and being a woman are given a different function. *DIVA* constructs a protagonist who emphatically is not like a girl or a woman is 'supposed' to be, but she still has a very traditional view of womanhood. The adulthood she imagines is a homogenous, predictable way of being in general and being a woman in particular. Diva envisions how she and a friend will run into each other as adults. They will kiss each other on the cheek, they will have 'become women enough to carry out a certain calculation correctly in [their] heads' (*DIVA* 1998: 403) and they will mime lines from a soap opera: 'The soap opera will be a code between us. Awareness that the conversation is not unique. But that will be exactly the point. It is the un-unique which will give us our security in our identities' (*DIVA* 1998: 403).[14]

At the same time Diva's mother tells her daughter to be new, fantastic and different. However, she changes her mind and says that Diva does not have to be anything in particular, but Diva herself likes to reiterate what makes her exceptional and extraordinary. Her mother's call for uniqueness

---

12 Definitionen på en humanist: den måste alltid tänka ut något fiffigare sätt att formulera sig (*DIVA* 1998: 144).
13 Karakteristiskt för en humanist är vidare, **enligt min mamma**, att **den inte har ordning på begreppen**. Den pratar och pratar och pratar sönder allt, detta gäller i synnerhet en humanist som försöker hänge sig åt kärleken (*DIVA* 1998: 38; see also 183, 186, 271).
14 Tvåloperan ska vara en kod mellan oss. Medvetenheten om att samtalet inte är unikt. Men det ska vara just det som är meningen. Just det o-unika ska ge oss vår trygghet i våra identiteter (*DIVA* 1998: 403).

stems from '[t]he horrible principle of duplication', that '[w]omen are kind of interchangeable', since the similarities between mothers and daughters are seen as more important than the differences (*DIVA* 1998: 184).[15] Diva's mother talks a lot about literature, like the poet she is. Diva should not read comics, she says; Diva should read Stendhal. The mother's poetry is as hard to understand as it is to write and her work frequently results in soliloquies on literary theory or the nature of art rather than poems, which are considered good when they finally do get written. Diva may not have much patience with her mother's literary commentary, but she describes her with sincerity and gives her ideas serious thought. The humanists are, as we have seen, described with a healthy dose of irony. Thus Diva's mother can be grouped with neither the humanists nor the hockey players' mothers; she is unique in the suburb of Värtbyhamn, much as Diva herself.

What *DIVA* does here, theoretically speaking, is discuss female voice by providing examples of literary strategies. In contrast to Diva's mother's struggle to find her literary voice and Diva's complete refusal of the same, Diva's brother Mellanbjörn (Middle-sized Bear, see Brothers Grimm's 'The Story of the Three Bears') successfully stages himself as a talented young *literatus*. He is a promising hockey player who also scores points with the adult world by writing and publishing poetry, reading Camus and Sartre and wrapping a scarf around his neck like a 'certain European thinker on a certain cover flap' (*DIVA* 1998: 79).[16] While Diva can let herself be impressed by her mother, the poetic project is so frustrating that it makes for an unreliable goal. The literary pursuits of Mellanbjörn are just as useless, since they are a pose and a representation of 'a certain kind of **young men, because they are eternal** [...] just as supreme as Mellanbjörn now is in his area' (*DIVA* 1998: 79). She does not see him as working towards an actual voice and yet he is granted exactly that.[17]

Much like the humanists, Mellanbjörn is described partly through references to individual authors/philosophers, but Diva also mentions his predilection for existentialism without delving into it; the point is not to say something about existentialism as such, but to parody certain types of young men with certain, befitting books in their pockets.[18] She refers to philosophy in a similar way: 'I turn to talking philosophy, like I sometimes do when I want to show that there is a brain too between these beautiful ears that are mine. So I say something apropos **Schopenhauer**' (*DIVA* 1998: 90).[19]

15 Den hemska duplikat-principen. Kvinnor är på sätt och vis utbytbara (*DIVA* 1998: 184).
16 [...] viss europeisk tänkare på en viss omslagsflik (*DIVA* 1998: 79).
17 [...] en viss sorts **ynglingar, för de är eviga**, [...] lika suveräna som Mellanbjörn nu är på sitt område (*DIVA* 1998: 79).
18 The majority of the authors mentioned in the novel are male and the only female philosopher Diva mentions is 'Hanna Arendt' (sic), to whom she refers as an author, p. 59. This lack – and misattribution – of female philosophers emphasizes the perceived lack of avenues for female voices.
19 Så att jag övergår till att prata filosofi, som jag ibland gör när jag vill visa att det finns en hjärna också mellan dessa vackra öron som är mina. Jag säger alltså något på tal om **Schopenhauer** (*DIVA* 1998: 90).

This appears to be a peculiar statement, since Diva has absolutely no problem enumerating everything that makes her fabulous, whether it is her intellect or her looks. However, in relation to her peers SannaMaria and Sebbe and the somewhat older Franses, whom her mother dismisses as an 'infatuation' (*DIVA* 1998: 59), Diva uses very un-teenage means to be herself: she refers to Schopenhauer and says he thought that empathy would save humanity, but really only got along with his little green dog (*DIVA* 1998: 90, 181, 274). Upon which whomever Diva is speaking to – or Diva herself – usually says that the green dog is a misprint, that she is misquoting and that she is an idiot. However, through (deliberately) misquoting she is also performing a philosophical conversation incorrectly. Thus, philosophy becomes something other than a way for Diva to prove that she is both smart and beautiful. She herself is rather convinced of the fact and the misquoting underlines how unsuccessful the strategy is. Instead philosophical discourse functions as a reversed domination technique[20] and thus as feminist practice.

The Novel as Theory – From How to Why

One of the phrases Diva uses the most is *a priori*, a philosophical term that describes knowledge independent of experience. She uses the phrase so often and so unconventionally that it changes from something a precocious teen might say to show off to something more meaningful:

> Franses draws [a picture of] THE HUNGER, it exists, if it does not exist anywhere else it now exists in Östra läroverket [Diva's school]. And a priori. (*DIVA* 1998: 97)[21]

> [A]s if sideburns looked good a priori. Sideburns do not look good a priori. (*DIVA* 1998: 133)[22]

> Nor will I ever write another book. A priori. (*DIVA* 1998: 252)[23]

> It is something about the hockey, or driving school, I do not know. On the whole I know nothing about this and that is a priori now. (*DIVA* 1998: 393)[24]

This use of *a priori*, like the failed philosophical conversation above, creates a destabilising humour, since the phrase connotes a philosophical practice – reasoning based on abstract concepts – that traditionally has been read as particularly male. By using unconventional grammar and applying the

---

20 See Berit Ås (1978, 2004) on master suppression techniques.
21 Franses tecknar HUNGERN, den finns, om den inte finns någon annanstans finns den nu i Östra läroverket./Och a priori (*DIVA* 1998: 97).
22 [S]om om det var snyggt med polisonger a priori. Det är inte snyggt med polisonger a priori (*DIVA* 1998: 133).
23 Jag kommer aldrig att skriva någon annan bok heller. A priori (*DIVA* 1998: 252).
24 Det är något med hockeyn, eller med trafikskolan, jag vet inte. Jag vet i stort sett ingenting angående detta och det är a priori nu (*DIVA* 1998: 393).

phrase to something slightly ridiculous like the attractiveness of sideburns, Diva highlights this tradition and subverts it. In other words, *DIVA* does theoretical work on a linguistic as well as a thematic level.

A priori moves from the trivial to the considerably more fundamental: THE HUNGER describes Diva's boundless and unconventional appetite for food and sex as well as the humanists' lack of the unruly and unpredictable in life. Diva's non-writing and her unwillingness to adapt is not defiance or lack of ambition and talent, but rather an ideological view of social and cultural conventions and the choices they allow.

Diva and *DIVA* operate largely in negations. The novel and its protagonist deconstruct traditional representations: it is slightly silly to be a humanist, futile to be an author and limiting to be a woman. However, it is good to be Diva. Unfortunately, this is a passing state. Diva says '**It never was anything else**. That is also a definition of adulthood. You figure that out, the paltry nothingness of everything' (*DIVA* 1998: 386).[25] With one of her childhood cohorts she laughs at 'the stupidity of childhood' (*DIVA* 1998: 442).[26] *DIVA* offers precious little in the way of comfort, in both senses of the word, and plenty of the scrambled interpretive moments both de Lauretis and Moriarty, by way of Barthes, call for in a text.

So far I have discussed *how* a novel can be read as a theoretical text, but the question of *why* one should do so remains. 'Is [women's writing] speaking the language of men or the silence of women?' de Lauretis asks and makes an extensive argument about language, theory and silence. Although her discussion is beyond the scope of this article, it serves as a reminder of how voice and narrative agency work in fiction (de Lauretis 2007: 242). My point is that *DIVA* stages theoretical arguments through the protagonist's relentless narration and commentary in layer after layer of time and experience.

Reading a text is, then, irrevocably reading *other-wise*, as de Lauretis put it (de Lauretis 2007: 259). Barthes provides another answer as to why one would read a novel as a theoretical text when he points out that the discourse on text happens in a social space, that the text in fact *is* a social space (Barthes 1977: 164). Thus, it can be argued that fiction cannot be excluded from discourse and theoretical inquiry. It is rewarding – a Barthesian pleasure – to read a novel parallel with relevant philosophical texts without placing them in different categories, not the least because they provide alternative approaches to the same questions. While the experiencing, first-person 13-year-old narrator in *DIVA* may not be a serious thinker as such, her commentary opens for meta-inquiry since she is a narrative choice made by an underlying narrating voice. The combined perspectives, as well as wide-ranging intertextuality and genre slippage, constitute a metafictive whole which, as has been shown, disturb traditional literary expectations.[27]

25 **Det var aldrig något annat.** Det är också en definition på vuxenhet. Man kommer underfund med det, alltings futtiga intighet (*DIVA* 1998: 386).
26 [...] barndoms dumhet (*DIVA* 1998: 442).
27 See Haasjoki 2012 and Kurikka 2005 for further discussion of narrative levels in *DIVA*.

This is where Barthes involves the reader, who creates the Barthesian text as a methodological field. *DIVA*'s thematic emphases in combination with its postmodern narrative excesses force the reader to re-evaluate the interpretive framework and thus connect to theoretical discourse.

References

Primary Sources

Fagerholm, Monika 1997: *Wonderful Women by the Water*. Transl. Joan Tate. Harvill Press, London.
Fagerholm, Monika 1998: *Diva. En uppväxts egna alfabet med docklaboratorium (en bonusberättelse ur framtiden)*. [DIVA. The Alphabet of Adolescence with a Laboratory of Dolls (A Bonus Tale from the Future)] Söderströms, Helsingfors.

Secondary Sources

Barthes, Roland 1977: From Work to Text. In *Image/Music/Text*. Ed. S. Heath. Fontana Press, London, 155–164. Originally published as 'De l'œuvre au texte', *Revue d'esthitique* 3/1971.
Björk, Nina 1998: Mitt val. [My Choice] – *Dagens Nyheter* 6.12.1998.
Haasjoki, Pauliina 2012: *Häilyvyyden liittolaiset. Kerronnan ja seksuaalisuuden ambivalenssit*. [Allies in Wavering. The Ambivalences of Narrative and Sexuality] Turun yliopiston julkaisuja, Annales Universitatis Turkuensis *Sarja – Ser. C Osa – Tom. 343*, Scripta lingua Fennica edita. Turun yliopisto, Turku.
Kurikka, Kaisa 2005: Tytöksi-tulemisen tilat. Monika Fagerholmin *Diva* utopistisena tekstinä. [The Spaces of Becoming-Girl. Monika Fagerholm's *Diva* as a Utopian Text] In *PoMon tila. Kirjoituksia kirjallisuuden postmodernismista*. [The Space of PoMo. Texts on Postmodern Literature] Eds. Anna Helle and Katriina Kajannes. Jyväskylän ylioppilaskunnan julkaisusarja 74. Kampus Kustannus, Jyväskylä, 56–72.
Kåreland, Lena 2004: Flickbokens nya kläder. Om Monika Fagerholms *Diva*. [The New Clothes of Girls' Books] In *Omklädningsrum. Könsöverskridanden och rollbyten från Tintomara till Tant Blomma*. [Changing Rooms. Gender Transgressions and Role Changes from Tintomara to Tant Blomma] Eds. Eva Heggestad and Anna Williams. Studentlitteratur, Lund, 121–138.
Lauretis, Teresa de 2007: *Figures of Resistance. Essays in Feminist Theory*. Ed. Patricia White. University of Illinois Press, Urbana & Chicago.
Malmio, Kristina 2012: Phoenix-Marvel Girl in the Age of *fin de siècle*. Popular Culture as a Vehicle to Postmodernism in *Diva* by Finland-Swedish author Monika Fagerholm. In *Nodes of Contemporary Finnish Literature*. Ed. Leena Kirstinä. Studia Fennica Litteraria 6. Finnish Literature Society, Helsinki, 72–95.
Moriarty, Michael 1991: *Roland Barthes*. Polity Press, Cambridge.
Ojajärvi, Jussi 2012: 'Benson & Hedges -sytyttimellä.' Kulutustavaroiden ja tavaramerkkikerronnan ulottuvuuksia vuosituhannen vaihteen suomalaisessa romaanissa. ['With a Benson & Hedges Lighter.' Perspectives on Consumerism and Consumer Goods in the Turn of the Century Finnish Novels] – *Kirjallisuudentutkimuksen aikakausilehti Avain* 2/2012, 52–75.

Solomin, Nina 1998: Ett livgivande storverk. [A Life-Giving Magnum Opus] – *Svenska Dagbladet* 13.12.1998.
Stenwall, Åsa 2001: *Portföljen i skogen. Kvinnor och modernitet i det sena 1900-talets finlandssvenska litteratur.* [The Briefcase in the Woods. Women and Modernity in Late 20th Century Finland-Swedish Literature] Schildts, Helsingfors.
Ås, Berit 1978: *Hersketeknikker.* [Master Suppression Techniques] – *Kjerringråd* 3/1978.
Ås, Berit 2004: The Five Master Suppression Techniques. In *Women In White. The European Outlook.* Ed. Birgitta Evengård. Stockholm City Council, Stockholm, 78–83.
Österholm, Maria Margareta 2010: *Ett slags kaos. Skeva flickor i svenskspråkig prosa från 1980 till 2005.* [A Kind of Chaos. Queer Girls in Swedish and Finland-Swedish Literature from 1980 to 2005] Lic. Diss., Uppsala University, Uppsala.
Österholm, Maria Margareta 2012: *Ett flicklaboratorium i valda bitar. Skeva flickor i svenskspråkig prosa från 1980 till 2005.* [A Girl Laboratory in Chosen Parts. Queer Girls in Swedish and Finland-Swedish Literature from 1980 to 2005] Rosenlarv förlag, Stockholm.
Österlund, Maria 2005: *Förklädda flickor. Könsöverskridning i 1980-talets svenska ungdomsroman.* [Girls in Disguise. Gender Transgression in Swedish Young Adult Fiction from the 1980s] Åbo Akademis förlag, Åbo.

Kristina Malmio

A Portrait of the Technological Sublime
DIVA and the History of the Digital Revolution

In a 1995 interview in a major Swedish daily newspaper following the publication of her debut novel, *Underbara kvinnor vid vatten* (1994; transl. 1997 by Joan Tate, *Wonderful Women by the Water*), Monika Fagerholm presented her views on the significant, yet intangible change that had taken place in Finland in a very short time, between the fall of the Soviet Union in 1991 and Finland's accession to European Union in 1995. For her, the most obvious examples of the new developments were to be found in Finnish culture in a wide sense: on Finnish television, self-assured, urbane, and daring people had replaced the shy and timid people that previously had exemplified the Finnish character. Besides this new mentality, the digitalisation had become so prevalent that, she argued, the ongoing 1990s, *nittitalet*, should be renamed *internettitalet*, or 'Internet decade' (Werkelid 1995).

Three years later, Fagerholm published *DIVA*, a novel with the intriguing subtitle: *En uppväxts egna alfabet med docklaboratorium (en bonusberättelse ur framtiden)* [The Alphabet of Adolescence with a Laboratory of Dolls (A Bonus Tale from the Future)]. Already the subtitle expresses an excess of information, a seemingly arbitrary and illogical flow of associations and allusions consisting of words, clichés, phrases and citations. The novel is primarily written in present tense, but even the past and the future are there as the protagonist moves back and forth freely between different times and story levels. The protagonist and storyteller Diva describes her own discourse as 'babbling' and herself as a mathematical genius, very beautiful and always hungry.[1] In a highly self-reflexive manner the novel thematizes subjectivity, identity, sexuality, femininity, truth versus fantasy and reality versus fiction; all these topics were prevalent in Finnish literature in the 1990s (see Sevänen 2013; Ojajärvi 2006: 7–20; Kurikka 2008).

The fragmented, mobile and multivalent identity of the protagonist of the novel, its heavy intertextuality referencing high and low culture and its consequent use of parody and irony aroused much interest among critics at the time it was published (Stenwall 2001: 229–234). It was called a masterpiece and a disappointment, a modern classic and an interesting failure (Kåreland

---

[1] All translations of *DIVA* from Swedish to English are mine.

2004: 122; Sundström 2004; Beckman 1998); furthermore, the protagonist was hailed as something not seen before: an extraordinary girl character in the history of the novel (see e.g., Möller 1998). Two literary models were identified as particularily important for *DIVA*, namely J.D. Salinger's *The Catcher in the Rye* (1951) and girls' books; both clues were promoted by the novel itself. The postmodern context of the novel was also emphasized (see e.g., Stenwall 2001: 221).² The reviewer Kaj Hedman (1998) pointed out that many of the features and literary strategies used by Fagerholm had already been employed in contemporary postmodern culture, especially in international and national literature and film. Hedman wrote: 'It [*DIVA*] can be apprehended as up to date, written after a favourite recipe. It is, however, not that simple. Rather one thinks that Monika Fagerholm in a skilful manner makes use of an up to date phenomenon for her own purposes'.³ On the whole, critics and scholars were united in their judgment that such a huge and experimental novel about a thirteen-year-old girl had never appeared before in Finland-Swedish, Finnish or Swedish literature.

What is most striking about this novel is the manifold excess and multiplicity, which it exhibits on a structural, discursive as well as thematic level. Words like 'stocktaking', 'machine' and 'a total recall' have been used when scholars describe the curious structure, variety of discourses and vast knowledge of *DIVA* and its protagonist (Haasjoki 2012: 109, 127–128; Malmio 2012).

What have not yet been explored are the structural and visual features Fagerholm's novel has in common with digital culture and the Internet. In my article I interpret *DIVA* as an expression of 'digital epistemology', a discourse where the digital marks its presence without necessarily being explicitly uttered (Ingvarsson 2015: 47) and provides a new explanation of the novel. Central to digital epistemology is the encyclopedic nature of the works of art created (Ingvarsson 2015: 47–49). They are organised according to an associative practice, a mosaique-like pattern instead of a linear logic and order (Ingvarsson 2015: 56). I argue, that the diversity and the structure of the novel becomes fully explained only after an analysis of *DIVA* in the context of digital culture and its development, a method that has its origin in Fagerholm's earlier discussion of the 'internetisation' of Western culture. Likewise, an analysis of this highly experimental novel shows the influence of new media on literature. Already Marxist scholar Fredric Jameson in his analysis of postmodern culture advances the idea of the relation of postmodernism to the 'Third Machine Age' and the development of new media during the era of global capitalism. He argues that computers, machines of reproduction, make new kinds of demands for aesthetic reproduction (Jameson 1991: 36–37). Furthermore, *DIVA* also casts light on Nordic society and culture in an age characterised by globalisation and new communication technology. The questions posed here are, then, why

---

2   In an interview by Marie Peterson in 2005, Fagerholm listed her literary 'household gods' as the following: Inger Edelfeldt, Kerstin Ekman, Jenny Diski, Janet Frame, Edmund White, and Marcel Proust.

3   The translation from Swedish to English is mine.

does Fagerholm use a networklike, multisequential structure and why does she situate her novel at the 1970s in Finland? How does it enter into a dialogue with the developments of digital culture in Finland and the Nordic countries?

Reading the novel in relation to digital epistemology and the development of Internetisation from the 1970s to the 1990s opens a slightly less optimistic interpretation of the novel than those presented in earlier research. *DIVA* has been interpreted as an utopian, feministic and queer novel, all about transgression of limits and boundaries connected to hegemonic discourses on gender, sexuality and girlhood (see e.g., Stenwall 2001; Kurikka 2005; Kåreland 2004). What I argue, however, is that the novel and its female, thirteen-year-old protagonist's hailed freedom from limits and transgressive potential might actually be a portrayal of a search engine and connected to the 1990s' developments of networks as the prevalent mode of communication and knowledge in the global era. As such, the novel depicts an 'early' phase in media history, as the development of the digital has in the 21st century entered a new period. Digitalisation is no longer presented in terms of machines or networks, but rather as 'ubiquitous computing' or for example mites, small particles that are now basically present everywhere in daily life, Jonas Ingvarsson argues (Ingvarsson 2015: 49). So this will be as much an interpretation of *DIVA* as an expression of digital epistemology as it is a depiction of the presence of the history of the Internet in a novel, which by the time it was published allowed a glimpse of what Jameson calls a 'postmodern or technological sublime', meaning 'a whole new postmodern space in emergence around us', a space created by new technology and a present-day multinational capitalism (Jameson 1991: 37).

Discoursive and Narrative excess in DIVA

Structural, discursive and thematic excess and diversity are indeed at the heart of *DIVA*. In the protagonist Diva's universe, nothing exists as 'neither/nor', but always 'both/and', as literary scholar Åsa Stenwall (2001: 208) has remarked. Already the subtitle – 'The Alphabet of Adolescence with a Laboratory of Dolls (A Bonus Tale from the Future)' – combines several heterogenic elements in a curious and highly personal style: 'Diva', the name of a praised and spoilt (female) artist; a story about the letters and growing up; scientific experiments with objects used for children's games and dolls that eventually look like human beings but are lifeless products. Furthermore, the novel also introduces itself as 'A Bonus Tale from the Future', a utopian extra story not yet seen, but about to come, a tale that includes an element of science fiction. The combinations are unexpected, abundant, all but conventional and at times even parodic. Already in the subtitle, it is obvious, then, that difference is not only exhibited but also thematized and even played with. Similarily, the novel is ambivalent in its production of discursive and narrative excess and freedom: it not only hails excess, difference and diversity, but even thematizes and parodies the same.

In the continuation, the reader is confronted with not one or two, but altogether five 'prologues', titled, in an ironic and self-reflexive manner as 'The Prologues', and called as follows: 'Phoenix-Marvel Girl'; 'Klafs[4] (en evig dag, kärleken föds)' [Klafs (An Eternal day, Love is Born)]; 'Dagboken' [The Diary]; 'Jag och mina vänner' [Me and My Friends] and 'Lilla döden'[The Small Death]. The names of the prologues evoke American popular culture, teen romances, adolescent girls' fiction, diaries and sexuality, as 'The Small Death' is an allusion to an orgasm. Similarly, wide-ranging are the novel's section titles, which represent the domains of philosophy, science fiction and experimental music, among others.

All in all, the novel embraces the discourses of popular culture, consumerism, teenagers, diaries, fairytales, philosophy and literature. *DIVA*'s abundance creates a protagonist whose range of knowledge obviously is beyond that of an average thirteen-year-old school girl, a feature that also raises questions about the actual identity of the protagonist. The richness and the diversity of the multiple discourses and the literary strategies used, like parody, in imitating and transforming these discourses, combined with a continuous repetition of words, phrases and thoughts already used in the story, create a textual 'web' typical of Fagerholm. This is a literary strategy she used already in her novel *Wonderful Women by the Water* (1994) and develops in her novels, *Den amerikanska flickan* [2005, transl. *The American Girl*, 2009] and *Glitterscenen och flickan hon går i dansen med röda gullband* (2009, transl. *The Glitter Scene*, 2010).

DIVA as an 'Imprint' of Digital Culture

The novel's dust cover, designed by Maria Appelberg, gives the first hint of *DIVA*'s relation to digital culture. It is a stylized portrait of a young girl laughing; her image is created with small dots in different colours. Only when the small dots and their interrelation are apprehended as a whole does the portrait of the protagonist emerge. Clearly, the cover image represents and imitates the fragmentary structure of the novel where all of the diverse parts and elements together create a network of pieces that form Diva, the protagonist, as well as *DIVA*, the novel. However, the small dots can also be read as pixels or as bytes – binary digits – that create digital 'data in the form of discrete elements' (Gere 2002: 11).

Although the recent digitalisation of culture has created many new forms of texts, there has always been so called 'ergodic', or interactive, literature that possessed similar features to today's digital texts (see e.g., Aarseth 1997; Svedjedal 2000: 56). As the scholar Espen J. Aarseth explains in his seminal work on ergodic literature:[5] 'Cybertext is not a "new", "revolutionary" form of text, with capacities only made possible through the invention of the

---

4 A word that depicts the sound of a pair of rubber boots against the sidewalk, in the rain.
5 Ergodic literature is by definition interactive and hypertext is a type of digital ergodic text (Aarseth 1997: 12).

digital computer. Neither is it a radical break with old-fashioned textuality, although it would be easy to make it appear so' (Aarseth 1997: 18). Rather, he argues, it is a 'broad textual media category' developed to describe the communication strategies of dynamic texts created both inside and outside the digital world (Aarseth 1997: 5). A cybertext is 'a machine for the production of variety of expression' and when people read from it, they are 'constantly reminded of inaccessible strategies and paths not taken, voices not heard' (Aarseth 1997: 3; see even Ryan 2004: 329).

Literary sociologist Johan Svedjedal (2000: 56) uses the concept 'hypertext' to describe the dynamic, multisequential texts that can be found in both digital media and literature on the Internet as well as in bound books.[6] He describes the characteristics of digital hypertexts in a similar manner to Aarseth and concludes: 'They may be called non-linear, multilinear, nonsequential, multisequential or multicursal, the point always being that traditional literary works are nearly always linear or monosequential' (Svedjedal 2000: 60). While monosequential texts are meant to be read from beginning to an end, multisequential texts consist of parts, each one monosequential but intended to be read in different sequences each time, sometimes even in random order (Svedjedal 2000: 54–55). The ideas and concepts of the literary theorist and linguist Roland Barthes have been adopted by hypertheorists; consequently, hypertexts have been seen as 'writerly' texts, intertextual by their very nature and linked to other texts in a vast web of connections (Koskimaa 1999: 117; see also Lahdenperä in this volume). Works of this kind have been described as open, fluid and interactive (Svedjedal 2000: 60).[7]

Although an e-book version now exists, *DIVA* is not a digital work, but was originally written and published in codex format. It does not, accordingly, offer its reader the choices offered by a *digital* hypertext, which can be read in several different sequences (Koskimaa 1999: 117; Ryan 2004: 329; Page and Thomas 2011: 9–10). Nevertheless, on several points, it 'behaves' like a hypertext. *DIVA* is profoundly intertextual as well as fluid. It is a writerly text and multisequential. Scholars have called attention to this even if they do not use the term in their descriptions. As literary scholar Kaisa Kurikka has noted, the narration of *DIVA* consists entirely of an 'indefinite, displaced middle'. One cannot draw a straight line through the novel's narration; rather, one can enter it at any point. Aside from the indicative page numbers and table of contents, the novel provides no clear beginning or end (Kurikka 2005: 59). Likewise, literary scholar Pauliina Haasjoki (2012: 127–128, 19) has shown in her analysis that the text, in a variety of ways, invites the reader to read not only horizontally (i.e., in the direction of the plot, knowledge and control), but also vertically (toward openness and ambivalence).

---

6   The use of terms varies in the books written about digital culture and literature. At times cybertext and hypertext seems to be used as synonymously, e.g., Aarseth 1997; Eskelinen 1999. According to David Bell (2009: 32), cyberspace and cyberculture were the terms used in the 1990s.

7   The difference between hypertexts and 'usual', monosequential literature is, as both Aarseth and Svedjedal emphasize, of course a question of level and quality, not of an ontological difference. See e.g., Svedjedal 2000: 84.

Other features of the novel that contribute to the multisequentiality of its structure and signal its hypertextual qualities are the visual markers and the spacing. The novel is divided into 'units of reading' that are separated from each other spatially. The following is the final passage from the chapter titled '**Franses at the edge of her fifth life** (sixth, seventh, eighth?)',[8] which is comprised of eleven units of reading:

'If you don't tell me anything, Franses, then I will have to tell you.'
I go to bed, crawl deep into the **cradle of Western culture**, with my dog, with Texye. If you don't tell me anything, Franses, I will tell.
This is what I tell.
The laboratory of dolls, the beginning of a tale from the future, a history forever buried within it, even though it has not yet happened. (*DIVA* 1998: 226)[9]

In this chapter, Diva sits at the kitchen table at her friend Franses' house doing her homework, when Franses arrives, sad and hostile, but she does not want to tell Diva what bothers her. The chapter, altogether five pages, consists of eleven minor passages – units of reading – that include Diva's philosophical reasoning and her fantasies, her perceptions and descriptions of what she and Franses do, their dialogue and several leaps in time and place. In the passage cited above, Diva talks to Franses (or, alternatively, is having an inner monologue). However, the units of reading that make up the chapter and all the other chapters as well, do not follow one another according to temporal, chronological structure, but are ordered in the same 'illogical' – that is, multisequential – way. This creates a story in which the reader follows the many paths of the protagonist and the story, so that even though the novel is read from beginning to end, the reader has the impression that these multiple paths exist multisequentially and side by side. Kurikka uses *rhizome*, a term borrowed from Gilles Deleuze and Félix Guattari, to describe the novel's structure. A rhizome forms a root system and creates unexpected meetings, bringing seemingly different elements together (Kurikka 2005: 61, 70; see also Österholm 2012: 84). The concept clearly depicts a central quality of Fagerholm's novel, the way in which the different units of reading are connected to each other in multiple ways and with no strict order.

Interestingly, the word *rhizome* also frequently occurs in the current discourse of digital culture and has been used by many scholars to describe the Internet (Gere 2002: 158–159).[10] The multisequential structure of

8 **Franses på randen av sitt femte liv (sitt sjätte, sjunde, åttonde?).** (*DIVA* 1998: 222).
9 Om du inte berättar något för mig, Franses, så får jag lov att berätta för dig./Jag går i säng, kryper djupt ner **i den västerländska kulturens vagga**, med hunden min, med Texye. Om du inte berättar något för mig, Franses, så ska jag berätta./Detta är vad jag berättar./**Docklaboratoriet**, början på en historia ur framtiden, en historia för evigt nerlagd i den, fast den inte än har hänt (*DIVA* 1998: 226).
10 Ingvarsson also points out that certain theories, such as posthumanism (e.g., Deleuze and Guattari, my remark) not only function as tools useful to analyse digital epistemology, but are actually also used as expressions of the same (Ingvarsson 2015: 48).

the novel, then, is similar to that of hypertexts. The use of the bold type enhances this impression. In a digital text, such as one published on the Internet, different pages of a site are connected to each other by links and anchors. An anchor is the spot where the link attaches, that is, at the beginning or the end-point of the link and is marked with a different colour and/or underlined (Koskimaa 1999: 117). The anchor makes it possible for the reader to acknowledge the existence of the link.

In *DIVA,* the words and sentences appearing in bold indicate that they exist on another level than the rest of the text. **'The laboratory of dolls'** in the passage above is but one of many citations frequently presented in bold type. The repetition and the bold type are, of course, used for emphasis. Furthermore, the recurring, bolded words can also be read as *a picture* of the possibility to link to somewhere else in the text and to enter another unit of reading. The recited words, sentences and citations in bold type in *DIVA*, then, function similarly to anchors and links in a digital text. They are the places where the multisequential structure of the novel opens up, as they steer the reader to another place in the novel's textual 'web'. If the reader views the words and meanings written in bold type as links and anchors, he or she sees that the pages in *DIVA* visually resemble pages on the Internet, where words are emphasized in order to signal their connection to other pages. The visual effect in *DIVA* is enhanced by the fact that some of the words in bold type that are continuously recited in the novel also occur as the headlines for the reading units that make up Diva's storytelling.

The recurrent words and sentences in bold type function as if they were Diva's own search words. The random logic of many of the words and citations in bold type are similar to the outcomes of a search engine. One does get results containing the words given the search engine, but they often occur in contexts and utterances unexpected and odd and they may be combined in strange ways, but they are always visually marked. What is more, the novel also demonstrates its ability to combine text, sound and pictures and shows a similar affinity for capital letters and abbreviations as digital culture does (Gere 2002: 8). Besides the bold type, the novel also includes other typographic and visual elements, such as vignettes of a small dog (possibly a picture or a symbol of Franses' dog Texye) at the beginning of chapters; words in all capital letters and words representing sounds, such as **'däpp'**, 'klafs', 'rasp', 'BANG BANG, 'OINK OINK OINK OINK' and 'GAP'.

Consequently, if Diva is apprehended not as a thirteen-year-old girl, but rather as a cybertext – 'a machine for the production of variety of expression' (Aarseth 1997: 3) – as well as a humorous, humanoid portrayal of the Internet, it is no longer astonishing that the protagonist is able to know all the facts and discourses she does, nor that she recites words and sentences. It explains the novel's network-like structure as well as its extensive use of bold type. This kind of reading of *DIVA* as an 'imprint' of digital culture and an expression of the development of new media at the time of its publication (see also Ingvarsson 2015: 47) can also be streched to the depictions of the protagonist, and time and place in the novel:

'Do not ever become such a tomboy,' my mom tells me. [...] 'One can also exist in another way', she continues. 'In several other ways. There are hundreds of ways to be, one can be as one likes. **'Surprise me'**, said Jean Cocteau to one of his friends, the name of whom I never pronounce right so it is no use to try. But it is a good motto'.

'That is how I want you to be for me, Diva. **New. Fantastic. Different**'. (*DIVA* 1998: 33)[11]

Diva and *DIVA* have in common the ambition to be extraordinary and the novel was, at the time of its publication, received as such. The declaration 'New. Fantastic. Different' has been interpreted as a testimony of a queer identity, a female utopian wish and a utopian portrayal of being a girl (Stenwall 2001; Österholm 2012; Haasjoki 2012; Kurikka 2005). On the other hand, the words have also been interpreted as an advertisement; consequently, they can be seen as a declaration promoting consumerism within the current global capitalism. Like a commodity *DIVA* and Diva must live up to the ever-changing demands of the consumer (Ojajärvi 2012: 62).

However, Diva's mother's statement offers yet another interpretation in line with my argument. The novel is a story about a girl growing up. There are two timelines to take into account in discussing Fagerholm's novel: that in which the novel is set, the 1970s and the time the novel is published in the late 1990s. The novel portrays an adolescent in the 1970s, which parallels what the Internet was at that time. The decade has been described as a crucial time for the development of the World Wide Web in the form it is known today, starting with e-mail and role-playing games through the use of Multi-User Domains (MUDs) (see Gere 2002: 145–146; Creeber and Martin 2009: 170–178; Castells 2001: 9–35). During the 1990s, the Internet grew rapidly worldwide and the Nordic region saw the breakthrough of home multimedia personal computers for Internet surfing (Svedjedal 2000: 24–25; Lindblom 2009).

The development of digital culture has had immense consequences for an understanding of time, space and identity and created a new world of communication (see e.g., Creeber and Martin 2009: 5; Castells 2001: 3). One could state, then, evoking the words of Diva's mother, that societal apprehension of time, space, identity and communication have, due to digital media and the Internet, become new, fantastic – in its senses of both 'strange' and 'incredible' – and different. In this expansive phase of its development, the growth in the popularity and significance of the Internet in the Nordic region may be described in terms similar to the protagonist of Fagerholm's novel: the one you thought did not exist, always hungry, filled with desire for everything in the world (*DIVA* 1998: 11, 25). This is

---

11 Bli aldrig en sådan där pojkflicka, säger min mamma till mig. [...] Man kan också vara på ett annat sätt, fortsätter min mamma. På flera andra sätt. Det finns hundra sätt att vara på, man kan vara som man vill. **'Överraska mig'**, sa Jean Cocteau till en av sina vänner vars namn jag aldrig uttalar rätt så det är onödigt att försöka. Men det är en bra devis./Så vill jag att du ska vara för mig, Diva. **Ny. Fantastisk. Annorlunda** (*DIVA* 1998: 33).

an explanation also in line with the reading of Diva's mother declaration as an incitement to consumerism (Ojajärvi 2012). As he describes the central features of postmodernism, among others its 'new depthlessness' and 'a whole new type of emotional ground tone', Jameson concludes that all these phenomena have a deep relationship to 'a whole new technology, which is itself a figure for a whole new world economic system' (Jameson 1991: 6).

A Meeting Point of Two Cultures

The emergence of new technology and new media has always influenced literary production and book publishing and produced novel forms of communication, textual structures, and consequently new readers. Scholars argue that ergodic hyperworks demand a new reading strategy, a 'hyperliterary competence' and a reader who is more active and participatory than previously. 'The defining characteristics of this hyperliterary competence does not have so much to do with new ways of interpretation as with different ways of navigating texts', Svedjedal explains (2000: 89; see also, Aarseth 1997: 20). He argues that due to digitisation older reading strategies, named by Rolf Engelsing as intensive and extensive reading, will be followed by 'zap reading' enacted by an impatient reader 'always on the move towards somewhere else in the textual universe' (Svedjedal 2000: 89–90).

Reading *DIVA* certainly stresses the reader's ability to navigate. Åsa Stenwall (2001: 238) asks if the novel actually demands a new, different kind of readiness of its reader, as it to an 'extreme degree' activates the reader to find patterns and meanings under the mass of words. In conclusion, she declares that *DIVA* does not demand a new kind of reading, but, rather, a revolution (Stenwall 2001: 241; see also, Österlund in this volume). I would like to modify her argument: *DIVA* not only demands, but also produces and exemplifies a new kind of reading as its multisequential structure produces effects like that of the hypertextual zap reading. The novel's portrayal of the protagonist's state of mind is akin to a 'zap': the protagonist surfs from one thought, domain, discourse and piece of information to another, freely, and without boundaries, like a person on the Internet. The prophecy of the subtitle of *DIVA* – A Bonus Tale from the Future – might also be a forecast of the novel's (maybe young female) readers of the 21st century, (more) familiar with zap reading than the readers who first struggled with it the 1990s.

Literature has had its own tradition of multisequential texts, namely avant-garde literature, which has in many ways questioned and broadened the limits of literary expression and has offered its own hypertexts long before the Internet existed (see e.g., Koskimaa 1999: 121–122; Gere 2002: 87–91). These texts have, Svedjedal (2000: 88) concludes, 'seldom been more than freak experiments, thrusts at the borders of what book format offers', but the situation has altered during the last thirty to forty years. Many of the strategies literary scholar Brian McHale has highlighted as typical of postmodern texts already have become everyday conventions in digital hypertexts (Eskelinen 1999: 135).

DIVA is, then, a meeting point of two cultures, literary and digital. It belongs to a postmodern literary trend, but it also imitates and transforms the multisequential structure and visual elements of the new media that came of age in the 1990s. There are many possible forms of intermediality;[12] for example, the illusion of the presence of another type of media can in literature be created by imitating the structure of the other media. The structural and visual features that *DIVA* has in common with the Internet can, then, be seen as forms of intermediality and signals of the presence of digital epistemology in a literary text. Similarly, the reading strategies put forward by the novel remind of those navigating on the WWW requests.

Fagerholm's novel is certainly not unique in its intermedial relation to the Internet and digital media, nor is it an especially early example of a literary text carrying the inscript of digitalisation. In all times there has been literature portraying, mimicking and admiring machines: Jameson exemplifies with high modernist literature and Ingvarsson finds traces of digital epistemology in Swedish literature from the 1960s. In 'weaker postmodern art works' can be found, according to Jameson, representations of the reproductive machines and reproductive processes on merely content or thematic level, for example narratives that include movie cameras, videos, tape recorders and so on. This kind of content or thematic level representation of reproductive processes dominates in Fagerholm's earlier novel *Wonderful Women by the Sea* in which cameras and photography play a central role in story telling. However, 'the most energetic postmodernist texts' have the power to evoke 'a whole new postmodern space in emergence around us', Jameson writes (Jameson 1991: 36–37). This is where the uniqueness of Fagerholm's novel *DIVA* becomes obvious. It allows the reader to 'glimpse into a postmodern or technological sublime', to grasp the central role of reproductive processes in postmodernist culture as the digital epistemology has become an integral part of the novel's overall structure.

Thus, two opposite tendencies seem to struggle with each other in Fagerholm's intriguing novel. On the one hand *DIVA*' s structural 'difficulty' and the demands it puts on the reader bear traces of an attitude typical of avant-garde literature and culture, an eagerness to explore the possibilities of new media (van den Berg 2012: 14). On the other hand, the affinities of the network of networks and the novel can be interpreted as a representation of the widely confusing spatial experience of the late modern society. As a result the 'immense communicational network', brought about by computers is actualised to the reader who also becomes a part of the 'web' created by the novel.

---

12 Intermediality is a subdivision of intertextuality and means the presence of another media in a media, e.g., literary texts that include references to photographs, films, paintings, music, and so on (Wolf 1999: 37–44).

Girls, Networks, and Knowledge in the Age of Globalization

In Fagerholm's literary world, the networks are *the* utmost form of communication and explicitly connected to the female protagonists. In spite of that, the cultural significance of networks is ambivalent: on the one hand, the discursive, narrative and thematic diversity of the novel with its affinities to the WWW, opens up a depiction of a fluid and free subjectivity, sexuality and identity. Presuming that this is a story about a thirteen-year-old schoolgirl, it offers utopian possibilities of identification and powers and spaces much larger and freer than those traditionally prescribed for young girls in the society. These might even be the possibilities offered by the Internet to its young, female users. On the other hand, if the information excess and diversity found in the novel is seen as a depiction of the heterogeneity of the Internet, readers are confronted with a 'protagonist' that is but an imitation and repetition of the endless discourses of the digital world. In this case, the novel might be read as a dystopic depiction of an 'empty' subject with only 'freedom' to imitate, but without an ability to distinguish between the trivial and the important. Finally, is *DIVA* also a parodic comment upon the transformation of knowledge in the time of digital communication technology? Is it a statement that both depicts and critically revaluates the knowledge offered by global networks?

These questions of knowledge and hierarchies of knowledge, could be approached through the phrase 'the cradle of Western culture', Diva's description of her bed and sleeping bag.[13] This idiom is, of course, usually used in the thoughts and ideas produced by male philosophers in ancient Greece, highly valued and appreciated and the basis of all Western knowledge. In Fagerholm's parodic use of the phrase, the metaphorical aspects (knowledge, general, and abstract, highly valued) are replaced by the concrete, everyday piece of furniture in which a 'baby', a young girl, sleeps, but obviously and metaphorically speaking, the new 'cradle of Western culture' today is the Internet. In the 'supertext' the global flow is created by computer networks:

> Every cultural expression, from the worst to the best, from the most elitist to the most popular, comes together in this digital universe that links up in a giant, a historical supertext, past, present and future manifestations of the communicative mind. (Castells 1996: 372)

What is of importance here is the transformation of *knowledge*, in the sense of 'facts that are of importance in (Western, Nordic, Finnish) society'. In the supertext and in *DIVA*, the hierarchies of knowledge are dissolved and new subjects have entered the arenas of knowledge and speech. The old male 'experts' have been substituted by 'ordinary' people, in this case by a thirteen-year-old school girl, with her in the Western culture less-valued knowledge. This is, of course, a revolution.

---

13 For another interpretation of this phrase, see Kurikka in this volume.

According to the sociologists, a major change took place at the end of the 1980s and at the beginning of the 1990s, when Finland turned rapidly from a state-centred nation into a competition society characterised by a new liberalist economy and became, to a higher degree than before, a part of the Western world and global, world market capitalism. The nation-state borders and the economic and political barriers became lower and the society opened up and developed in a multicultural direction. Not only people's values changed, but also a discursive transformation took place; a discourse on freedom and competition became predominant and replaced an earlier one on security and continuity (Sevänen 2013; Heiskala 2006: 35–36). Similar economic, social and discursive developments had already been occurring for a while elsewhere in the Western world. It is not a coindicence, then, that *DIVA* occured as late as the end of the 1990s. By that time, Finland had finally become a part of the social, economic and cultural developments that had brought about postmodernism elsewhere. A discursive, thematic and narrative diversity had entered the former, relatively uniform Finnish culture and literature and the apprehensions of time, place and identity had lost their former anchorage in the nation state.

Postmodernism has been read as the cultural expression of globalization (see e.g., Connell and Marsh 2011: 94) and *DIVA* is a postmodern text. As has been pointed out, the poststructuralist ideas of literature as an endless web of citations and allusions to other texts, comes very near the ideas of hypertext as a 'nonlinear' writing, but many other, parallel lines of thought centreing on webs were developed simultaneously in humanities, social sciences and art along side the formation of digital culture and the World Wide Web. The network was *the* model of reality when scholars and writers grasped the world of late modernity until the 21st century, eventually still one more imprint of digital epistemology (see also Ingvarsson 2015: 48).

Simultaneously, the status of networks has changed during the last thirty to forty years. In history, networks were preserved for the private sphere, and 'centralized hierarchies were the fiefdoms of power and production', Manuel Castells writes (2001: 2). According to him, global capitalism, the development of computing and telecommunications and the societies in which individual freedom and open communication were a demand of high interest, made the networks the supreme form in all domains of economy and society, 'outcompeting and outperforming vertically organized corporations and centralized bureaucracies' (Castells 2001: 1). The network is associated with flexibility and adaptability, capacities of central importance in order to survive in a rapidly changing world (Castells, 2001: 1–2). However, seen from this perspective, the excess and diversity to be found in *DIVA* are not only an expression of a new, Utopian freedom, beneficial, good and correct, but also as a product of certain historical, economic, social and medial conditions and an allegorical portrayal of a digital epistemology ready to invade every part of human life.

References

Primary Sources

Fagerholm, Monika 1998: *DIVA. En uppväxts egna alfabet med docklaboratorium (en bonusberättelse ur framtiden)*. [DIVA. The alphabet of Adolescence with a Laboratory of Dolls (A Bonus Tale from the Future)] Söderströms, Helsingfors.

Secondary Sources

Aarseth, Espen J. 1997: *Cybertext. Perspectives on Ergodic Literature*. The John Hopkins University Press, Baltimore and London.
Beckman, Åsa 1998: Skapa ett eget alfabet. [Creating One's Own Alphabet] – *Dagens Nyheter* 23.10.1998.
Bell, David 2009: On the Net: Navigating the World Wide Web. In *Digital Cultures. Understanding New Media*. Eds. Glen Creeber and Royston Martin. Open University Press, Maidenhead, 30–38.
Berg, Hubert van den 2012: Preface. In *A Cultural History of the Avant-Garde in the Nordic Countries 1900–1925*. Eds. Hubert van den Berg et al. Rodopi, Amsterdam, New York.
Castells, Manuel 1996: *The Rise of the Network Society*. The Information Age: Economy, Society and Culture. Volume I, The Rise of the Network Society. Blackwell Publishers, Oxford, Malden.
Castells, Manuel 2001: *The Internet Galaxy. Reflections on the Internet, Business, and Society*. Oxford University Press, Oxford.
Connell, Liam and Marsh, Nicky 2011: *Literature and Globalization. A Reader*. Routledge, London and New York.
Creeber, Glen and Martin, Royston 2009: Introduction. In *Digital Cultures. Understanding New Media*. Eds. Glen Creeber and Royston Martin. Open University Press, Maidenhead, 1–10.
Creeber, Glen and Martin, Royston 2009: Appendix. New Media: A Timeline. In *Digital Cultures. Understanding New Media*. Eds. Glen Creeber and Royston Martin. Open University Press, Maidenhead, 170–178.
Eskelinen, Markku 1999: Digitaalinen dominantti, bioteksti ja psykosomaattinen käyttöliittymä. [Digital Dominants, Biotexts, and Psychosomatic User Interfaces] In *Johdatus digitaaliseen kulttuuriin*. [Introduction to Digital Culture] Eds. Aki Järvinen and Ilkka Mäyrä. Vastapaino, Tampere, 129–143.
Gere, Charlie 2002: *Digital Culture*. Reaktion Books Ltd., London.
Haasjoki, Pauliina 2012: *Häilyvyyden liittolaiset. Kerronnan ja seksuaalisuuden ambivalenssit*. [Allies in Wavering. The Ambivalences of Narrative and Sexuality] Turun yliopiston julkaisuja, Annales Universitatis Turkuensis *Sarja – Ser. C Osa – Tom. 343*, Scripta lingua Fennica edita. Turun yliopisto, Turku.
Hedman, Kaj 1998: Fagerholm ser allt ur 'Divas' synvinkel. [Fagerholm Views Everything through Diva's Perspective] – *Österbottningen* 11.11.1998.
Heiskala, Risto 2006: Kansainvälisen toimintaympäristön muutos ja Suomen yhteiskunnallinen murros. [The Change in International Operational Environments and the Social Rupture in Finland] In *Uusi jako. Miten Suomesta tuli kilpailukyky-yhteiskunta?* [New Deal. How Finland Became a Competition Society] Eds. Risto Heiskala and Eeva Luhtakallio. Gaudeamus, Helsinki, 14–42.
Ingvarsson, Jonas 2015: BBB vs WWW. Digital epistemologi och litterär text från Göran Printz Påhlsson till Ralf Andtbacka. [BBB vs WWW. Digital Epistemology

and Literary Text from Göran Printz Påhlsson to Ralf Andtbacka] – *Tidskrift för litteraturvetenskap* 1/2015, 45–60.

Jameson, Fredric 1991: *Postmodernism, or, The Cultural Logic of Late Capitalism*. Duke University Press, Durham.

Koskimaa, Raine 1999: Digitaaliset tekstit ja kirjallisuus. [Digital Texts and Literature] In *Johdatus digitaaliseen kulttuuriin*. [Introduction to Digital Culture] Eds. Aki Järvinen and Ilkka Mäyrä. Vastapaino, Tampere, 113–128.

Kurikka, Kaisa 2005: Tytöksi-tulemisen tilat. Monika Fagerholmin *Diva* utopistisena tekstinä. [The Spaces of Becoming-Girl. Monika Fagerholm's *Diva* as a Utopian Text] In *PoMon tila. Kirjoituksia kirjallisuuden postmodernismista* [The Space of PoMo. Texts on Postmodern Literature] Eds. Anna Helle and Katriina Kajannes. Jyväskylän ylioppilaskunnan julkaisusarja numero 74. Kampus Kustannus, Jyväskylä, 56–72.

Kurikka, Kaisa 2008: To Use and Abuse, to Write and Rewrite: Metafictional Trends in Contemporary Finnish Prose. In *Metaliterary Layers in Finnish Literature*. Eds. Samuli Hägg, Erkki Sevänen and Risto Turunen. Studia Fennica Litteraria 3. Finnish Literature Society, Helsinki, 48–63.

Kåreland, Lena 2004: Flickbokens nya kläder. Om Monika Fagerholms *Diva*. [The New Clothes of Girls' Books] In *Omklädningsrum. Könsöverskridanden och rollbyten från Tintomara till Tant Blomma*. [Changing Rooms. Gender Transgressions and Changes of Roles from Tintomara to Tant Blomma] Eds. Eva Heggestad and Anna Williams. Studentlitteratur, Lund, 121–137.

Lindblom, Tomi 2009: *Uuden median murros Alma Mediassa, Sanoma Osakeyhtiössä ja Yleisradiossa 1994–2004*. [The Break Through of New Media in Three Finnish Media Companies] Viestinnän laitos, Viestinnän julkaisuja 16. Tampereen Yliopistopaino, Tampere. http://urn.fi/URN:ISBN:978-952-10-5472-3 (Accessed 2.3.2016)

Malmio, Kristina 2012: Phoenix-Marvel Girl in the Age of *fin de siècle*. Popular Culture as a Vehicle to Postmodernism in *Diva* by Finland-Swedish Author, Monika Fagerholm. In *Nodes of Contemporary Finnish Literature*. Ed. Leena Kirstinä. Studia Fennica Litteraria 6. Finnish Literature Society, Helsinki, 72–95.

Möller, Anna-Lena 1998: En finlandssvensk Diva. [A Finland-Swedish Diva] – *Vasabladet* 23.10.1998.

Ojajärvi, Jussi 2012: 'Benson & Hedges-sytyttimellä.' Kulutustavaroiden ja tavaramerkkikerronnan ulottuvuuksia vuosituhannen vaihteen suomalaisessa romaanissa. ['With a Benson & Hedges Lighter.' Perspectives on Consumerism and Consumer Goods in the Turn of the Century Finnish Novels] *Kirjallisuudentutkimuksen aikakauslehti Avain* 2/2012, 52–75.

Ojajärvi, Jussi 2006: *Supermarketin valossa. Kapitalismi, subjekti ja minuus Mari Mörön romaanissa Kiltin yön lahjat ja Juha Seppälän novellissa 'Supermarket'* [In the Light of Super Market. Capitalism, Subjectivity, and the I in the Novel of Mari Mörö and the Short Story 'Super Market' by Juha Seppälä] Suomalaisen Kirjallisuuden Seura, Helsinki.

Page, Ruth and Thomas, Bronwen 2011: Introduction. In *New Narratives. Stories and Storytelling in the Digital Age*. Eds. Ruth Page and Bronwen Thomas. University of Nebraska Press, Lincoln and London, 1–16.

Peterson, Marie 2005: Monika Fagerholm. Flickornas försvarare. [Monika Fagerholm. Defender of Girls] – *Dagens Nyheter* 1.3.2005.

Ryan, Marie-Laure 2004: Digital Media. In *Narrative across Media. The Languages of Storytelling*. Ed. Marie-Laure Ryan. University of Nebraska Press, Lincoln and London, 329–335.

Sevänen, Erkki 2013: Nykykirjallisuuden yhteiskunnallinen kehys. [The Social Framework of Contemporary Literature] In *Suomen nykykirjallisuus 2. Kirjallinen elämä ja yhteiskunta* [Finland's Contemporary Literature 2. Literary Life and

Society], ed. Mika Hallila et al. Suomalaisen Kirjallisuuden Seura, Helsinki, 11–36.

Stenwall, Åsa 2001: *Portföljen i skogen. Kvinnor och modernitet i det sena 1900-talets finlandssvenska litteratur.* [Briefcase in the Woods. Women and Modernity in Late 20th Century Finland-Swedish Literature] Schildts, Helsingfors.

Sundström, Charlotte 2004: Mellan allt och inget. [Between Everything and Nothing] – *Ny Tid* 51–52/2004.

Svedjedal, Johan 2000: *The Literary Web. Literature and Publishing in the Age of Digital Production: A Study in the Sociology of Literature.* Acta Bibliothecæ regiæ Stockholmiensis LXII. Publications from the Section for Sociology of Literature at the Department of Literature, Uppsala University 42. Kungliga Biblioteket, Stockholm.

Werkelid, Carl Otto1995: 'Mellanfallarna' får upprättelse. [Those In-Between Get their Revenge] – *Svenska Dagbladet* 15.5.1995.

Wolf, Werner 1999: *The Musicalization of Fiction. A Study in the Theory and History of Intermediality.* Internationale Forschungen zur Allgemeinen und Vergleichenden Literaturwissenschaft 35. Rodopi, Amsterdam & Atlanta GA.

Österholm, Maria Margareta 2012: *Ett flicklaboratorium i valda bitar. Skeva flickor i svenskspråkig prosa från 1980 till 2005.* [A Girl Laboratory in Chosen Parts. Queer Girls in Swedish and Finland-Swedish Literature from 1980 to 2005] Rosenlarv Förlag, Stockholm.

New Forms of Pleasure, Anxiety and Writing

II

Anna Helle

When Love and Death Embrace
Monika Fagerholm's *The American Girl* and *The Glitter Scene* as Postmodern Melodrama

'But Eddie, what a fascinating personality', said Doris Flinkenberg. [...] 'You could really fall in love with her. And that's what he [Björn] did. Head over heels. So in love that he didn't know left from right. You know what it can be like, right? We know. Young love. A violent end'. (*The American Girl* 2009: 150)[1]

In this passage, Doris Flinkenberg, one of the protagonists of Monika Fagerholm's *The American Girl* (*Den amerikanska flickan* 2004), talks to her friend Sandra about a dead American girl, Eddie, and about a boy, Björn, who was in love with Eddie. In Doris's view it is evident that death and true love have a kind of complementary relation. With this passage, I therefore wish to introduce my reader to the themes of love and death in Fagerholm's novels *The American Girl* and *The Glitter Scene* (*Glitterscenen* 2010).

Fagerholm is known as an experimental writer and a postmodernist (cf. Kurikka 2005; Malmio 2012). Her style is original and recognizable and the storylines of her novels are multi-layered. The experimental novel – and postmodernism in particular – is often highly cerebral and therefore difficult to understand. Nevertheless, Fagerholm herself does not prefer to label her works as intellectually challenging. Especially when it comes to her award-winning novels, *The American Girl* and *The Glitter Scene*, she argues in an interview that the novels are first and foremost about sentiments (Miettinen 2004: 9).

In this essay, I aim to take notice of both the experimentalism and sentimentality of the two novels in which the two themes, love and death are central. What is more, the composition based on love and death is essential to the Western literary tradition in general, as in *Romeo and Juliet* or *Die*

---

1 'Men alltså, fascinerande', sa Doris Flinkenberg. 'Man kunde verkligen bli förälskad i henne [Eddie]. Och det var det han [Björn] blev. Upp över sina öron. Så förälskad att han inte visste ut eller in. Du vet hur det kan vara, eller hur? Ung kärlek. Ond bråd död'. (*Den amerikanska flickan* 2005: 149). Part of this passage is later repeated in another context and slightly transformed (*Den amerikanska flickan* 2005: 160/ *The American Girl* 2009: 162).

Leiden des jungen Werthers. I suggest that love and death are entangled in Fagerholm's novels in a multitude of ways. Eddie, for example, is presented as a lovely and fascinating young girl who attracts the aforementioned boy Björn and his cousin Bengt. The boys love Eddie passionately, but the triangle drama has an extremely violent end. As the citation at the beginning of this article indicates, the tragic ending makes the story of the American girl appear ever more intriguing to Doris, who is only a child at the time of the tragedy.

This article approaches the themes of love and death in the novels at hand from the viewpoint of melodramatic imagination (Brooks 1995). The aim is to discuss to what extent the novels fit in the melodramatic frame. I examine the melodramatic traits of the novels, and doing so, I also tackle the question of importing melodrama into the postmodernist context.

The End of the Glitter Scene

The American Girl and *The Glitter Scene* form a diptych titled, *The End of the Glitter Scene*. The novels share the same milieu and some of the same characters. Time is one of the central elements that differs between the novels. Neither novel has a chronological time frame but the novels' timelines partly overlap each other. However, *The American Girl* is situated in an earlier time, around the 1970s, whereas the events of *The Glitter Scene* take place in a period lasting from the 1980s to the first decade of the 2000s. The diptych is experimental in many ways. It is typical of the two novels to reiterate events repeatedly from different perspectives and in changing manners. This style creates ambiguity, making it difficult for the reader to decide what to believe.

There are dozens of characters in *The End of the Glitter Scene* novels. The most important ones are girls or women living in a fictional place called the 'District'. The story begins with the death of a young girl, Eddie, under mysterious circumstances in the District. The protagonists of *The American Girl* are Sandra Wärn and Doris Flinkenberg who are schoolgirls and close friends. They play dramatic games, one of them about the American girl and immerse themselves in the mystery of her death (cf. Österholm 2012: 266–268). Suzette Packlén and Maj-Gun Maalamaa form a similar pair in *The Glitter Scene*. In comparison with Doris and Sandra, however, their relation to the tragedy of the American girl is more distant.

The twins, Rita and Solveig, also have a major role in both novels. They are children in *The American Girl* and adults in *The Glitter Scene*. As it turns out at the end of *The Glitter Scene*, Rita and Solveig have always known what happened when Eddie died (*Glitterscenen* 2009: 394–395; *The Glitter Scene* 2010: 501–504). Among other characters are the boys Bengt and Björn, and the so-called 'cousin's mama', Astrid Loman, who is the foster mother of Doris, Solveig, Rita, Bengt and Björn. In the same household there is also a man called 'cousin's papa' who has a minor role in the tragedy of the American girl.

The bipartite novel reiterates its binary structure by introducing a great number of characters that come in pairs. What is interesting in this regard is that Eddie is alone; she comes from America and is an outsider. Due to her short stay in the District, Eddie remains something of an enigma to the other characters. She is considered a 'stranger' (*The American Girl* 2009: 3) who is 'like a question mark, a mystery' (*The Glitter Scene* 2010: 49). In addition to Eddie, many other characters also meet their ends. This applies to Bengt who dies in a fire, to Ulla Bäckström who falls out of a window, to the parents of Rita, Solveig and Bengt who die in a car accident and many others. The fact that there are so many deaths points to exaggeration instead of tragic tones (cf. Helle 2008: 61–62). Nevertheless, due to the numerous deaths and because of the interwoven relationship between love and death, it is fruitful to consider the novels' relationship with melodrama.

The Melodramatic Mode and Postmodern Melodrama

Melodrama has several different definitions. Originally, it was the term for a certain kind of 19th century musical drama in Paris and London that appealed to the emotions of the receiver (Nemesvari 2011: 2–4). However, in contemporary research, melodrama is used in a broader sense to describe the 'melodramatic mode' of a play, movie or novel (Brooks 1995: xiii–xvii). Used in this sense, it does not strictly define a genre but rather is a description of a work's style, its artistic means or even its tone or attitude (cf. Mercer and Shingler 2004; Zarzosa 2010: 236). In the context of Hollywood films or TV series, for instance, melodrama may also have pejorative connotations referring to unrealistic, romantic stories addressed mainly to female viewers (Brooks 1995: 12; Neale 1993: 66–67).

I am not claiming that *The American Girl* and *The Glitter Scene* should be read as representatives of the traditional melodrama genre; it would not even be possible due to the experimental characteristics of the novels. The more traditional melodramas in the novel genre include those written by such authors as Charles Dickens (1812–1870), Thomas Hardy (1840–1928) and Henry James (1843–1916) and it is evident that Fagerholm's novels are not melodramatic in the same sense. Nevertheless, the melodramatic mode is a useful notion when approaching *The American Girl* and *The Glitter Scene*. The novels make use of typically melodramatic traits such as excess, over-sentimentality, innocence and a polarized division between good and evil (cf. Singer 2001: 37–58). Rather than traditional, I would characterize these novels as postmodern melodrama.

How is this shown in *The American Girl* and *The Glitter Scene*? First of all, there is a certain tone of melodramatic fatality in *The American Girl* and *The Glitter Scene*. Death is present at all times: innocent young girls die violently and many good things seem to fall into decay. The multiplicity of deaths in the novels – already on the first six pages, three main characters die – generates an experience of excess. Furthermore, as this essay will show, some of the characters have an excessively vivid emotional life, which points to over-sentimentality. This applies especially to Doris who is very dramatic by nature. The excess also contributes to the hyperbolic characteristics of the novels in the form of abundant repetition, as I will show later on.

When it comes to the polarization between good and evil in *The End of The Glitter Scene* novels, it is best crystallized in the epigraph provided by the American director David Lynch at the beginning of *The Glitter Scene*: 'There is goodness in blue skies and flowers, but another force – a wild pain and decay – also accompanies everything'. This epigraph catches the ambivalence of *The American Girl* and *The Glitter Scene* for the novels combine death and fear on one hand and joyful play and beauty on the other. The characters Sandra and Doris are innocent children who, in spite of their young age, are fascinated by Eddie's death and continue to play the American Girl game they have created. While love is usually seen as good, in these novels it is closely related to death.

It is worth noticing, however, that while melodrama in the traditional sense underlines the importance of moral questions and the idea that justice will prevail in the end (Brooks 1995: 20), Fagerholm's novels are vaguer in this regard. In traditional melodrama, the distinction between good and evil typically manifests itself through characters that are either virtuous or villainous (cf. Singer 2001: 45–46; Brooks 1995: 11). In *The American Girl* and *The Glitter Scene*, however, this distinction is blurred. As this essay will show, this is due to the experimental nature of the novels.

Furthermore, music also plays an important role and this can be seen as a reference to the traditional melodrama. The very first words of *The American Girl* refer to music: 'This is where the music begins. It is so simple. It is at the end of the 1960s, on Coney Island in New York. There is a beach and boardwalk, a small amusement park, some restaurants, fun slot machines, and so on' (*The American Girl* 2009: 1).[2] Here the music refers to a record that the American girl makes in a music recording machine:

> She [Eddie] steps into the machine just for fun and randomly starts feeding coins into it.
> You can select background music, but she does not. She pushes Record and then she sings.
> *Look, Mom, they've destroyed my song.*
> It does not sound very good. It really does not. But it does not mean anything.
> *Look, Mom, what they've done to my song.*
> The words do not fit very well with reality. It is such a beautiful day out there.
> (*The American Girl* 2009: 2)[3]

The lyrics of Eddie's song that are repeated several times in the novels refer to Melanie Safka's song 'Look what they've done to my song, ma' from the late

---

2   Här börjar musiken. Det är så enkelt. Det är i slutet av 1960-talet, på Coney Island, utanför New York. Här finns simstränder och picknickplatser, ett litet tivoli, några restauranger, roliga spelautomater, så (*Den amerikanska flickan* 2005: 1).
3   Hon går in i automaten på skoj. På måfå börjar hon mata in slantar i den./Man kan välja musik som bakgrund, men hon avstår. Hon trycker inspelning och sedan sjunger hon./*Titta mamma, de har förstört min sång.*/Det låter inget vidare. Det gör det inte. Men det betyder ingenting./*Titta, mamma, vad de har gjort åt min sång.*/ Orden rimmar inte så bra med verkligheten. Det är en sådan vacker dag där ute (*Den amerikanska flickan* 2005: 7–8).

1960s. The song is not particularly sad, but in the context of *The American Girl* the words sound sinister. The ambivalent tone of the novels is apparent already at the beginning: the American girl sings about destruction but the sun is shining and she feels happy (*The American Girl* 2009: 1).

Eddie's Death

The whole story of the novels begins with the death of the American girl, Eddie: 'IT HAPPENED IN THE DISTRICT, AT BULE MARSH. EDDIE'S DEATH. She was lying at the bottom of the marsh. Her hair was standing out around her head in thick, long strands like octopus tentacles. Her eyes were wide open'. (*The American Girl* 2009: 3)[4] The death of the young girl is the prime mover behind all the events and actions that follow. From the very beginning it is clear that Eddie's death is neither natural nor suicide. Therefore, someone must be responsible for her death, and there is a killer in the District.

Now, this is a beginning typical for murder mysteries, and there is also something very typical to Western culture in this vision of a dead young girl. As a matter of fact, it is a cliché. Edgar Allan Poe already noted that the death of a beautiful woman is the most poetic topic in the world (Bronfen 1996: 59). The image also recurs in the tradition of Western art (Bronfen 1996) and more recently in numerous TV series. The image of the American girl in the water may remind one of Laura Palmer who is found dead by the water at the beginning of the television series *Twin Peaks* (1990–1991), created by the aforementioned David Lynch,[5] even though Palmer did not die in the water; her body had been brought to the shore in a plastic bag. It may also remind readers of the girl called the Wild Rose, played by Kylie Minogue in the music video of Nick Cave's and Minogue's duet, the murder ballad 'Where the Wild Roses Grow' (1996). Then again, many of the contemporary images of dead young girls by the water can be seen as references to *Hamlet*'s Ophelia who, however, is not murdered but dies either accidentally or by her own hand. Particularly the images are reminiscent of a painting called *Ophelia* (1852) by the Pre-Raphaelite artist John Everett Millais (1829–1896).

Why build the whole story of the American girl on such a worn-out scene if not to underline its frequency in Western culture? In my view both of these novels utilise two common cultural themes – the murder mystery and the dead young girl – and manipulate them in a postmodern way. It would not be the first time for a postmodernist novel to recycle the notion of murder mystery or detective story, quite the opposite. The formula of

---

4   *Det hände sig i Trakten, vid Bule träsket. Eddies död. Hon låg på träskets botten. Håret spretade kring huvudet i tjocka, långa slingor, som bläckfiskarmar, ögonen var stort uppspärrade* (*Den amerikanska flickan* 2005: 9).
5   According to Fagerholm, she was inspired by *Twin Peaks* when writing the novels (Helle 2008: 62).

a (failing) detective story has been utilized by such postmodernist authors as Umberto Eco or Thomas Pynchon (Tani 1984: 148–151).

Thus, the opening of *The American Girl* hints at murder mystery, but no detectives or policemen emerge in the novels. The police investigations are passed over incidentally in a few lines (*The American Girl* 2009: 165). Instead, there are rumours and unofficial investigations of the death of the American girl. Many of the characters seem to think that Eddie's death has got something to do with love, and of course, there are the two boys, Bengt and Björn, who are both in love with Eddie. The triangle around the American girl is doomed from the very beginning, because Björn and Bengt are cousins living in the same household and would not want to share Eddie. The triangle breaks the close bond between the boys:

> Björn and Bengt: together they made an amusing, odd couple. People would sometimes say *the collected silence*. Bengt, thirteen years old, and half a head taller than Björn, the older, thoughtful one. The cousin's mama used to say 'the apples of my eyes' about the boys.
>
> So that is the way it was before Eddie came, before Bencku met Eddie and everything changed. And once everything started changing, everything happened very quickly. In less than one year everything that had been would be destroyed. (*The American Girl* 2009: 17–18)[6]

What is it, then, that happened so quickly? At the beginning of *The Glitter Scene*, the tragedy of the American girl is told in a version in which Björn is the killer:

> The American girl who was pushed into the water from a cliff in the summer of 1969 by her jealous boyfriend, was sucked into the whirlpool and disappeared, and when her boyfriend understood what he had done he became so beside himself he went off and hanged himself. (*The Glitter Scene* 2010: 15)[7]

Björn is most often presented as the one to blame for Eddie's death, but there are also other versions of the story. In *The Glitter Scene*, the already mentioned young girl, Ulla Bäckström suspects that the death may well have been Bengt's fault:

> 'You know, with that story. The American girl. You start thinking of other possibilities.'

6 Björn och Bengt; tillsammans utgjorde de ett udda, lustigt par. *Den samlade tystnaden,* sa man om dem ibland. Bengt, tretton år, halva huvudet längre än Björn, den fem år äldre, eftertänksamma. 'Mina ögonstenar' brukade kusinmamman säga om de båda pojkarna./Så var det alltså innan Eddie kom, innan Bencku mötte Eddie och allt förändrades. Och när förändringen väl hade kommit igång, hände allting mycket snabbt. På mindre än ett år skulle allt som dittills varit vara ödelagt (*Den amerikanska flickan* 2005: 23).

7 Den amerikanska flickan som sommaren 1969 blev skuffad i vattnet från en klippa av sin pojkvän som var svartsjuk, sögs upp i vattnets virvlar och försvann och när pojkvännen förstod vad han hade gjort blev han så ifrån sig att han gick iväg och hängde sig (*Glitterscenen* 2009: 19).

'Björn who killed himself. Her boyfriend, after she had died. But Bengt, the other boy, the one in the woods, who loved her too. Who was he?'

'*If* it was him... And then, when you start thinking like that you sort of became unsure of everything'. (*The Glitter Scene* 2010: 30)[8]

Many girls who come along later, including Maj-Gun and Ulla, see Eddie's death as resulting from a passionate or unconditional love: "'They say she died from love", Ulla Bäckstöm whispers. The one who killed her loved her too much'" (*Glitterscenen* 2009: 22/*The Glitter Scene* 2010: 20). The young girls tend to think that the tragic ending adds to the romanticism of the love story and they admire the mythical American girl for having been so fascinating that someone wanted to kill her. In my opinion this peculiar and yet well-trodden longing for a romantic death is one of the essential questions in Fagerholm's novels. But when the American girl dies, Björn commits suicide and Bengt stops talking. The beautiful young love ends in two deaths. However, it is possible that Eddie's death has little to do with Björn and Bengt. At the end of *The Glitter Scene*, Solveig tells her 'truth' of what happened when Eddie died. According to her it is the cousin's mama who is responsible for Eddie's death for reasons that remain unclear. This is what Solveig says about the incident:

> The American girl who ran out onto Lore Cliff, the cousin's mama after her, and the American girl couldn't get any farther.
> The cousin's mama on the cliff who remained standing there. (*The Glitter Scene* 2010: 505)[9]

Prior to the final scene on the Lore Cliff, the cousin's mama had met Eddie in the garden, and they had had an argument. The cousin's mama had been very angry and she had treated Eddie roughly. Solveig's description of the events is quite cryptic and she does not claim that the cousin's mama killed the American girl. However, she does imply that it was the cousin's mama who led Eddie to her premature death, albeit unintentionally. According to this interpretation Björn dies before Eddie, not the other way around. Björn commits suicide after an argument he has with the cousin's papa, a violent alcoholic. Cousin's mama finds his dead body but does not have the courage to accuse cousin's papa of Björn's death. She therefore targets Eddie who coincidentally happens to come around looking for the boys (*The Glitter Scene* 2010: 494–500).

This interpretation is central for reading Fagerholm's novels as postmodern melodrama. Peter Brooks (1995: 15) has argued that melodrama

---

8 Du vet, med den historien. Den amerikanska flickan. Man börjar tänka på andra möjligheter./Björn som tog livet av sig. Hennes pojkvän, efter att hon dött. Men Bengt, den där andra pojken, han i skogen, som älskade henne också. Vem var han?/*Om* det var han... Och sen, när man börjar tänka så blir man liksom osäker på allt (*Glitterscenen* 2009: 30).
9 Den amerikanska flickan som sprang ut på Loreklippan, kusinmamman efter och den amerikanska flickan kom ju inte längre./Kusinmamman på berget som stod kvar (*Glitterscenen* 2009: 396).

was born in a situation where the traditional notions of ethics and truth had lost their power because of secularization. According to him '[w]e may legitimately claim that melodrama becomes the principal mode for uncovering, demonstrating, and making operative the essential moral universe in a post-sacred era' (Brooks 1995: 15). In the secularized world, melodrama is a way of representing moral questions. Elisabeth Bronfen (1996: 219) has stated that the death of a woman in Western literature often helps to 'regenerate the order of [a fictional] society' and 'eliminate destructive forces' threatening it. The woman who dies may well be innocent, as in the case of the American girl. Interpreted from this angle, the American girl as an outsider is sacrificed by cousin's mama for the sake of bringing back the order of the District society after Björn's suicide. *The End of the Glitter Scene* addresses the question of dead young women in Western culture and as a postmodern melodrama it muddles up the moral categories to revivify the problem.

'Death's Spell at a Young Age'

Doris Flinkenberg also dies at the Bule Marsh, just as Eddie did, but years later in the story line:

> *It happened in the District, at Bule Marsh, death's spell at a young age.* [...]
> Doris came to Bule Marsh and she walked up Lore Cliff. She stood there and counted to ten. She counted to eleven, twelve, and fourteen, too, and to sixteen, before she had gathered enough courage to raise the pistol's barrel to her temple and pull the trigger. (*The American Girl* 2009: 5–6)[10]

To begin with, the descriptions of the deaths of both Eddie and Doris begin with the same words: 'It happened in the District, at Bule Marsh' thereby drawing a parallel between the two deaths. The Swedish words 'Det hände sig' ('It happened') refer to the sort of language used in the Bible, and also allow for associations to the phrases used in fairy tales and legends. They open up a supernatural dimension to the story together with such unrealistic ideas as 'death's spell' and make one think of 'another force' of pain and decay mentioned in the Lynch quote at the beginning of *The Glitter Scene*. The words can also be read as a rhetorical figure that emphasizes the legendary nature of the stories about dead young girls.

First it seems that Doris's death only imitates the circulating story about the American girl. Sandra and Doris create their own American girl game and they pretend to be solving the mystery of her death (e.g., *Den amerikanska flickan* 2005: 13/*The American Girl* 2009: 8), yet later in the novel the

---

10 *Det hände sig i Trakten, vid Bule träsket: dödens förtrollning vid unga år.* [...]/Doris kom till Bule träsket, hon gick upp på Loreklippan, hon stod där och räknade till tio. Hon räknade till elva, tolv och fjorton också, och till sexton, innan hon hade samlat tillräckligt mod för att höja pistolmynningen mot tinningen och trycka av (*Den amerikanska flickan* 2005: 11–12).

connection between the deaths of Doris and the American girl turn out to be complicated. From the outset, there is an ominous aura surrounding Doris that the reader cannot ignore. Already at the very beginning of *The American Girl*, it is revealed that Doris will end up committing suicide. However, in *The American Girl* her story is narrated as if the reader is unaware of the tragic end and her forthcoming death is repeatedly foreshadowed. This is interesting, because the reader does not need these omens in order to predict or deduce Doris's fate; the reader already knows it. This is why these 'omens' need to be explained differently, and one explanation is that from the viewpoint of the atmosphere or the affective force, it is important to keep the death motif constantly present. The incessantly surrounding death is like the already-mentioned horrifying 'another force'; it always exists behind the good things or as their counterforce.

What, then, are Doris's omens like? In the girls' game, for example, Doris repeats the words '[y]oung love, a violent end' (*Den amerikanska flickan* 2005: 160/*The American Girl* 2009: 162) to Sandra. With them she refers to the American girl and the boys who were in love with her, but also to the budding love between herself and Sandra. The words disturb the reader, because Sandra and Doris do not yet know what the reader knows from the beginning: that Doris herself will end up facing a 'sudden evil death'.[11] Another phrase Doris keeps on repeating is the Latin '[m]emento mori' (e.g., *Den amerikanska flickan* 2005: 159, 161, 164/*The American Girl* 2009: 161, 163, 166) which means 'remember that you will die' or 'remember your mortality'.[12]

Doris repeats '*memento mori*' to Sandra who is playing the part of Bengt. She does this to create a horrendous atmosphere surrounding the American girl game. One of the games ends surprisingly when the words are pronounced by someone other than Doris and to Doris herself: '"Remember that you're also going to die", could be heard from somewhere in the darkness behind them and two of the women from the house on the First Cape stepped out of the darkness' (*Den amerikanska flickan* 2005: 164/*The American Girl* 2009: 166). The women from the First Cape are summer residents of the District. Just as in the above citations, the characters do not know the real horror of their words although they are pronounced in order to create a dramatic effect because only the reader knows that Doris is about to die.

There is a lot of repetition in *The American Girl* and *The Glitter Scene* and some of the repeated passages undergo transformations. The altering repetition creates ambivalence and ambiguity. Based on this, it is not important to fully understand what happens in the novels. Not knowing and accepting one's ignorance is actually an essential part of the reading experience of the novels and most likely a presupposition for a pleasurable experience.

---

11 The original Swedish '*ond bråd död*' also has a religious meaning. In the old Lutheran church prayer, God is prayed to protect one from a sudden evil death.
12 According to a legend, the saying originates from the Roman Empire where a slave was to whisper these words to the ear of a war hero during the triumph. *Memento mori* also refers to the kind of art that deals with human mortality.

The excessive number of deaths draws the reader's attention to the question of death in these novels. This question can be approached with the help of the French philosopher Maurice Blanchot (1907–2003). According to him, for a human being death is the outside of life. It is therefore something completely other. It cannot be grasped by reason or consciousness and a human being cannot comprehend death (Bourassa 2009: 33–34; Alanko 2001: 213; Critchley 1997: 73). Inside the fictional world of Fagerholm's novels, death is no doubt this kind of an incomprehensible idea the characters are forced to encounter.

The presence of death affects all the residents of the District in some way. Doris, for example, is captured by the idea of death because she has a close and continuous relationship with the death of the American girl in her new foster family, in her games and finally when she finds the dead body of the American girl five years after the disappearance (*Glitterscenen* 2009: 150/ *The Glitter Scene* 2010: 184). The surrounding death is also an important reason for Doris's death because Doris gets so intensively and so complexly stuck with the death of the American girl. The recurrent phrase 'death's spell at a young age' (*Den amerikanska flickan* 2005: 11, 15/*The American Girl* 2009: 5, 9; *Glitterscenen* 2009: 25/*The Glitter Scene* 2010: 23) refers to the influence of Eddie's death on the young girls. It is used for the first time when Doris's suicide is described.

The deaths agitate many other residents of the District as well, as if they were caught in the slipstream of death. This is shown in the different opinions about the death of the American girl that circulate in the District. They also fascinate people younger than the American girl. In *The Glitter Scene* there is even a passage saying, '*The American girl who died, and all the death that gathered around her*' (*Glitterscenen* 2009: 20/*The Glitter Scene* 2010: 17), which reveals the central role of the death in the lives of the residents of the District. A more humorous example of the presence of death in the lives of the characters (and in the novel) is the postcard that Maj-Gun keeps on the wall of her kiosk. It has a small and innocent text printed on it: '*Today is the first day of the rest of your life*' (*Glitterscenen* 2009: 115, 133/*The Glitter Scene* 2010: 138, 162). This citation may refer to an optimistic possibility of beginning a new life each day, but it can also be taken to mean that today begins the rest of your life that will sooner or later end up in death.

There is still one more essential point to consider about Doris's death. Despite the similarities between Eddie's and Doris's deaths there is a crucial difference between them. Eddie is either killed or dies accidentally while Doris commits suicide. In *Over Her Dead Body. Death, Femininity and the Aesthetic* (1992) Elisabeth Bronfen writes about female characters who choose to commit suicide. According to her, 'suicide implies authorship with one's own life, a form of writing the self and writing death that is ambivalently poised between self-construction and self-destruction' (Bronfen 1996: 142). From this viewpoint the difference between the ways in which the two characters die is significant. Eddie is a victim of a murder or manslaughter and as I suggested earlier, she can be seen as a kind of 'sacrificial lamb', a term that is even mentioned at the beginning of *The American Girl* (2009: 5). Doris may also be a victim, but of violent and unloving parents and she dies by her own hand. Doris admires the dead American girl and confuses death with love; she is enthralled by death's spell and little by little begins to long for death.

Melodramatic Sentiments

Strong emotions are always an essential part of melodrama and romantic melodramas are fuelled by passionate love affairs; *The American Girl* and *The Glitter Scene* are not exceptions to the rule. There is the triangle drama among Eddie, Björn and Bengt, but the young girls Sandra and Doris also fall in love. The budding love between the girls is first presented in *The American Girl* when the girls accidentally end up kissing and hugging (*Den amerikanska flickan* 2005: 152–153/*The American Girl* 2009: 154). This is what a minor character called Tobias reports about Doris and Sandra in *The Glitter Scene* years later in the story time:

> And she [Doris] finds her way to the house in the darker part, completely new then. And a girl the same age lives there. Her name is Sandra Wärn and she becomes like fat on bacon with Doris for many years. A friendship that becomes love for Doris and that Doris enters into hook, line, and sinker. But it ceases, a fight, some misunderstanding, as can happen between two who are close, maybe too close – and when it suddenly ends Doris is skinless. (*The Glitter Scene* 2010: 79)[13]

The relationship between Doris and Sandra can be explained as on what Adrianne Rich has called 'the lesbian continuum'. According to Rich, the lesbian continuum consists of various kinds of relations between women and they cannot be reduced to sexuality. What is more, women can participate in the continuum regardless of whether or not they identify themselves as lesbians (Rich 1986: 51, 54). The relation between Doris and Sandra participates in the lesbian continuum in this sense,[14] but eventually their relationship also contains an element of tragedy. As it turns out, Doris would be more willing to devote herself exclusively to Sandra, whereas Sandra is also attracted to relationships with boys. Feeling abandoned by Sandra, Doris begins to 'court death' instead of the absent friend and lover (cf. Bronfen 1996: 158). The painful break with Sandra is given as one of the many possible explanations for Doris's suicide (*Glitterscenen* 2009: 28/*The Glitter Scene* 2010: 28). The young love between the two girls ends up with Doris's death.

13 Och [Doris] hittar till huset i den dyigare delen, alldeles nybyggt då. Och där bor en flicka i samma ålder, hennes namn är Sandra Wärn och henne blir Doris ler och långhalm med i många år. En vänskap som blir kärlek för Doris och som Doris går in i med hull och hår. Men den upphör, ett gräl, något missförstånd, som det kan vara mellan två som är nära, kanske för nära – och den upphör plötsligt är Doris utan hud (*Glitterscenen* 2009: 68).
14 In Rich's (1986: 51) view politics and a struggle against the patriarchy are an important part of the lesbian continuum, but this does not apply to the relation between Doris and Sandra.

Over-sentimentality, typical to melodrama, also shows in individual characters. This applies first and foremost to Doris, who is very passionate in love and also dramatic by nature. She loves the cousin's mama very much and admires Sandra endlessly. She is described as a lovely, adorable girl – 'Doris-light' – who brings hope to the cousin's house after Björn's death: 'And at the cousin's property, in the cousin's house, there is something about Doris. Her mood, her joy, her *light*. Which infects everything and brings about a change' (*Glitterscenen* 2009: 66/*The Glitter Scene* 2010: 75). Doris brings joy and laughter to the house of mourning.

On the other hand, there is also a violent side to Doris's life (cf., Österholm 2012: 117). She has been constantly beaten and abused by her parents and she is addicted to violent stories about real life crimes. As a child, she has the habit of reading *True Crimes* magazines together with the cousin's mama, as can be seen in the following quote: "'He killed his lover with fifteen hammer blows to the head", Doris Flinkenberg read aloud with her best Sunday school voice and later she said, innocently and surprised like the child she actually was, "Jealousy can cause all sorts of things, can't it?"' (*Den amerikanska flickan* 2005: 45/*The American Girl* 2009: 41).[15] Doris is a contradictory character, combining cuteness and violence.

Unfortunately, Doris's happiness turns out to be fragile: when she loses Sandra and finds Eddie's dead body, she breaks down and commits suicide. Finding Eddie's body is traumatic for Doris, because in her childhood she has witnessed Eddies' death caused by cousin's mama. The twins Rita and Solveig have lied to Doris about what happened. Doris sees Eddie fall from the cliff, but the twins try to convince her that Eddie did not die:

> Rita alone, who came home.
> Told Doris Flinkenberg that it was a game, 'she came up again later.' You can believe that sort of thing if you want to, if you're young and a child.
> Even if it still doesn't leave you, it remains there. (*The Glitter Scene* 2010: 505)[16]

When Doris finds Eddie's dead body she collapses, because the discovery unveils the truth. Everyone with whom she has lived has lied to her, even her beloved foster mother, cousin's mama Astrid Loman. After Doris's death, Solveig finds Doris's half-finished crossword puzzle:

> There is a last name in the row where the correct word is supposed to be filled in: 'Astrid a pop song for the day'. And it is the idea that you're supposed to fill in the surname of the singer who had sung that song the time during the 60s I guess it was. 'A song for the day.'

---

15 'Han dödade sin älskade med femton hammarslag i huvudet', läste Doris Flinckenberg högt med bästa söndagsskoleröst och sedan sade hon, oskyldigt och förvånat som det barn hon faktiskt också var: 'allt möjligt kan svartsjukan ställa till med, eller hur?' (*Den amerikanska flickan* 2005: 45).

16 Rita ensam, som kom hem./Sa till Doris Flinkenberg att det var en lek, 'hon kom nog upp därifrån sen'. Sånt kan man tro på om man vill tro på det, om man är liten och ett barn./Även om det ändå inte lämnar en, det stannar kvar (*Glitterscenen* 2009: 397).

> I don't remember that song. Doesn't mean anything to me.
> But it is the name, Astrid. And after the name, in straggling angry teenage letters there is a long word that doesn't fit in the boxes following it, there are only four of them. Letters on top of each other, a terrible word, I'm not going to say it, but something with *m*. (*The Glitter Scene* 2010: 506)[17]

In her adolescence Doris becomes aware of her foster mother's role in the death of the American girl and she begins to see her as a murderer. This breaks her heart but also makes her very angry. All in all, Doris's emotional life is anything but tame.

In addition to Doris, Bengt also undergoes strong sentiments. He has an emotional but strongly polarized relation to Eddie. When Eddie is still alive, he adores her and shares many of his secrets with her, which is exceptional because Bengt is an extremely shy boy, but after Eddie's death – also after the death of his cousin Björn – Bengt begins to dread the memory of Eddie. This is what Bengt thinks about Eddie after her death:

> When Eddie was gone all of this would be turned against him. Eddie's mystique, the entire environment. It would be transformed into a dark, threatening force, one filled with questions. *Nobody knew my rose of the world but me.*[18] But what did that mean?
> And he would be surrounded by a desertlike loneliness: Eddie cursed.
> And Bencku: something inside would turn against him. He would be defenceless in the face of the threatening and the inexplicable. (*The American Girl* 2009: 25–26)[19]

The memory of his beloved Eddie turns into a dark, threatening force in Bengt's experience. Death transforms the idea of the living wonderful American girl into something terrifying and difficult to understand. Since Eddie has been such an important figure for Bengt, her death influences him very strongly: he stops talking.

---

17 Det står i rutan efter vilken rätt ord ska fyllas i rutorna ett efternamn: 'Astrid en schlager för dagen.' Och där är det mening att man ska fylla i rätt efternamn på den sångerskan som sjöng just den sången, nångång på sextiotalet var det väl. 'En schlager för dagen.'/Inte minns jag den sången. Säger mig ingenting./Men det är namnet, Astrid. Och efter namnet står i spretiga och fula tonårsargsinta bokstäver ett långt ord som inte ryms i de där rutorna efter, som är bara fyra. Bokstäver på varandra; ett hemskt ord, jag tänker inte säga det, men någonting på m (*Glitterscenen* 2009: 397).

18 This phrase is also the epigraph of *The American Girl*. It is a reference to the American author and playwright Tennessee Williams (1911–1983) and originally it was related to Williams's special relationship to his sister. In this context the phrase refers to the relationship between Eddie and Bengt, because Eddie compares their relationship to Williams's relation to his sister (*Den amerikanska flickan* 2005: 30).

19 När Eddie var borta skulle allt detta vändas emot honom. Det som var Eddies aura, hela atmosfären. Den skulle förvandlas till en hotfull, mörk kraft, en full av frågetecken. *Ingen kände min ros i världen utom jag.* Men vad betydde det?/Och han skulle omges av en ökentomhet: Eddie olycksfågel./Och Bencku: någonting i honom själv skulle vända sig emot honom. Han skulle vara försvarslös inför hotfullheten och det oförklarliga (*Den amerikanska flickan* 2005: 31).

Must All Beauty Die?

In this article I have read *The End of the Glitter Scene* novels from the viewpoint of the interwoven relationship between love and death. The theme is widely discussed in criticism of Western literature, but Fagerholm's novels bring new perspectives to the topic. I have focused especially on the deaths of Eddie and Doris. At first they seem quite similar, but a closer look reveals crucial differences.

Eddie is a young girl, an outsider, who comes from America. The boys Bengt and Björn fall in love with her, but the triangle ends in two deaths. Throughout the novels and in the voices of various characters it is repeatedly suggested that Eddie dies because of love. Ever since Eddie's death the whole society of the District seems to be surrounded and haunted by death, which is why Bengt sees Eddie as 'cursed' (*olycksfågel* in Swedish). There is, however, another side to Eddie's death, because she dies involuntarily as a victim of either an accident or a murder. Because of her premature death, Eddie becomes a mythical figure, an incarnation of a beautiful girl who meets a violent end. This is interesting considering that, according to some, death and femininity are the two central enigmas of the Western discourse (Bronfen 1996: 255).

Due to Eddie's exceptional fate, many of the characters of the diptych tend to see her as something larger than life. However, her story would not be as fascinating to the other characters without the circulating rumours about the love affairs between Eddie and Björn, but also between Eddie and Bengt. Although Bengt dies years later than the other two, the fact that all three die young increases the excitement. The novels do not tell whether or not it is because their lives end at the heyday of their youth. Nevertheless, the triangle love-death-youth is at the very heart of the tragedy of the American girl.

However, Eddie's death can also be seen differently when scrutinized outside the romantic frame. It is possible that her death was caused by cousin's mama Astrid Loman. This line of interpretation leads to a conclusion according to which the American girl as an outsider was sacrificed and had to die to bring social order back to the District. According to Elisabeth Bronfen (1996: 219), this is one of the most frequent motives for the death of a young girl in the Western tradition.

Doris's death is different in many ways and not least because she dies by her own hand. Doris admires the dead American girl and sees love and death as the two sides of the same coin: you cannot have one without another. Doris is a mistreated young girl who has lived through different kinds of violence. She is a vulnerable and dramatic person and she adjusts her need to be loved into the model that the culture and the surrounding District society keep on offering her: that of a dead young girl. Doris commits suicide and her death becomes one more link in the legendary line of dying young girls in the District.

I have approached *The American Girl* and *The Glitter Scene* from the viewpoint of features typical to the melodramatic mode. The excess takes many forms in the novels: It is present as an enormous number of deaths. It also shows in the abundant repetition related to the deaths, but also to other factors. The exaggeration, so typical to these two novels, can also be seen as a form of excess, and Doris is no doubt the character who distinguishes herself in this regard. One of the features of the melodramatic mode is over-sentimentality, and as I see it, *The American Girl* and *The Glitter Scene* are loaded with enormous emotions. However, far from fitting into the frame of traditional melodrama, the novels recycle the features typical of it, play with them and even deconstruct some of them. As Ulla Bäckström, one of the girls from the District, ironically describes the recurring deaths: 'Are on the cliff and die of love, fall fall, every time the same way . . . that, well, it becomes a bit monotonous' (*Glitterscenen* 2009: 30/ *The Glitter Scene* 2010: 30).

The deconstructive approach applies first and foremost to the moral emphasis that is central to traditional melodrama: the moral aspect is scattered in Fagerholm's novels. The novels ask moral questions about who is responsible for the deaths, but they offer only partial, contradictory or incomplete answers and therefore leave the reader in a state of confusion. The uncertainty muddles the conceptions of innocence and guilt. To conclude, *The American Girl* and *The Glitter Scene* are not representatives of the traditional melodrama genre, but they introduce many melodramatic features and transform them into an essential part of their postmodernist aesthetics.

The American Girl and *The Glitter Scene* form a mysterious whole in which love and death continue to circulate. The novels combine a sense of threat to alluring stories about love and desire. They use appealing imagery to fascinate the readers, but at the same time they tend to exhaust it by excessive use. When writing about contemporary American female authors such as Sylvia Plath or Angela Carter, Bronfen states that even female authors use images of dying women. Relying on Linda Hutcheon (1989) she claims, however, that female authors often use postmodern strategies 'to point out the [...] historical power of those cultural representations, while ironically contextualising both in such a way as to deconstruct them' (Bronfen 1996: 40). This is exactly what I think *The American Girl* and *The Glitter Scene* do. The exaggeration together with the excessive repetition underlines the notion of a dying young girl and therefore poses the question: Why is the death of a young girl so fascinating in Western culture? The problem, however, remains unsolved. Instead of offering answers, the novels keep the questions open. In this sense, *The American Girl* and *The Glitter Scene* resemble the Bule Marsh: a treacherous but enticing maelstrom of love and death.

References

Primary Sources

Fagerholm, Monika 2005/2004: *Den amerikanska flickan*. Femte tryckningen. Albert Bonniers Förlag, Stockholm.
Fagerholm, Monika 2009: *The American Girl. A Novel*. Transl. by Katarina E. Tucker. Other Press, New York.
Fagerholm, Monika 2009: *Glitterscenen och flickan hon går i dansen med röda gullband*. Söderströms, Helsingfors.

Fagerholm, Monika 2010: *The Glitter Scene. A Novel.* Transl. by Katarina E. Tucker. Other Press, New York.

Secondary Sources

Alanko, Outi 2001: Maurice Blanchot ja kirjallisuuden oikeus kuolemaan. Kirjallisuus (filosofian) ulkopuolena. [Maurice Blanchot and Literature's Right to Death. Literature as the Outside (of Philosophy)] In *Elämys, taide ja totuus. Kirjoituksia fenomenologisesta estetiikasta.* [Experience, Art, and Truth. Texts on Phenomenological Aesthetics] Eds. Arto Haapala and Markku Lehtinen. Yliopistopaino, Helsinki, 205–240.

Bourassa, Alan 2009: *Deleuze and American Literature. Affect and Virtuality in Faulkner, Wharton, Ellison, and McCarthy.* Palgrave Macmillan, London & New York.

Bronfen, Elisabeth 1996: *Over Her Dead Body. Death, Femininity and the Aesthetic.* Third Edition. Manchester University Press, Manchester.

Brooks, Peter 1995: *The Melodramatic Imagination. Balzac, Henry James, Melodrama, and the Mode of Excess.* Yale University Press, New Haven and London.

Critchley, Simon 1997: *Very little…Almost Nothing. Death, Philosophy, Literature.* Routledge, London.

Helle, Anna 2008: 'Kuoleman lumous nuorella iällä'. Tytöt ja kuolema Monika Fagerholmin *Amerikkalaisessa tytössä*. ['Death's Spell at a Young Age'. Girls and Death in Monika Fagerholm's *The American Girl*] – *Kirjallisuudentutkimuksen aikakausilehti Avain* 2/2008, 59–64.

Kurikka, Kaisa 2005: Tytöksi-tulemisen tilat. Monika Fagerholmin *Diva* utopistisena tekstinä. [The Spaces of Becoming-Girl. Monika Fagerholm's *Diva* as a Utopian Text] In *PoMon tila. Kirjoituksia kirjallisuuden postmodernismista* [The Space of PoMo. Texts on Postmodern Literature] Eds. Anna Helle and Katriina Kajannes. Jyväskylän ylioppilaskunnan julkaisusarja numero 74. Jyväskylä, Kampus Kustannus, 56–72.

Malmio, Kristina 2012: Phoenix-Marvel Girl in the Age of *fin de siècle*. Popular Culture as a Vehicle to Postmodernism in *Diva* by Finland-Swedish Author, Monika Fagerholm. In *Nodes of Contemporary Finnish Literature.* Ed. Leena Kirstinä. Studia Fennica Litteraria 6. Finnish Literature Society, Helsinki, 72–95.

Mercer, John and Shingler, Martin 2004: *Melodrama. Genre, Style, Sensibility.* Wallflower Press, London.

Miettinen, Niina 2004: Tekijä X. [Factor X.] – *Parnasso* 7/2004, 7–9.

Neale, Steve 1993: Melo Talk: On the Meaning and Use of the Term 'Melodrama' in the American Trade Press. *The Velvet Light Trap* Number 32, Fall 1993.

Nemesvari, Richard 2011: *Thomas Hardy, Sensationalism, and the Melodramatic Mode.* Palgrave Macmillan, New York.

Rich, Adrianne 1986: Compulsory Heterosexuality and Lesbian Existence. In Adrianne Rich: *Blood, Bread, and Poetry. Selected Prose 1979–1985.* W.W. Norton & Co, New York and London, 23–75.

Singer, Ben 2001: *Melodrama and Modernity. Early Sensational Cinema and its Contexts.* Columbia University Press, New York.

Tani, Stefano 1984: *The Doomed Detective. The Contribution of the Detective Novel to Postmodern American and Italian Fiction.* Southern Illinois University Press, Carbondale & Edwarsville.

Zarzosa, Agustin 2010: Melodrama and the Modes of the World. – *Discourse* 32.2./2010, 236–255.

Österholm, Maria Margareta 2012: *Ett flicklaboratorium i valda bitar. Skeva flickor i svenskspråkig prosa från 1980 till 2005.* [A Girl Laboratory in Chosen Parts. Queer Girls in Swedish and Finland-Swedish Literature from 1980 to 2005] Rosenlarv förlag, Stockholm.

Maria Margareta Österholm

The Song of the Marsh Queen
Gurlesque and Queer Desire in Monika Fagerholm's Novels *The American Girl* and *The Glitter Scene*

Imagine: Sandra Wärn after her friend's death. Among all the fabric, in the waterless swimming pool. Colourful, shimmering lengths she wrapped herself in, and fell asleep. Slept and slept, in sorrow, inconsolable, wrapped in fabric. But from them, like from a cocoon, the Marsh Queen was born, the one who went out into the world, to the music. Never returned, but – forgot nothing. All of it, the house, the swimming pool, her and her friend's world, all of the fabric, she took them with her to the music. Wrote songs about them, such as one called 'Death's Spell at a Young Age'. (*The Glitter Scene* 2010: 28)[1]

After Doris Flinkenberg's death, which disrupts the friendship between her and Sandra Wärn, Sandra grows up to be a rock star called The Marsh Queen writing songs about her friend and love Doris Flinkenberg, of a world of their own, full of desire and imagination. All this takes place in the District, a fictional place in Finland. The two novels *Den amerikanska flickan* (2004, *The American Girl*) and *Glitterscenen* (2009, *The Glitter Scene*) unfold the girls' relationship mainly by stories they stage and tell each other based on events in their lives and surroundings. The most important story is the one about the unsolved murder of a young girl in the District, called Eddie de Wire or The American Girl. The murder of Eddie forms a mystery plot that runs through the two novels. In my thesis *Ett flicklaboratorium i valda bitar. Skeva flickor i svenskspråkig prosa från 1980 till 2005* (2012, A Girl Laboratory in Chosen Parts. Queer Girls in Swedish and Finland-Swedish Literature from 1980 till 2005), I explore femininity in literature

---

1 *Föreställa sig*: Sandra Wärn efter väninnans död. Bland alla tygerna, i den vattentomma simbassängen. Färggranna, skimrande längder som hon rullade in sig i, och somnade. Sov och sov, i sorg, otröstlig, invirad i tyger. Men ur dem, som ur en kokong, föddes Träskdrottningen, som begav sig ut i världen, till musiken. Återvände aldrig, men – glömde ingenting. Allt det där, huset, simbassängen, hennes och väninnans värld, alla tygerna tog hon med sig, till musiken. Gjorde sånger om det, till exempel en som heter *Dödens förtrollning vid unga år* (*Glitterscenen* 2009: 28–29).

from 1980 to 2005.² In this article I return to the girls Doris and Sandra in *The American Girl*. This time I follow their story again in *The Glitter Scene*, a novel that was not part of my earlier study. My aim is to elaborate on the story about the two girls, their love and struggle, via the concept of the *gurlesque*, which is an aesthetic mixing feminism, femininity, cuteness and the grotesque.

Doris, Sandra and their fantasy world consists of gurlesque aesthetics and queer desires. Their story is scattered in both books, and told in a kaleidoscopic way. Fagerholm experiments with chronology and draws on classical mystery stories while mixing in popular songs and quotes from all sorts of places. I treat the two novels as one story, pieced together by fragments from the two books. The style of my academic writing is also intentionally influenced by the novels. As a method I want the literary worlds and languages of the girls and the texts I am examining to be present in the way I write. As literature influences theory, literature simultaneously becomes theory. I want the literary world and language of the text to be visible also in the way I am telling Sandra's and Doris' story as it is presented in the diptych *The End of the Glitter Scene*.³ The purpose of this method is to create a queer style of academic writing. Therefore, one of the most appealing aspects of the gurlesque aesthetic is its intertextual trait that fuels an academic approach to this type of literature.

The Gurlesque and the Marsh Queens of Literature

Imagine: The Marsh Queen and the District. Doris loves Sandra. Sandra loves Doris. The music begins with these places, names and loves; this particular music could be called gurlesque.

Arielle Greenberg, poet and literary critic coined the term *gurlesque* to label a tendency in American contemporary poetry. Thus, the gurlesque is a way of bringing girls and girliness to the forefront in literature:

---

2   In my thesis (Österholm 2012) I use a variation, hybrid and/or translation of queer – *skev* in Swedish – in my exploration of how gender is subverted and called in to question in the works of Fagerholm and others. The word *skev* draws on the original meaning of queer, strange or twisted; its coinage was influenced by Norwegian and Danish attempts to translate queer. Using *skev* as a variation and translated hybrid of queer, I also hope to capture forms of normativity not strictly tied to sexual desire – taking queer one step further, but also back to the original meaning of the word. *Skev*, as I write about it, is a way to talk about subversive or uncomfortable girlhoods that are not easily pinned down. In the term gurlesque I found another way of thinking about and beyond proper girlhoods. In this article gurlesque is my main focus, but in my view gurlesque texts subvert gender in a way that sometimes can be called queer in the broadest sense of the word. For the sake of clarity, I use the English term *queer* here.

3   I am inspired by the works of Donna Haraway, Rosi Braidotti, Teresa de Lauretis, Annelie Bränström Öhman, Nina Lykke and Mona Livholts as well as Gilles Deleuze and Félix Guattari when developing this method.

> [This style is] ... not ... limited to this work or this author, because the particular brand of sensuality/sentimentality at work here is one which I believe is in the zeitgeist: a 'gurlesque' aesthetic, a feminine, feminist incorporating of the grotesque and cruel with the spangled and dreamy. (Greenberg 2010: 2)

I noticed the same tendency in literature written in Swedish. Gurlesque is a way of highlighting some of the more outspoken features of the girlhoods in contemporary Swedish literature. Girlhood is a recurring theme in contemporary Swedish and Finland-Swedish literature. The writings of Monika Fagerholm, Mare Kandre and Inger Edelfeldt among other Nordic authors are full of girls who do not want to or are not able to be Proper Girls. Contemporary literature written in Swedish is rich with gurlesque themes: bad girls, swamp creatures, eating disorders, periods, rape, diaries, food, angels, hair and other experiences of girlhoods. These literary girls are not comfortable within heteronormativity and they try to tell alternative stories about girlhood. I return to these gurlesque girls because I cannot get them out of my mind; there are so many and they do such exciting things with the concept of girlhood. In Fagerholm's novel, Sandra and Doris' relationship is a great point of departure for an overview of what the gurlesque can be in late modern fiction.

The Gurlesque is situated in the Riot Grrrls movement in the nineties with ties to queer femme theory. The gurlesque was born at the end of the last millennium, but has a long heritage and has been taking place in different parts of the world such as the United States, Japan and Korea. This means that most texts that could be labelled gurlesque do not work with the concept. As the title of the volume *Gurlesque. The New Grrly, Grotesque, Burlesque Poetics* suggests, the concept takes its inspiration from a wide range of feminist theory and aesthetics occupied with the notion of femininity. As Greenberg writes in her contribution to the Gurlesque anthology:

> It's not a movement or a camp or a clique. Most of these women don't even know each other, never went to school together. They'd rather not belong to a club that would blah blah blah. Frankly, Lara and I were surprised any of these bad-asses would agree to be in this book. (Greenberg 2010: 3)

During recent decades the idea of femininity, seen as a possibility, not only a problem, has emerged within feminist theory and activism (Dahl 2011). Perhaps femininity is not just a sign of oppression and maybe being feminine is not synonymous with ciswomanhood.[4] The gurlesque is part of

---

4   Wibke Straube explains cis as 'A term that I use to describe a person who has not altered the gender or sex to which they were assigned at birth. I use this term to address a position that is assumed to hold gender privilege in comparison to a Trans position'. Straube also mentions the critique against the term: 'In this critical discussion, cis is argued to maintain an essentialising dualism between trans positions and non-trans positions that present gender as stable and coherent (cis as the position that has not changed since birth) and seem to ignore queerfeminist critiques of all genders as a "doing", a performative, embodied and continuously re-embodied practice' (Straube 2014: 23–24). See even Enke (2012).

an elaboration of femininity, put forward by Chloë Brushwood Rose and Anna Camilleri, the editors of *Brazen Femme. Queering Femininity*:

> Instead, femme might be described as 'femininity gone wrong' – bitch, slut, nag, whore, cougar, dyke, or brazen hussy. Femme is the trappings of femininity gone awry, gone to town, gone to the dogs. Femininity is a demand placed on female bodies and femme is the danger of a body read female or inappropriately feminine. We are not good girls – perhaps we are not girls at all. (Brushwood Rose and Camilleri 2002: 13)

Bad girls, good girls, perhaps no girls – the categories blur borders. But who is to decide who is outside the norm and who is inside? Who is appropriately feminine and when? Bodies produce different meanings over time and place, class, gender and race. Even though theories of femininities often focus on subversion, it is difficult to decide what subversion is and in what context it occurs (Dahl 2011). In my way of reading through the gurlesque, I am thinking of femininity as a dress that fits no body, even though it may look better on some, but mostly I am curious about the feeling of being uncomfortable in femininity and how different literary girls feel and talk about that feeling of discomfort. Femme theory is a crucial part of critical femininity studies and the recent increased interest in femininity is a development making way for gurlesque thoughts. Queer femme theory has been an inspiration in my thinking about the gurlesque as an aesthetics. I think of femme and gurlesque as branches on the same tree, exploring femininities in literature, art and life. Even though I will not dwell further on the concept of the femme in this article, femme theory still leaves its lip stick traces on my theoretical dress.

There is an extensive number of girls in contemporary literature who feel that they cannot fulfil the expectations of Proper Girlhood; they experience how the dress tightens, threatens to explode. Even though the concept of Proper Girlhood is ambivalent, a girl who is at first perceived as fitting the norms can in another context or situation be found outside them. Maria Österlund (2005: 339) uses a girl matrix in *Förklädda flickor. Könsöverskridning i 1980-talets svenska ungdomsroman* [Girls in Disguise. Gender Transgression in Swedish Young Adult Fiction from the 1980s] to explain this flexibility in girlhoods, placing the Proper Girl on one side and the Bad Girl on the other, with the tomboy in between. Sandra M. Gilbert and Susan Gubar (1979: 267–269) also discuss Frances in Emily Brontë's *Wuthering Heights* (1847) as 'a model young lady'; however, her properness is only on the surface.[5] Although the Proper Girl is not a fixed concept, the gurlesque relates to the idea of girlhood and calls it into question. The gurlesque takes inspiration and feeds on a long heritage of girlhoods in literature, art and popular culture. One early incarnation of the gurlesque is described by Greenberg, when she suggests a biography in 'Some Notes on the Origin of the (Term) Gurlesque':

---

5   See even Fyhr (2003: 186).

> Her aunts were Angela Davis and Nan Goldin and Hello Kitty and the Guerilla Girls and Dolly Parton and Exene Cervenka and Cindy Sherman and Poly Styrene, the fifteen-year-old multiracial girl with braces on her teeth screaming '*Some* people say little girls should be seen and not heard, but I say: *Oh, bondage, up yours!*' as she fronted the band X-Ray Spex in a 1977 punk club in London. She was a pink and black and yellow and red and brown and rainbow-colored silver baby, and she was a girl baby except when she was a boy baby, which was sometimes. (Greenberg 2010: 1)

The writings of Monika Fagerholm draws on similar heritage and have made an impact on literature in Sweden and Finland that cannot be underestimated. Fagerholm's books can be seen as a kind of gurlesque mother ship, a home for lost girls, offering cherries in the snow and naughty flowers, letting down their hair so they can climb down to the bottom of an empty pool. This imagery with its recurring details, motifs and narrative devices is where Fagerholm's characters Doris and Sandra exist. The ship might be called the Marsh Queen, and I would say that a large part of Swedish and Finland-Swedish contemporary literature has joined her journey, at least some parts of it.

Every journey must have music, as I mentioned at the beginning; the music that could be called gurlesque, begins with Doris and Sandra. Several years later, when their relationship is long lost, Sandra is an almost-famous rock star in New York. A few more years after that Johanna, also from the District, does a school project about Sandra, The Marsh Queen. The project is supposed to be about something that touches you, the teacher says, and to be inspired by the myth of Orpheus and Eurydice. Johanna chooses music as her subject: 'Patti, Debbie, Ametiste and the Marsh Queen. Who once grew up here in the District in the house in the darker parts of the woods: her name was Sandra Wärn' (*The Glitter Scene* 2010: 11).[6] This school project eventually becomes more important to Johanna and she calls it Project Earth. In her room she collects bits and pieces:

> *The Marsh Queen who rose from the mire.* The material that will be made into a story is constantly growing. Quotations, clippings, informations. All over the place, everywhere.
> Write her into the story. There aren't many women in the history of music. At least make her a footnote in *The History of Punk Music*.
> It is Råttis J. Järvinen, a music teacher, who said that to Johanna in school. (*The Glitter Scene* 2010: 9–10)[7]

---

6   Patti, Debbie, Ametiste och Träskdrottningen, som en gång växte upp här i trakten i huset i den dyigare delen: hennes namn var Sandra Wärn (*Glitterscenen* 2009: 15).

7   *Träskdrottningen som reste sig ur dyn.* Själva materialet som ska göras historia av växer hela tiden. Citat, klipp, informationer. Huller om buller, överallt./'Skriv in henne i historien. Det finns inte många kvinnor i musikhistorien. Gör henne åtminstone till en fotnot där. I Skräpmusiken historia.'/Det var Råttis J. Järvinen, en musiklärare som sagt det till Johanna i skolan (*Glitterscenen* 2009: 14–15).

The Marsh Queen is more than a footnote in music history; according to Johanna the Marsh Queen is history and vision, dreams, a boat you can float on. Her cultural heritage is connected to the gurlesque and to cultural phenomena mentioned by Greenberg in the biography she sketches. At the same time, the Marsh Queen is a tale to come and a backdrop for two fictional girls and an aesthetic made of feminism, femininity, poetry and popular culture. Johanna's method for telling her story in Project Earth is reminiscent of Fagerholm's poetics in the two novels and is also an inspiration for my own method.

A Girl's Room of Their Own

What Sandra in Fagerholm's novels turns out to be in her grown up life has everything to do with Doris, their love for each other and their games at the bottom of a waterless swimming pool in Sandra's house. The swimming pool is their own world, a place where they play with femininity and make up stories based on their own experiences:

> Down in the swimming pool too, when the Marsh Queen was a child, was just a square, sloppily tiled hole in the ground, never filled with water – there was so much about that house that in some way was unfinished. The girl hung out down there in the swimming pool, it became her world. And a moment in her life, childhood, *the only world*, for a time she came to share with a friend who became everything to her, they were always there. (*The Glitter Scene* 2010: 28)[8]

Fagerholm tells different stories about girlhoods than are usually told; thus, she changes how the world – in fiction and beyond – perceives girls. In Fagerholm's novels the girl's room is treated as a mythical place, a room of one's own, reminiscent of the one Fanny Ambjörnsson describes in her cultural study of the colour pink in a Swedish context. As Ambjörnsson writes, the girl's room is a place of which dreams are made, including desire, toys and over the top-aesthetics, but the freedom there is restricted (Ambjörnsson 2011: 95–96). The room that girls inhabit can be seen as a place in which they are trapped, but it can also be a room of their own, a kind of dream world with its own set of rules and a sense of freedom. Similarly, Kajsa Widegren uses the girl's room as a feminist metaphor in her thesis. The contemporary Swedish artists she writes about create 'another girl's room', built on the duality between having a room of one's own, on the one hand and being invisible and shut-in on the other (Widegren 2010: 24). Fagerholm is also experimenting with these ambivalent associations of girls in her portrait of Doris and Sandra.

8   Också ner till simbassängen som när Träskdrottningen var barn bara var ett fyrkantigt slarvigt kakelbelagt hål i marken, aldrig vattenfyllt – det var så mycket med det där huset som blivit liksom på hälft. Därnere i simbassängen höll flickan till, det blev hennes värld. Och ett slag i livet, barndomen, *den enda världen*, som hon en tid kom att dela med en väninna som blev allt för henne, de var alltid där (*Glitterscenen* 2009: 28).

Sandra and Doris are not alone in inhabiting this kind of a girl's room in contemporary literature. In my thesis I write about girls who create rooms of their own through play, dolls, imagination and writing. In Fagerholm's novels the girl's room is sometimes called The Glitter Scene, which is also alluded to in the name of the diptych, *The End of the Glitter Scene*. Sandra's experiences with Doris and their joint imagination becomes an inspiration and a necessity for her creativity. Sandra's songs and her life story fuel Johanna's dreams and fill her with longing for something more than ordinary teenage life. Doris and Sandra's room might be theirs, but it affects a lot of other people over time; Johanna is one of them.

Doris and Sandra's relationship is larger than life; that is obvious from the beginning. Doris discovers the new girl that has moved into the neighbourhood and decides that they are going to be friends. Sandra is unsure, even afraid of Doris straightforward way of following her around, but Doris is stubborn. One morning Sandra hears snoring from the pool, a noise that sounds as if it comes from something large, but not grown up, maybe a mammoth baby, she thinks. But it is Doris who, when she wakes up, proclaims that she is hungry, as if it was the most common thing to wake up in someone's empty swimming pool: 'Terribly *Dorisly* hungry. I could eat a house' (*The American Girl* 2009: 101).[9] From that moment there is a certainty for Sandra too about their relation. Together the girls build a world of their own and use a language that can be called gurlesque, filled with desire for food, fabrics and each other. Terribly Dorisly hungry could be the theme of their world, the planet called Doris. Sandra lands on the planet and the game begins. This is a game of femininity, a most serious one because it begins and ends with death. A few years later, when their relationship is over, Doris kills herself in the woods. Her suicide is linked to the murder of the American girl Eddie, a secret that is revealed when Sandra has moved away from the District.

The mystery of Eddie is one of the founding stories in the Sandra and Doris relationship. They want to walk in her moccasins, sing her songs and experience her desires, in order to get to the bottom of what really happened when she died. Sandra plays the role of the American girl, Eddie while Doris portray the men in Eddie's life, some of them still living in the District by the time of their fantasy. They discover a tape that Eddie recorded in a recording booth in Coney Island. She sings '*Look, Mom, what they've done to my song*' (*The American Girl* 2009: 2) and the song becomes a vital part of the game.[10] This is a trigger for Sandra's transformation to the Marsh Queen but the song also expresses many of the unspoken experiences Sandra and Doris have in common, such as unresolved relationships to the adult women in their lives; they have both been abandoned by their mothers. Doris and Sandra try to find different ways to walk the path from girl to woman. The adult women

---

9   Förskräckligt *doriskt* hungrig. Jag skulle kunna äta upp ett hus (*Den amerikanska flickan* 2005: 103).

10 *Titta, mamma, vad de har gjort åt min sång* (*Den amerikanska flickan* 2005: 8). Fagerholm is referring to Melanie Safka, 1970, 'What They've Done to my Song, Ma', *Candles in the Rain*, Buddha Records.

in their lives become important on that journey and the girls incorporate them in their fantasies.

Many of the girls' fantasies include desire. The heterosexual love story is in focus but is somewhat subverted while Doris is in drag as a sometimes dangerous lover. For her part, Sandra performs a scandalous and sexually outspoken femininity when she plays the role of Eddie or her absent mother Lorelei Lindberg. Thus, roleplaying becomes a way of staging feelings of attraction. All of a sudden the girls slip out of their fantasy and kiss as two girls in love. The kiss is described as wet and sweet but it is also the first step on the path to adulthood where decisions have to be made and love has to be named:

> Was it the road toward the definite and the limited, which also had a name? That which was not open to all possibilities like the winding road they were now on? If it was like that, in that case, did you want to take that step? Already now? (*The American Girl* 2009: 155)[11]

Becoming an adult marks the end of girlish freedom and is therefore a threat to the relationship. The girls do not take the leap right then; they return to their haven of childhood a few seconds after the kiss. Later, this subject will be further discussed.

Some of the girls' games remain secret; the novel never reveals the contents of them; thus, they remain the hidden room of Doris and Sandra. For a while the girls wear T-shirts with the words Loneliness&Fear printed in green and call themselves SisterNight and SisterDay.[12] The game is connected to the poltergeist phenomena. Thus, Fagerholm allows the girls some privacy, a true room of their own within the novel. However, it could be quite the contrary: is the reader invited to imagine their game and become a part of it? I often find myself daydreaming about the clothes, words and sisterhood of this particular fantasy. The game in the novel continues in my mind and expands beyond fiction. My fantasy is also triggered by other events that take place in broad daylight in the novel: fights, sexuality, pleasure and anxiety. Even though the attraction between the girls is obviously queer, it is based on their inability to feel comfortable with the idea of girlhood, to be Proper Girls; an intangible feeling pulls them together. Doris, also called the 'marsh child', coloured of roads and violence, a runaway girl with an overbite and Sandra with a harelip and braces, fragile and always an outsider to her parent's love as well as in their divorce. 'So, you are a girl with a backpack?' they say to each other, and then they were two:

---

11 Var det vägen mot det bestämda och det avgränsade, det med ett namn också. Det som inte var öppet för alla möjligheter som den kringliga väg de tog sig fram på nu?/ Om det var så, i så fall, ville man faktiskt ta det steget? Redan nu? (*Den amerikanska flickan* 2005: 154).

12 The names are written together in the original.

The one backpack and the other backpack and everything inside them, games and stories, stories and games, would occupy Doris and Sandra for many, many years. And would be elevated, little by little, into another reality. (*The American Girl* 2009: 107)[13]

The backpacks constitute the beginning of their own world. They spread the contents of their backpacks and their minds in a small rectangle, the swimming pool, where for a moment in time it is possible to negotiate the meanings of girlhood until their fantasy comes to an end and Sandra has to live on without Doris. Still, after her death Doris is always present, laughing in Sandra's head. Sandra strives to be normal, hypersuperextranormal, hanging out with Birgitta, daughter of a dentist and a Proper Girl. They do their homework together, watch TV and talk about boys. Still, Doris-in-her-head is laughing at Sandra's attempts to be a Proper Girl. To be around Birgitta is something totally different from being with Doris:

> There were things that never arose, which they had done with Doris Flinkenberg, in their world. Things that never swelled over the borders, that never became larger than, larger than life, everything. That never burst. Burst. Exploded. (*The American Girl* 2009: 379)[14]

In this new proper world, Sandra tells Birgitta that she wants to be a clothing designer. She knows she is lying to Birgitta and feels dizzy and crazy. Thus, she becomes the same insecure girl she was before she entered Doris' universe. Birgitta is so far away from the relationship with Doris, less gurlesque; Sandra pretends hard to be normal. Still people can tell: 'That there was something about her. Something really twisted' (*The American Girl* 2009: 388).[15] Birgitta cannot bring the words about Sandra's twistedness to her tongue, so she says that she doubts Sandra is telling the truth, but Sandra wonders what the truth really is. She has two parallel voices in her head, one that tries to act normal and one that is more twisted – the voice of Doris. Sandra's relationship to girlhood and femininity is complex; she tries to fit in but even her body reacts against her as she faints. In Sandra's case the gurlesque part of her life and the troublesome feeling of not being able to be a Proper Girl, becomes a very real bodily experience.

---

13 Den ena kappsäcken och den andra kappsäcken och allt som fanns däri; av detta uppstod lekar och berättelser, berättelser och lekar, lekar som var berättelser, som skulle sysselsätta Doris och Sandra i många många år. Och föras upp, småningom, i en annan verklighet (*Den amerikanska flickan* 2005: 108).

14 Det var saker som aldrig jäste, som de hade gjort med Doris Flinkenberg, i deras värld. Saker som aldrig svällde över sina ramar, som aldrig någonsin blev större än livet, hela allt. Som aldrig sprängde. Sprängdes. Detonerade (*Den amerikanska flickan* 2005: 366–367).

15 Att det var något med henne. Något riktigt skevt (*Den amerikanska flickan* 2005: 375).

Girlhood and Storytelling

If there is one lesson Sandra has learned from her time with and her loss of Doris, it is to tell stories and thereby make herself and her awkwardness comprehensible. At least to herself. In the part of *The American Girl* that deals with Doris' death there is a page with the heading 'Sandra Night/Doris Day, Doris Night/Sandra Day', encapsulating the girls' different relationships to storytelling. However, the title also hints at the fact that the two girls' approaches to storytelling are intertwined. The heading alludes to their fantasy called Loneliness&Fear. Doris could go on about her life in colourful and sparkling language, always keeping to the truth. Sandra, on the other hand, is said to be a certain kind of mythomaniac, making up various tales about herself, but never lying. There is always a hint of truth in her fantasies, games and memories. I understand this vague attitude towards make believe as the beginning of Sandra's future as The Marsh Queen performing on the glitter scene, singing gurlesque songs of love and loss, of an empty swimming pool and a girl, a silver lining of true stories. As Fagerholm presents it:

> And Sandra learned something about stories and storytelling.
> That the fireworks, that the flip side of mythomania was emptiness.
> One, or many, holes in the day, a hole in reality.
> And it was her. (*The American Girl* 2009: 484)[16]

There is a hole, a queer space, marked by Doris in Sandra's head. Sandra, like so many of Fagerholm's girls, turns to storytelling in order to become comprehensible. She twists stories about girls and gives them alternative meanings. This act is one of the main features of the gurlesque: using traditional and maybe even normative images of girlhoods – movies, fairy tales, feminist theory and popular culture – to investigate and displace the gender called girl.

The American Girl and *The Glitter Scene* deal with questions of truth and fiction, of how myths and mysteries influence and even invent realities. Sandra and Doris's relationship circles around the murder of Eddie and years later other girls tell stories about them and Doris's death. Sandra also mythologises herself as the Marsh Queen, and inspires Johanna in creating her Project Earth. These literary girls and their destinies also contribute to my thinking about what the gurlesque can be and I consider it a concept still in the making. A crucial point of departure in this development is the collaboration between literature and theory and especially how literature can be seen as theory and a way of creating knowledge. Fagerholm's literary texts bring to mind the views of Teresa de Lauretis on feminist writing and fictional figures:

---

16 Och Sandra lärde sig något om berättelser och berättande./Att fyrverkeriets, mytomanins frånsida var tomheten./Ett, eller många, hål i vardagen, ett hål i verkligheten./*Och det var hon* (*Den amerikanska flickan* 2005: 467).

> [T]hey also construct *figures*, at once rhetorical and narrative, that in resisting the logic of those conceptions, point to another cognition, a reading *other-wise* of gender, sexuality and race. This is the sense in which these texts 'do' feminist theory and are not simply feminist fiction. (de Lauretis 2007: 258–259)

This also applies to *The American Girl* and *The Glitter Scene*; the novels do feminist theory: Fagerholm reads girlhood other-wise. Doris, Sandra, and the past, present and future girls that emerge from them in the novels and their counterparts in fiction, are in that sense intertwined with gurlesque theory. The gurlesque existed before its naming and continues to grow in diverse literary texts as well as in theory, blurring the boundaries between the two, creating an ongoing gurlesque space. The gurlesque aesthetics and what girlhoods, types of bodies and experiences it relates to are dependent on equal parts of fiction and theory. The debate of what the gurlesque could be is an ongoing conversation. Fagerholm's girls are a few of the participants, telling their story about girlhood from their time and place. I am learning about the gurlesque from them and at the same time I am using the concept to understand them.

As mentioned earlier, this particular gurlesque space and possibility of negotiating girlhoods does not last forever in Fagerholm's novels. Before Doris's death ends the love story between Sandra and Doris, there is a tentative sense of something new and unknown called adulthood in the novel, with all the demands of being a proper heterosexual woman. Towards the end Sandra thinks about adulthood in these words:

> A language that they had already been in the process of outgrowing for a long time now in this puberty that had just started and that would never lead them back to a fun childhood where there were their own worlds, many lives, many games and personalities. But just the opposite, out into the real world to become grown-ups like the Islander, the cousin's mama, Lorelei Lindberg, and the Bombshell. And yes, all had their good sides, but in the grand scheme of things you still had to say, yuck. (*The American Girl* 2009: 254–255)[17]

Doris and Sandra's play dates are most serious, in a gurlesque time and place. The world of their own and its ambiguities, word play and venturous fantasies, are contrasted to adulthood. The girls leave a queer time and place in the words of Jack Halberstam in *In a Queer Time and Place. Transgender Bodies, Subcultural Lives* (2005). Heteronormativity, Halberstam writes, is not only a description of proper sexual desire and bodies; it also demands certain kinds of lives. It can be a linear story with reproduction as the main plot: a person is born, becomes a playing child then an irresponsible youth;

---

17 Ett språk som de egentligen hade hållit på att växa ur under en lång tid i denna pubertet som nyss hade börjat och som aldrig skulle leda dem tillbaka till någon rolig barndom där det fanns egna världar, många liv, många lekar och personligheter. Utan tvärtom, upp i den riktiga världen för att bli vuxna som Älänningen, kusinmamman, Lorelei Lindberg och Bombnedslaget. Och ja, de hade ju sina sidor allesammans, men i det stora hela måste man ändå säga att, yäk! (*Den amerikanska flickan* 2005: 248).

he or she grows up and forms a couple, lives a responsible life with children and then grows old. Queer lives often tell a different story, according to Halberstam (2005: 2): 'Queer subcultures produce alternative temporalities by allowing their participants to believe that their futures can be imagined according to logics that lie outside of those paradigmatic markers of life experience – namely, birth, marriage, reproduction, and death'.

Sandra and Doris are very aware of this paradigmatic narrative, even though they do not bring it to the surface, as they know that girlhood is not supposed to continue forever, but the passage to womanhood is painful. If the position of the girl holds its own kind of femininity, one that allows imagination and freedom, then the thought of growing up is frightening and absurd. That is why Sandra's and Doris' serious kiss in the woods outside their make believe world and role play, is a threat to their relationship. When seriousness enters the arena, when Sandra and Doris begin to have sex, to be in love like grown-up people, they are happy at first, but simultaneously it is also the beginning of the end. The girls' games are erotic, filled with sexual attraction, but when the girls leave their girl universe and become caught up in the norms of adult relationships, the feeling is no longer the same. Now they have a word for their relationship and it is not a word they made up themselves. Curled up together and exhausted after their first night of love making, Sandra feels, for the first time, that there are too many words and the words will soon come between them when they get into a fight that cannot be fixed. When Doris dies, the girls are barely on speaking terms.

Woman is another word towards which the girls are ambivalent. One of the adults in the story is The Bombshell Pinky Pink, a strip tease dancer who performs an excessive girliness that becomes part of Sandra's and Doris's games. At first the thought of being called a woman, by the Bombshell Pinky Pink, makes Sandra feel special, but she wonders what Doris would say about that:

> Sandra. Woman. Hmm. An interesting thought. But God, so entertaining. And Doris would then start laughing and Sandra would also start laughing. Because they did not want to become anything, either of them, just be together, like they were. (*The American Girl* 2009: 196)[18]

To use the word woman about oneself is absurd in Sandra's and Doris' universe. A few years later, when the girls are not together anymore, Doris is called a woman and also a child of nature. This happens in bed, after her first heterosexual experience, when Doris tries to talk to her boyfriend Micke about the scraps of songs singing in her head, newspaper clippings and small parts of sentences she cannot forget. However, Micke knows nothing about the world of girl fantasies, words that are able to create a world. To be a woman, which Micke wants her to be, is something totally different, and

---

18 'Sandra. Kvinna. Hm. En intressant tanke... Men gud så underhållande.' Och hur Doris sedan skulle börja skratta och hur hon också skulle börja skratta. För de ville ju egentligen inte bli till något, någondera; bara vara tillsammans, som de var (*Den amerikanska flickan* 2005: 193).

something Doris does not find very interesting. This time it is her turn to yearn for fewer words, like Sandra did before. Doris misses her girl space. She has not changed; she is still full of sabotaged songs and hot-headed ideas, but now there is no room, no one to talk to about her fantasies. She tries the word woman out for herself, confirming that this was her very first sexual experience, that heterosexual sex makes her a woman: 'Now I'm not a VIRGIN anymore' (*The American Girl* 2009: 325).[19] Girlhood is not just a question of age, following Halberstam's line of thought; it is also about lives outside the reproductive framework, producing an alternative temporality – if only for a moment. Thus, girlhood can be seen as a queer time and in the story of Sandra and Doris, girlhood is also connected to desire outside the heteronormative order.

Sandra's and Doris's exit from girlhood also marks the end of their relationship and a shift to heterosexuality. At least that is what it looks like. Neither of them is happy and Doris's suicide is connected to her loss of Sandra and the world of girlhood. Doris refuses to grow up; she chooses death over adult womanhood. Sandra grows up to be the Marsh Queen and she brings Doris and their joint girlhood into her music and performance. Sandra lets Doris and their story live forever. Their love keeps singing in her head; Doris's laughter is there too and Sandra tells the world about their romance.

After Doris's death, Sandra tries to be normal; she tries heterosexuality with overgrown and drunk boys: 'She used sex to evoke something in herself – and was it even sex, in that case?' (*The American Girl* 2009: 431).[20] She even tries Bencku, one of the boys in the District who was involved with the mythic American girl Eddie and who also was a part of her and Doris's fantasy world, but she is in no way comforted: 'Maybe she met something of herself in those rooms. Something worse than shame and promiscuity' (*The American Girl* 2009: 431).[21] By wallowing in heterosexuality she brings Doris even closer to her; Doris comments on her every move. She realizes that she has to live with Doris-in-her-head. Anything else is impossible.

The heteronormative narrative is not such a straight line in the case of Sandra and Doris (see Ahmed 2006). Pinky teaches the girls the art of dance and seduction, which magazines to read and other important facts for making femininity. The education she gives in femininity becomes the foundation for their imaginative universe. The teaching also results in Doris's school essay 'Profession: Striptease Dancer', somewhat of a gurlesque shock for her teacher and the community. Bringing that kind of knowledge into the classroom is not being a Proper Girl. During the day, when Sandra's father, the Islander, who Pinky dates, is not throwing parties, Pinky is one of the girls. It seems that Pinky has decided to live against her age and is happy to do so but her girliness is also part of her profession as

---

19 Nu är jag inte OSKULD mer (*Den amerikanska flickan* 2005: 315).
20 Hon använde sex för att framkalla något i sig – och var det ens sex, i så fall? (*Den amerikanska flickan* 2005: 417).
21 Kanske mötte hon något av sig själv i de där rummen. Något som var värre än skam och promiskuitet (*Den amerikanska flickan* 2005: 417).

a striptease dancer. Pinky shares an ambivalence toward adulthood with the girls. She is the one who tries to call Sandra a woman and she gives Doris and Sandra lessons about femininity. Despite her teachings in seduction, she is more relaxed and comfortable together with the girls than with the men and the parties at night, when she becomes someone else and the girls feel the age gap. For Pinky womanhood is like a game you can be good at. Ambjörnsson has interviewed queer activists that use the colour pink and girliness as resistance. To play with pink is to question the connections between femininity and infantilism, make a different interpretation of what childishness means, according to Ambjörnsson. To perform a pink and childish femininity is also a challenge to the heteronormative life line, a way to avoid and subvert expectations of maturity and adulthood (Ambjörnsson 2011: 201). Though Pinky is very much a part of a heteronormative order in her role as girlfriend and hostess of the parties for Sandra's father's hunting team, she also undermines heteronormativity by exaggerating girliness and not acting her age.

The kind of over the top-femininity that Pinky presents is also the main ingredient in the gurlesque. It consists of feminism, femininity, cuteness and grotesque disgust but always exaggerated. The name 'the Marsh Queen' is a good example of the gurlesque with its associations to smelly swamps and dashing (queer) queens full of confidence deeply rooted in shame. The border-crossing ambivalence of the name is a queer strategy, a way of talking back to the limitations of heteronormative femininity. To say: Do you think I am too much? Then I am going to show you too much of everything. This strategy is also embedded in the shift of the word 'queer' from invective to activism and theory. The queer activists took a word covered in shame and violence and made it their own. Pinky uses this strategy and passes it on to Doris and Sandra, but it is a risky strategy. At the beginning they are not aware of the jeopardy in which Pinky's heart and femininity is. They see her as a heroine and think she knows everything a girl is supposed to know, but soon it is revealed that everyone does not agree and Sandra's father is leaving Pinky, who is devastated. She feels how the men look upon her and almost calls herself a whore:

> 'Never become a who – striptease dancer,' the Bombshell said to Doris Flinkenberg with quivering lips and did everything she could to act impartial, but her face was red from crying, her makeup was in streaks of dark green and dark brown and black everywhere, and in the next moment, when she had said that, her face wrinkled up and she started crying again. (*The American Girl* 2009: 209–210)[22]

---

[22] 'Bli aldrig en ho… stripteasedansös', sa Bombnedslaget till Doris Flinkenberg med darrande läppar och gjorde sitt allt för att se saklig ut, men hennes ansikte var rödgråtet och sminket låg i strimlor av mörkgrönt och svart överallt, och i följande sekund, när hon sagt det, skrynkladdes hennes ansikte till gråt igen (*Den amerikanska flickan* 2005: 205).

The great and tragic love stories are also a crucial part of the stories Sandra and Doris tell each other; Pinky's sad departure fits right in. Even though the girls' loyalties are with Pinky through thick and thin, the novel shows that her kind of femininity is not wanted on the heterosexual market in the long run: 'The heart is a heartless hunter, Pinky./Love does not save on humiliation, Pinky./That is the way it is' (*The American Girl* 2009: 208).[23] This sentence is repeated several times as Pinky leaves the house and the story of Sandra and Doris, marking the tragedy that sometimes clings to girls who cannot be Proper Girls.

The risk and pleasure in making a spectacle out of oneself also brings to mind Mary Russo's *The Female Grotesque. Risk, Excess and Modernity*. Russo (1994: 12) notes that the idea of female grotesque might be a tautology, since femininity is defined against masculine norms and hence always deviant. Femininity can be understood as a hyperbolic act in itself, however undistinguished it is made. Pinky's expressions of femininity may seem innocent, but they are also on the verge of crossing boundaries. The hyperbole is one part of it; not acting according to one's age is another. Russo (1994: 60) writes: 'In other words, in the everyday indicative world, women and their bodies, certain bodies, in certain public framings, in certain public spaces, are always already transgressive – dangerous and in danger'. Actually, this is a risk the grotesque shares with the aesthetic of the cute. Sianne Ngai writes in 'The Cuteness of the Avant-garde' that cuteness in all its vulnerability and passivity also includes sadistic desires, but there is also a threat of violence hidden in cuteness, according to Ngai (2005). Lara Glenum (2010) discusses the gurlesque through Ngai in 'Theory of the Gurlesque. Burlesque, Girly Kitsch and the Female Grotesque' and suggests that girls' attraction to all things cute mirrors a sense of deformity and 'reflects the degree to which they have already found themselves stripped of significant social agency'. In the aesthetic of the gurlesque, cuteness and the grotesque come together and offer a way to feel, think and rage about the boundaries and vulnerabilities of girlhood. For a spectacular girl like Pinky, the infractions are severe as they will be in Doris's case. If the gurlesque seems cute and innocent, it should also be remembered that the stakes are high when it comes to not passing as a Proper Girl. Doris is one of many contemporary literary girls that do not make it into adulthood alive and sane.

The Rise of the Marsh Queen

> They put on makeup. They were preparing themselves for the moment when the ugly duckling would become a swan, or like this: the moment when the marsh child would become Marsh Queen, also a pun that meant nothing then, yet. That moment did not seem so far away. In any case, not if you looked at one of them.

---

23 Hjärtat är en hjärtlös jägare, Pinky./Kärleken sparar inte på förödmjukelser, Pinky./ Så är det med den (*Den amerikanska flickan* 2005: 204).

In other words at Doris. And it was only Doris, not Sandra, who was also a surprise. You had thought it would be the other way around. (*The American Girl* 2009: 272)[24]

Doris grows up, ahead of Sandra, but she will never be older, as her life ends. Still, as Marsh Queen, she will live forever in Sandra's head and in the songs that spring from her memory. Actually, right before her death Doris performs with Micke's Folk Band. There are a few recordings fuelling the myth of young death in the District several years later when *The Glitter Scene* takes place. Doris is one of many girls that passed away early; thus, her story is a source of gossip and fascination. As the artist the Marsh Queen Sandra has told about Doris in interviews, but she always stops talking before the remembering hurts. She hides behind more pedestrian dreams of moving far away and romantic notions of being an American girl. She tells the story of the ugly duckling from a small town who came to live among the glamorous and interesting people: 'Maybe I left because I wanted to be with people called Jack, Vanessa, Andy, and Cathe' (*The Glitter Scene* 2010: 28).[25] Right before she actually meets some of these people and begins her punk star journey, she is in a singing booth on Coney Island, maybe even the one where Eddie recorded her song. Sandra also wants to record that song, the one she sang with Doris, but she cannot remember the words:

> 'Look, Mom, what they've done to my song.'
> They've destroyed it.
> But it is so stupid. Suddenly she has forgotten the words. The words to THAT song, it is almost unbelievable!
> She stops singing, stops completely. Suddenly sees herself from the outside.
> What in the world is she doing standing there in the booth howling, all alone?
> (*The American Girl* 2009: 502)

Then she meets A, who soon will write a New Year's resolution: 'The Marsh Queen and I, in the month of August play in Wembley Arena./It did not turn out quite like that. But almost' (*The American Girl* 2009: 503).[26] This brief episode of the novel is called 'The day the music died and I started living'.

---

24 De målade sig. De förberedde sig för den tidpunkt när ankungen skulle bli svan, eller såhär: den tidpunkt när Träskungen skulle bli Träskdrottning, också en ordlek som inte betydde någonting då, än. Den tidpunkten verkade inte vara så långt borta. I alla fall inte om man tittade på den ena av dem./Alltså på Doris. Och det var just Doris, inte Sandra, det var också en överraskning. Man hade tänkt sig att det skulle vara tvärtom (*Den amerikanska flickan* 2005: 264).
25 Kanske for jag iväg bara för att jag ville vara med folk som heter Jack, Vanessa, Andy och Cathe (*Glitterscenen* 2009: 29).
26 Titta mamma, vad de har gjort åt min sång./De har förstört den./Men det är ju så dumt. Plötsligt har hon glömt orden. Orden i DEN sången, det är nästan oerhört!/ Hon slutar sjunga, kommer av sig helt och hållet. Ser sig plötsligt utifrån./Vad i all världen står hon där i kiosken och håjlar för, i enslighet och mol allena? [...] 'Träskdrottningen och jag, i augusti månad spelar vi på Wembley Arena.'/Det blev ju inte riktigt så./ Men nästanåt (*Den amerikanska flickan* 2005: 483–484).

Does this mean that Sandra is finally over Doris, or is it a way for her to let Doris-in-her head sing and become the queen she could have been?

Thus, the Marsh Queen rises from the fantasy worlds of girls and from the many novels and artworks performing feminist and queer theory of femininity. Gurlesque is one of her names. In 'Figures of Resistance', Teresa de Lauretis explains that feminist literature can be feminist theory. Literature, she writes, not only describes identities outside the norms; realistic or not, fiction can also transfigure reality, transform it (de Lauretis 2007: 258–259). In another essay, 'Eccentric Subjects' she argues that feminism, both as a movement and as consciousness, should try to imagine resistance to and disidentification with femininity as something other than masculinity to think outside heteronormative dichotomies. Feminism can dream and act from personal/political positions outside of such dualisms (de Lauretis 2007: 163). The tale of Sandra and Doris, as told in Monika Fagerholm's *The American Girl* and *The Glitter Scene*, is part of such feminist imagination that creates girlhood otherwise. Doris and Sandra are participating in and part of creating a gurlesque time and place in literature, art, activism and theory; they are trying to rethink stories about girlhood.

References

Primary Sources

Fagerholm, Monika 2005/2004: *Den amerikanska flickan*. Albert Bonniers Förlag, Stockholm.
Fagerholm, Monika 2009: *The American Girl. A Novel*. Translated by Katarina E. Tucker. Other Press, New York.
Fagerholm, Monika 2009: *Glitterscenen och flickan hon går i dansen med röda gullband*. Söderströms, Helsingfors.
Fagerholm, Monika 2010: *The Glitter Scene. A Novel*. Translated by Katarina E. Tucker. Other Press, New York.

Secondary Sources

Ahmed, Sara 2006: *Queer Phenomenology. Orientations, Objects, Others*. Duke University Press, Durham & London.
Ambjörnsson, Fanny 2011: *Rosa. Den farliga färgen*. [Pink. The Dangerous Colour] Ordfront, Stockholm.
Brushwood Rose, Chloë and Camilleri, Anna 2002: *Brazen Femme. Queering Femininity*. Arsenal Pulp Press, Vancouver.
Dahl, Ulrika 2011: Ytspänningar. Feminismer, femininiteter, femmefigurationer. [Surface Tension. Feminisms, Femininities, Femme Figurations] – *Tidskrift för Genusvetenskap* 1/2011, 7–27.
Enke, Anne Finn 2012: The Education of Little Cis. Cisgender and the Discipline of Opposing Bodies. In *Transfeminist Perspectives. In and Beyond Transgender and Gender Studies*. Ed. Anne Finn Enke. Temple University Press, Philadelphia, 234–246.

Fyhr, Mathias 2003: *De mörka labyrinterna. Gotiken i litteratur, film, musik och rollspel.* [The Dark Labyrinths. The Gothic in Literature, Film, Music and Role Play] Ellerströms, Lund.

Gilbert, Sandra M. and Gubar, Susan 1979 [2nd Ed 2002]: *The Madwoman in the Attic. The Woman-Writer and the Nineteenth-Century Literary Imagination.* Yale Nota Bene, New Haven & London.

Glenum, Lara 2010: Theory of the Gurlesque, Girly Kitsch and the Female Grotesque. In *Gurlesque. The New Grrly, Grotesque, Burlesque Poetics.* Eds. Lara Glenum and Arielle Greenberg. Saturnalia Books, Ardmore, 11–23.

Greenberg, Arielle 2010: Some Notes on the Origin of the (Term) Gurlesque. In *Gurlesque. The New Grrly, Grotesque, Burlesque Poetics.* Eds. Lara Glenum and Arielle Greenberg. Saturnalia Books, Ardmore, 1–8.

Halberstam, Judith/Jack 2005: *In a Queer Time and Place. Transgender Bodies, Subcultural Lives.* New York University Press, New York & London.

Lauretis, Teresa de 2007: *Figures of Resistance. Essays in Feminist Theory.* University of Illinois Press, Urbana & Chicago.

Ngai, Sianne 2005: The Cuteness of the Avant-Garde. – *Critical Inquiry* 4/2005, 811–847.

Russo, Mary 1994: *The Female Grotesque, Risk, Excess and Modernity.* Routledge, New York & London.

Straube, Wibke 2014: *Trans Cinema and its Exit Scapes. A Transfeminist Reading of Utopian Sensibility and Gender Dissidence in Contemporary Film.* Linköpings universitet, Linköping.

Widegren, Kajsa 2010: *Ett annat flickrum. Kön, ålder och sexualitet i Maria Lindbergs, Anna-Maria Ekstrands och Helene Billgrens flickbilder.* [Another Girls' Room. Gender, Age and Sexuality in Maria Lindberg's, Anna-Maria Ekstrand's, and Helene Billgren's Pictures of Girls] Mara förlag, Göteborg.

Österholm, Maria Margareta 2012: *Ett flicklaboratorium i valda bitar. Skeva flickor i svenskspråkig prosa från 1980 till 2005.* [A Girl Laboratory in Chosen Parts. Queer Girls in Swedish and Finland-Swedish Literature from 1980 to 2005] Rosenlarv förlag, Stockholm.

Österlund, Maria 2005: *Förklädda flickor. Könsöverskridning i 1980-talets svenska ungdomsroman.* [Girls in Disguise. Gender Transgression in Swedish Young Adult Fiction from the 1980s] Åbo Akademis förlag, Åbo.

Transformations and Forms of Reading

Ann-Sofie Lönngren

Oppression and Liberation
Traditional Nordic Literary Themes of Female Human-Animal Transformations in Monika Fagerholm's Early Work

Ego, identity, collectivity and subject-hood, most often in relation to young girls, have been central themes in Monika Fagerholm's authorship as far back as her debut short story collection *Sham* (1987). The literary characters attempt one position, then reconsider, change, assess, move forward, or go back in a movement that is constantly renewed (Sandin 1991: 2–4). In this article I will focus on a specific aspect of this identity-related instability in two texts from the early phase of the authorship, namely its possible intertextual relationships to Nordic folklore regarding female human characters' transformations into animals. Indeed, the cultural representations of woman-animal transformations points toward the posthumanist critique of the Enlightenment idea of a cohesive, pre-established human subject clearly separated from the animal (Wolfe 2009: xiii–xiv).

The figure of a human being turning into an animal is an ancient trope and can be found worldwide. The Western literary canon includes a few early and heavily influential examples such as *The Odyssey* (c. 700 BCE), where the witch Circe transforms Odysseus' men into pigs and Ovid's *Metamorphoses* (c. 0), which contains a variety of transformations. Within a specifically Nordic context, the presence of such motifs and storylines is historically so rich that the question is not whether they exist, but rather, as H.R. Ellis Davidson (1978: 126) notes, where to begin investigating them. In everything from Sámi shamanism to the Old Norse sagas, from the Finnish epic *The Kalevala* to Swedish folk tales, there is an abundance of stories about human-animal transformations.

Interestingly, this transformation figure has continued to be represented up to the present day, with uncountable variations and forms of expression. This has been discussed by George Ferzoco and Miriam Gill, who claim that in modern times, metamorphosis is a relevant area of study both because of its persistence in European culture and because it is a 'pervasive concept to raise fundamental questions about the nature and agency of radical change'. Moreover, the simultaneous conservative *and* subversive potentials in this figure, in that the transformation can be both voluntary and liberating or forced and oppressive, ultimately mean that the figure is essentially about agency, social change, politics and power (Ferzoco and Gill 2005: 1–2). In the modern context, such stories are often found within the frames of what

Gilles Deleuze and Félix Guattari have called 'minor literature', characterized by political and collective qualities. In their discussion, this literature is exemplified by Franz Kafka's authorship in general and *The Metamorphosis* (1915) in particular (Deleuze and Guattari 1987: 16–27).

Thus, the figure of the human-animal transformation is interesting because it *both* consists of intertextual traces from Western, literary history *and* has the potential to point out acute contemporary political problems.[1] Moreover, it entails the potential to be both liberating and oppressive. In relation to this discussion, Fagerholm's authorship stands out as particularly relevant, as it is generally considered to be one within the contemporary, Nordic context that most consistently uses mythological and old folklorist motifs. Thus, it underscores an assertion made by W.M.S. and Claire Russell (1978: 145), namely that folklore is an integral part of literature, not an intrusive element of it, something that may affect the language, structure and themes of outstanding works in both poetry and prose.

However, Fagerholm does not use the folklorist material randomly; rather, I argue, she uses it in ways that highlights the fact that, as Aili Nenola (1993: passim) points out, gender and sexuality are aspects that concern folklore overall.[2] More specifically regarding the literary figure of human-animal transformations, Fagerholm clearly employs its inherently political potential in order to highlight the significance of these categories. On a wider scale, this can be understood from the perspective of ecofeminist lines of thought, according to which there is a Western, discursive connection between 'woman' and 'animal' that reaches back to Aristotle.[3] Moreover, as Cary Wolfe (2003: 8) has stated, 'the humanist discourse of species will always be available for us by some humans against other humans as well, to countenance violence against the other of *whatever* species – or gender, or race, or class, or sexual difference'. This indicates that the category of 'human being' is not a neutral one but, rather, a fiction created in the intra-action between different axes of power.[4]

In this essay, I set out to explore potential intertextual connections between two texts from Fagerholm's early literary production and mythology and

---

1   I understand the concept *intertextuality* not as a phrasing of the ways in which authors influence one another or the sources of a literary work, but rather as a concept that contains the idea that the literary text is always already an ideological 'permutation of texts'. See Roudiez, 'Introduction,' (1980: 15), and Kristeva (1980: 36–38).
2   This is a phrasing that should not be misunderstood. 'Gender' and 'sexuality' are historically situated concepts, intimately bound up with the development of modern, Western societies (Davidson 1987:1; Laqueur 1990; Butler 1990). Although the application of these terms before or beyond this sphere is thus essentially anachronistic, it still points out a historical reality of the distribution of power between different bodies as well as the continuum of inter-dependence between norm and deviance, between power and resistance.
3   See, for example, Gaard 1993; Adams 1993; Soper 2000.
4   See also Fuss (1996: 1). I chose to employ Karen Barad's term 'intra-activity' to open up the possibility that this process happens in the dynamic relationship between both human- and non-human factors. See Barad (2008: 132–135), and Lykke (2010: 51).

folklore within the Nordic sphere, specifically with regards to the construction of the 'human' in relation to gender and sexuality. The discussion will focus on two different variations of the figure of transformation in relation to two female literary characters: Patricia in the short story 'Patricia Rabbit' from the collection of short stories *Patricia* (1990) and Isabella in the novel *Wonderful Women by the Sea* (1994). My hope is that such a study will serve several purposes. First, I aim to understand how the intertextual relationship between folklore and literature can manifest itself in the twentieth century. Second, I wish to discuss the significance of norms regarding gender and sexuality in the discursive construction of the human literary character in Fagerholm's authorship. Finally, I strive to deepen the understanding of some particularly significant aspects of Fagerholm's fiction.

Patricia Becoming-Rabbit: A Line of Escape

Patricia. Berättelser, a collection of short stories, was published in 1990 and has not received much attention in previous research.[5] In *Portföljen i skogen* (2001: 201), Åsa Stenwall claims that the collection as a whole is 'characterized by disgust and hysteria, escape and pessimism in the world of girls',[6] while Fagerholm ('Fagerholms nya kretsar': 2009) herself has argued that *Patricia* is over-theorized and 'probably the most boring book in the world'.[7] In general, I agree with Fagerholm that the narratives in her novels are more intriguing than the ones in this collection, but I nevertheless want to maintain that the short story 'Patricia Rabbit' makes up in complexity for what it possibly lacks in aesthetic qualities.

In 'Patricia Rabbit', the main character Patricia Blanck, a young university student, lives in a room she rents in the house of two eccentric sisters, Edith and Marnie. The sisters are very curious about Patricia and her life, in particular her love life. Pressured, Patricia lies and says that she has a boyfriend named Björn, a man who definitely exists and with whom Patricia has had sex a few times but is not in love with. Rather, as I have claimed in a previous article (Lönngren 2011: 61–64; see even Österholm 2012: 211), Patricia is more likely to be in love with Björn's girlfriend Monica, something that Patricia does not dare to confess, even in her own diary, except on one occasion: 'M, beloved [...]. It is the first and last time she spells it out' (*Patricia* 1990: 141).[8] This unacknowledged same-sex desire is continually, throughout the story, conceptualized as 'Rabbit', an intrusive presence in Patricia's life, who even sometimes thinks 'inside her

---

5 This collection of short stories has not been translated into English. The translation of the title and all the quotes in this article are mine.
6 [...] 'drag av äcklad hysteri, av flykt och svartsyn i flickvärlden'.
7 'Fagerholms nya kretsar kring brott och myter', (*Dagens Nyheter* 19.9.2009, http://www.dn.se/dnbok/fagerholms-nya-kretsar-kring-brott-och-myter/ accessed 12.12.2013, 'nog världens tristaste bok.'
8 M, älskade [...]. Det är första och sista gången hon skriver ut det. (*Patricia* 1990: 141)

head. The thing which is thinking is independent and unspeakable' (*Patricia* 1990: 134).⁹ Apparently, it is the 'love that dares not speak its name' that is haunting Patricia in the shape of Rabbit.[10]

In her room, Patricia struggles to make Rabbit disappear and thus hacks with a pen in the palm of her hand until she bleeds, then 'lies down on the bed, presses her still-tightened fist against the cheek, tries to shut her eyes and close her ears. It doesn't help. Rabbit is there' (*Patricia* 1990: 140).[11] However, the situation does not get completely out of hand until Patricia gets fed up with all the lying and tells the sisters that the relationship between her and Björn is over. The helpful sisters then invite the nice youth pastor Erik from their congregation to their home, in an apparent attempt to bring the two young people together. Patricia has no choice but to play along with the charade, but when she returns to her room in the evening, the transformation she has been trying to prevent is completed: 'The change is painful. Her ears jerk around: it feels like knives through her head, her eyes enlarge, change their shape and position: like knives through her head, her skin becomes light and shaggy fur: that is the worst of all' (*Patricia* 1990: 152).[12]

When the sisters and Pastor Erik discover Patricia's change, they tend to her as well as they can. Her room is now more like a cage and she is given lettuce to eat. All this appears proper since Patricia's transformation concerns both body and mind: 'Rabbit shivers, strives for cleanliness. Rabbit whines but does not give any other signs of life. Rabbit is shy. When the door opens Rabbit hides as well as it can, under the bed or on the window sill behind the curtain' (*Patricia* 1990: 154).[13]

Patricia's way back to human-hood is depicted as a convalescence, in which long walks with Pastor Erik play an important part, along with the books about Christian love that he lends her, with titles such as *The Joy of Being a Woman (and What a Man Can Do)* and *I Married You* (*Patricia* 1990: 154).[14] After a period of time, Patricia says to Erik: 'Did you know that I am Rabbit at night? Before it was every night, then all the time, now only sometimes. Almost never' (*Patricia* 1990: 155).[15] When Erik then 'ironically asks her/if she eats dandelion leaves as well/it is as if a magic wand tapped

---

9   Det är någonting som tänker i hennes huvud. Det som tänker är fristående och onämnbart (*Patricia* 1990: 134).
10 This is an often referred to quote by Oscar Wilde regarding homosexuality.
11 [...] lägger sig på sängen, trycker sin ännu knutna näve mot kinden, försöker sluta sina ögon och stänga sina öron. Det hjälps inte. Kanin är där. (*Patricia* 1990: 140.)
12 Förvandlingen är plågsam. Öronen saxar: det känns som knivar genom huvudet, ögonen förstoras, ändrar form och läge: som knivar genom huvudet, huden blir ljus och ruggig päls: det är det allra värsta (*Patricia* 1990: 152).
13 Kanin darrar, bemödar sig om renlighet. Kanin gnyr, men ger annars inga livstecken ifrån sig. Kanin är skygg. När dörren öppnas gömmer sig Kanin så gott det går, under sängen eller på fönsterbrädet, bakom gardinen (*Patricia* 1990: 154).
14 English in original text.
15 [...] vet du att jag är Kanin på nätterna. Förut varje natt, sedan hela tiden, nu bara ibland. Nästan aldrig (*Patricia* 1990: 155).

Patricia./She ceases to be Rabbit altogether' (*Patricia* 1990: 155).[16] Just as in the fairy tale, the prince comes along to save the woman in need and gives her cultural meaning within a context of compulsory heterosexuality.[17] However, as 'fully recovered' and engaged to Erik, Patricia does not act the way she used to. Instead of being a bit quiet and withdrawn, she now likes to speak loudly (especially when feminists are listening) about how lovely it feels to wear lace undergarment for the sake of a man. Thus, instead of the Rabbit she first transforms into – an act which certainly suggests resistance against heteronormative expectations of heterosexuality – she has now become more like a conventional feminine *Playboy* bunny.[18]

There are several interesting aspects of Patricia's transformation in 'Patricia Rabbit'. The first one I would like to point out is that it is part of a long mythological and folklorist tradition, previously discussed by Marina Warner (1994: 353–356), of female literary characters becoming animal in order to escape sexual advances from men.[19] In relation to this assertion, it is interesting to note that it is also possible to understand Patricia's transformation as a 'becoming animal', along the lines of thought of Gilles Deleuze and Félix Guattari. Indeed, just as I have previously discussed in relation to Finnish author Aino Kallas's novel *The Wolf's Bride* (1928),[20] Patricia's change can be conceptualized as a female 'line of escape', a means to resist the oppressive triangular constellation under which she suffers (Deleuze and Guattari 1987: 12): the curious sisters, the male lover (Erik/Björn) and herself.

Moreover, I would like to highlight the intertextual relationship between 'Patricia Rabbit' and texts produced in a pre-modern sphere. As Fagerholm herself has acknowledged in an interview in 1991, this story was inspired by the above-mentioned Ovid's *Metamorphoses* (Sandin 1991: 4), but I would also like to claim that, specifically in relation to folklore from the Northern European sphere, Patricia has a clear forerunner in the destiny of the young girl Aino, who is depicted in the Finnish national epic *The Kalevala*.

---

16 [...] ironiskt frågar henne/om hon äter maskrosblad också/är det som om ett trollspö vidrört Patricia./Hon slutar vara Kanin helt och hållet (*Patricia* 1990: 155).
17 This concept comes from Adrienne Rich (1993). Of course, *heterosexuality* is a concept just as dated as *gender* and *sexuality*, a fact that I discussed in footnote 2 (Katz 1995).
18 Interestingly, this distinction seems possible to conceptualize in line with the one between 'metaphor' and 'figuration' suggested by Rosi Braidotti (2002: 3).
19 Sometimes, turning into an animal might not just mean that a female literary character can escape gender-based expectations but also that she can defend herself. This is the case, for example, in Fagerholm's novel *DIVA* (1998), where the female protagonist at one point becomes a 'dog-girl' who yaps, bites and goes down on all fours when threatened by unwelcome male advances.
20 See chapter 3 in *Following the Animal. Power, Agency, and Human-Animal Transformations in Modern, Northern-European Literature* (Lönngren 2015).

Resisting Different-Sex Coupling and Marriage: Patricia and Aino

The Kalevala was collected and recorded into a coherent story during the nineteenth century, but draws on old traditions of Finnish songs, tales, legends and myths. One of these is the story of Aino, who is betrothed by her brother Joukahainen to be the wife of the much older Väinämöinen. Aino is very sad about this and sits down to cry beside the sea. Then she sees three young women bathing, which makes her want to do the same. She goes into the water, and then she climbs up on a rock, which sinks and takes her down with it into the depth of the sea. Aino is mourned as dead, but the next time Väinämöinen is out fishing he captures a strange fish. He takes out his knife to kill it, but then it escapes into the water again. From the water it speaks to him, with Aino's voice, saying the last words he will ever hear from her:

> I am not a water-salmon,
> Not a perch from deepest water,
> But a young and lovely maiden,
> Youthful Joukahainen's sister
> Whom thou all thy life hast longed for
> Whom thou hast so long desired. (*The Kalevala* 1985: 57)

There are several possible intertextual connections between the story of Aino and 'Patricia Rabbit'. The first one is apparent from the brief description above: they both employ similar lines of escape, *becoming animal*, in order to flee gender-based expectations for different-sex relationships. These are expectations that are clearly so rigid that the only way to escape them is to give up the very foundation of being 'woman' altogether – humanity. Thus, both Patricia and Aino can be understood through the lens of Judith Butler's (1993: 7) claim that 'the matrix of gender relations is prior to the emergence of the "human"'.[21] Moreover, as Aino in fact risks drowning; this story, clearer than Fagerholm's modern one, points out that a flight line is far from a refuge (Deleuze and Guattari 1987: 41)[22] but might, rather, be a dangerous

---

21 The strategy of becoming animal in order to avoid sexual advances from men is also employed in Swedish author Birgitta Trotzig's short story 'The Girl and the Butterfly', where a girl who is to marry instead is touched by a butterfly and pupates (This has not been translated into English. The translation of the title is mine. Orig. 'Fjärilen och flickan', in *I kejsarens tid. Sagor* [*In the Time of the Emperor: Fairy Tales*] (Trotzig 1975: 113). Another example can be found in Swedish author Sofia Rapp Johansson's horrifying prose poem *Silverfish*, in which a four-year-old girl who is regularly raped by her father eventually turns into a silver fish (this has not been translated into English. The translation of the title is mine. Orig. *Silverfisken* [2005]).
22 This fact is also experienced by the grown-up Renée in the end of Fagerholm's novel *Wonderful Women by the Sea*. Just as for Aino, Patricia and Isabella, water is Renée's sanctuary and her private sphere, far off from her destructive relationship with her best friend's boyfriend (which, interestingly, within the context of the human/animal transformation, includes BDSM practices in which Renée is led on a leash). But water is also the element that finally causes her death: she drowns. Also as a child, Renée at one point tries to employ a line of escape, becoming animal, to

and unpredictable strategy with a high price. The acknowledgement of the intertextual connection with *The Kalevala* helps acknowledge the desperation and danger that characterizes Patricia's situation in 'Patricia Rabbit'.

The second possible intertextual connection between these two stories is the significance of *water*, an element that comes across as that which bell hooks (1990: 41–49) has called a 'site of resistance'. In both *The Kalevala* and 'Patricia Rabbit', water is a collective, feminine sphere, where women meet and form relationships that not only go beyond the heterosexual norm but might also, in fact, pose a threat against it. As I made clear above, the reason why Aino goes into the water is because she sees three young women already bathing in it, and she thus chooses the company of other women rather than the different-sexed pairing. Indeed, the possibility of female same-sex desires, practices and relationships inherent in this choice is, as we have seen, the central theme in 'Patricia Rabbit'.

However, water is also a significant feature in Fagerholm's story. Repeatedly, Patricia is referred to as a 'mermaid', and she makes frequent visits to the bath house. This is the only place where she feels at home, where she can hide away from the demands of the outside world. Just like Aino, Patricia is attracted to the water because of the presence of female bodies in or near it, an attraction that does not have to be primarily erotic; indeed, Patricia 'loves to look at the old women's spectacular physiognomies, at breasts and veins and grey, wide-open genitalia in the sauna' (*Patricia* 1990: 133).[23] Water is the element in or near which the un-demanding, non-judgmental female community can be found.

Finally, there is a third aspect that stands out as meaningful in both *The Kalevala* and 'Patricia Rabbit', thus suggesting an intertextual relationship between the two, namely the significance of *hair* in regards to gender and sexuality. When Aino is betrothed to Väinämöinen, she mourns the fact that as a married woman, she will be forced to hide her hair:

> Therefore have I cause for weeping,
> Weeping for the beauteous tresses,
> Now my youthful head adorning,
> And my hair so soft and glossy,
> Which must now be wholly hidden,
> While I still am young and blooming. (*The Kalevala* 1985: 37)

---

get away from the oppressive context characterized by the adult's power over the child. She does that by escaping into the forest and staying away for days. In the latter part of Fagerholm's authorship, the line of escape of becoming-animal is at one point explored in yet a different manner by Maj-Gun Maalamaa in *The Glitter Scene* (2009). During a crisis, caused by the belief of having killed her best friend, this female literary character becomes the 'child-animal', stays indoors, in the dark for days, and eats cat food.

23 [...] älskar att se på de gamla kvinnornas vidunderliga fysionomier, på bröst och blodådror och grå, uppsprängda kön på bastulaven (*Patricia* 1990: 133).

In *The Kalevala*, long flowing hair apparently signifies youth and freedom, an idea that is both echoed and inverted in 'Patricia Rabbit'. At the bath house, Patricia refuses to use a bathing cap when she visits the swimming pool because she thinks that her long, flowing hair makes her look like a mermaid when she is swimming. However, the night she turns into Rabbit, she dreams that she is swimming and suddenly discovers that she has lost all her hair. Dream and reality merge when the reader, immediately after having been told about this dream, learns that the night after Patricia's transformation, her hair had to be swept up from the floor. After Patricia's 'recovery', she again lets her hair grow long, an act that is strongly encouraged by her boyfriend Erik.

Thus, in both *The Kalevala* and 'Patricia Rabbit', female hair is an important feature, apparently related to expectations regarding sexuality. This suggests an intertextual relationship between the two, but in 'Patricia Rabbit', the significance of hair also clearly points beyond this connection and towards other possibilities. As we saw in the quote above, when Patricia changes into Rabbit, she develops hair all over her body, a change that has no counter-part in *The Kalevala*. Rather, this can be understood in relation to Maria Margareta Österholm's (2012: 214) claim that the animal theme in 'Patricia Rabbit' contains traces from the fairy-tale world, and can thus be related to an assertion previously made by Warner (1994: 353–354), that the development of body hair is an important aspect for the female mythological or folklorist figure turning animal in order to escape sexual advances from men.

Moreover, just as in traditional fairy tales, and in contradiction to the freedom the long hair signifies for Aino in *The Kalevala*, for Patricia, long hair is instead associated with expectations of traditional femininity and different-sexed sexual desire (cp. Warner 1994: 363–364). The connection between heteronormativity and Patricia's long hair is apparent in the fact that when she at one point meets her secret love Monika for coffee, she hides her hair under a scarf. Moreover, Monika is the only one who likes Patricia's short hair-cut and Monika's own photo exhibition features female heads, shaved and tattooed. Not surprisingly, this exhibition is not much appreciated by Erik. Here, a twentieth-century, Western, lesbian sub-culture is suggested, in which short hair on women signifies non-heteronormativity and female emancipation. This is an interesting application and subversion of an ancient conceptualization of women's hair as significant in relation to norms regarding gender and sexuality.

Together, these three points of comparison between *The Kalevala* and 'Patricia Rabbit' concerning the woman-animal transformation, the significance of water, and the meaning of hair certainly suggest an intertextual relationship between the two stories, but also point out possible connections between Fagerholm's story and the wider sphere of fairy tales and modern societal norms. Before I draw any more extensive conclusions, I would like to complement this discussion with one about Fagerholm's use of the folklorist figure of the swan maiden.

Isabella, Sea Maiden. A Contemporary Swan Maiden

In *Underbara kvinnor vid vatten* (1994, *Wonderful Women by the Sea* 1997), the course of events primarily takes place in the Finnish archipelago during three summers in the 1960s, where Isabella (Bella), her husband Kajus and their son Thomas socialize with another family: mother Rosa, father Gabbe and their two daughters Nina and Renée. While sunbathing, water-skiing and drinking cocktails, complicated relationships develop between the two families, primarily between Bella and Rosa, who eventually run off to Copenhagen together. From that trip only Rosa returns, while Bella leaves her husband and son for good and eventually gives birth to a child she has conceived with Rosa's husband Gabbe.

In relation to the discussion above, it is interesting to note that one of the main characters in this novel, Bella, can in fact be seen as a modern version of the ancient folklorist motif of the swan maiden. This is a global figure that has been extensively discussed by Barbara Fass Leavy (1994: 11), who, in her influential study *In Search of the Swan Maiden,* claims that tales about swan maidens are particularly interesting since they 'contrast the pleasures of a magic realm with the harder facts of real life, which for woman include minimal (if any) autonomy in her existence'. Moreover, Fass Leavy (1994: 37) identifies the Old Norse text *The Lay of Volund* in *Poetic Edda* (c. 800–1000) as one of the oldest sources of this kind of tale. The story begins with three young maidens flying through the air and stopping to spin fine linen on a beach. There, they meet three men, whom they follow away from the sea and into their houses. However, what the men do not know is that the swan maidens have only come to stay for a period of time, or, more precisely, seven years:

> but all the eight they suffered anguish,
> and in the ninth necessity parted them;
> the maidens hastened through Mirkwood,
> the strange, young creatures, to fulfill their fate. (*The Poetic Edda* 1996: 103)

Seven years is, interestingly, about the time Bella is happy to stay with Kajus, after which she experiences a period of anxiety and stress before she finally leaves him. Of course, it takes more than this similarity to identify Bella as a contemporary swan maiden and I will now discuss two different features that suggest an intertextual relationship between traditional tales about the swan maiden and *Wonderful Women by the Sea*.

Just as in *The Kalevala* and 'Patricia Rabbit', the first feature is *water*, an element that is mentioned even in the novel's title, *Wonderful Women by the Sea* and then immediately referred to again in the title of the first chapter: 'Isabella, sea-maiden'. Here, a connection is explicitly made between water and Bella; moreover, the reference to her as a 'sea-maiden' means that she is conceptualized as a sort of liminal creature, a mythological figure that only *appears* as completely human, while *really* being something else. In this chapter, Bella is certainly introduced as a being who, just like the swan maidens, is levitated above the water surface: As a young woman, Bella works one summer at an amusement park as a sea maiden sitting on a small shelf above a swimming pool. The visitors pay to throw balls at a red button below the shelf, which, if hit, makes the shelf give way and causes the sea maiden to fall into the water. Kajus comes to the amusement park time and again to try and make Isabella fall and he succeeds over and over, but he also makes her fall for him and just as in the *The Lay of Volund*, she strips herself of her non-human features (feathers/the sea-maiden costume) and follows him away from the water into the life they create as a married couple.

Throughout the novel, however, the presence of the sea at the summer resort is a constant reminder of the opportunities of another kind of life that Bella lost when she chose to marry Kajus. As she spends most of her time on the beach with her best friend at the resort, Rosa, the draw of the water appears to be constant. Indeed, it is by the sea that the two women become close and discover that they not only share a similar longing to escape life as married with children (*Wonderful Women by the Sea* 1997: e.g. 49), but also develop some kind of erotic or romantic feelings for each other. In fact, when it is clear that Bella is pregnant with Rosa's husband's child, Rosa expresses the desire to raise this child together with her. These circumstances make water come across as an element with similar significance as the one in 'Patricia Rabbit', as a space for a female community and for desires outside the heterosexual norm. Apparently, however, Rosa is not a swan maiden; at the end of the novel, it is only Bella who abandons husband and son.

This line of analysis leads to a second feature that makes it possible to understand Bella as a contemporary swan maiden, namely the fact that along with her husband Kajus, she also abandons their son, Thomas. This circumstance introduces into *Wonderful Women by the Sea* that which Fass Leavy (1994: 63) has described as one of the more disturbing elements of the swan maiden, namely that she leaves not only her husband behind, but also her children. However, Bella does not do so with a light heart. In a painfully drawn-out process in the novel's latter half, she tries repeatedly to speak with Thomas before she leaves, but in his childish way he refuses to listen to what he instinctively knows is bad news:

> 'Hello, Only Child. Are you asleep?' Bella will say. Thomas does not reply. But his silence will not stop Bella.
> 'We must have a talk.'
> 'I am going to tell you everything now. I want you to listen, Thomas.'
> 'Thomas dear. Wake up. We must have a talk.'
> Thomas turns over on his stomach and buries his face in the comforter, grunting in a way he believes is usual for him when he is fast asleep. (*Wonderful Women by the Sea* 1997: 199)[24]

---

24 'Hej Endabarnet, sover du?' kommer Bella att fråga. Thomas kommer inte att svara. Men Bella kommer inte att sluta prata för det./'Vi måste prata'./'Nu tänker jag berätta allt för dig. Nu vill jag att du lyssnar, Thomas'./'Thomas snälla. Vakna. Vi måste prata'./Thomas vänder sig på mage, borrar ansiktet i dynan, grymtar som han har för sig att han brukar göra när han sover djupt. (*Underbara kvinnor vid vatten. En roman om syskon* 1994: 195)

Time and again, Bella tries to talk to Thomas, but he turns away and eventually, it is only in writing he gets her message: she has left the family. Interestingly, this agony for leaving the children behind in particular (but sometimes also for leaving the human husband) is typical for the swan maiden and a forerunner to Bella's and Thomas's relationship within Nordic folklore can, in fact, be found in depictions about a close literary relative to this literary figure: the seal woman or female *selkie*.[25]

These folkloristic creatures occur most commonly in Orkney Islands and Scottish folklore, but they also exist in Australia and Northern America; within a Nordic context, they can be found in folklore of the Farœ Islands and Iceland.[26] In *The Seal's Skin*, an Icelandic story transcribed in the 1860s (but orally told since ancient times), the narrative basically follows the one in traditional swan maiden tales, albeit with the significance of the feathers exchanged for a seal's skin. A young man walks by a cave outside of which many seals' skins hang. He takes one home and comes back to the cave the day after, only to find a young, beautiful woman searching for the skin he took. They marry, live in harmony and have children, but the woman often looks at the sea. One day the husband leaves behind the key to the chest in which he has locked her skin at home. The woman finds the key and opens the chest out of curiosity, but upon finding the skin, she bids her children farewell and plunges into the sea with the words:

Woe is me! Ah, woe is me!
I have seven bairns on land,
And seven in the sea. (*Favorite Folktales from around the World* 1986: 310–311)[27]

These strong emotions before abandoning the children strongly resemble Bella's anguish regarding Thomas in *Wonderful Women by the Sea*, but the fact that Bella leaves treats behind for him also suggests an intertextual connection to another Nordic tale about the *selkie*, the Farœ story *The Seal Woman*. Here, the woman's concern for the children she leaves behind is highlighted, as, upon having found her skin, she puts out the fire and hides sharp objects so that they will not hurt themselves before their father comes home (Hammershaimb 2007). Thus, she reveals a concern for the well-being of her children after she has left, that strongly resembles that of Bella. However, one common feature of the swan maidens in *The Lay of Volund*, the *selkies* in the two Nordic stories, and Bella, is that despite the anguish

---

25 The similarity between the swan maiden and the female *selkie* was previously pointed out by Fass Leavy (1994: 39).
26 Folkloristic motifs and mythologies involving animals tend to be altered according to the species available in the immediate surroundings. The swan exists globally, but in some places, where other species are abundant (like seals in Iceland), this other species is employed instead. Moreover, being creatures living in the sea and on land with a face and body almost the size of humans', seals appear as particularly fitting for these kinds of tales.
27 'Bairn' is an old Scottish word for children. See also *Icelandic Folktales and Legends* (1972: 100–102).

they all feel before leaving their children and husbands, they all succumb to the temptation to escape when given the opportunity. Moreover, the female characters all choose to leave at exactly the same time in all of these stories: when the husband is temporarily away from home.

Thus, when comparing *Wonderful Women by the Sea* with pre-modern folklore within the Nordic sphere, possible intertextual relationships are revealed, and a continuum is made visible regarding the tension between the expectations of motherhood and family on the one hand and the longing for female independence on the other. It is an interesting fact that the prerequisites for this split within the female literary characters are depicted as far back as *The Lay of Volund*, in which it is made clear that the maidens leave their families because they long to go to battle. As Fass Leavy (1994: 37) notes, this signals a significant duality in their characters in relation to gender. At the beginning of the poem, the swan maidens are spinning, an activity that in ancient Nordic texts is associated with both female magic and traditional female chores. As female warriors, however, they instead present themselves as Valkyries, female spirit beings who, on the battle fields of Midgard, chose which warriors were to die and brought them to Valhalla.

To a contemporary reader the co-existence of spinning and warfare in one figure might appear somewhat paradoxical. However, rather than personal characteristics, these should be seen as metaphors for the swan maidens' unreliability as wives and mothers (Fass Leavy 1994: 37). Clearly, aspects of these characters simply do not comply with expectations regarding gender and sexuality; indeed, within the Western, modern sphere, Bella is only one among many who has this female warrior inside of her.[28] As Fass Leavy (1994: 293–302) notes, Nora in Norwegian dramatist Henrik Ibsen's play *A Doll House* (1879) is a swan maiden, leaving both husband and children behind. More recent examples are Sally in Swedish author Sara Stridsberg's Novel *Happy Sally* (2004), and Mrs. Brown in American author Michael Cunningham's *The Hours* (1998), novels in which the symbolism of water helps to identify the motif of the swan maiden.

Conclusions

In this essay I have, by placing parts of Fagerholm's authorship in a wider context, been able to point out possible intertextual relationships between Patricia in 'Patricia Rabbit' and Isabella in *Wonderful Women by the Sea* and a global as well as more specifically Nordic context of folklore, mythology, and motifs common in fairy tales. Thus, my investigation enlightens the

---

28 Swedish author Inger Edelfeldt's *Kamalas bok* (1986) [Kamala's Book] contains an interesting variation of the swan maiden motif. There a young woman, who throughout the story struggles with expectations regarding beauty norms and heterosexuality, at the end is replaced by her inner wolf as the story's first-person narrator.

ways in which ancient figures, tropes and themes can be innovatively re-employed within twentieth century literature. In the examples I chose from Fagerholm's early authorship, this re-production appears both on thematic levels and in connection with specific features of certain literary characters.

More specifically between the characters of Patricia and Isabella, it is apparent that the ancient figure of the woman/animal transformation is employed in different ways and produces different textual effects. While Patricia's change into a rabbit, which means a significant manifestation of nonhuman agency and in fact entails a suggestion of a post human becoming, the aspects of Isabella that are possible to understand in relation to folkloristic depictions of swan maidens rather comes across as a metaphor for the oppositions and tensions that, within the frame of the 'feminine', are produced by gender-specific oppression. Regarding both of these characters, it is interesting to note the ways in which their construction relies on the intra-activity between norms regarding gender, sexuality, human and animal, an observation that points out a relevant area for further investigations. If the 'human' is not, in Fagerholm's authorship, a stable identity or category, but rather the effect of a power-laden process of qualification,[29] then it makes sense, from a range of different perspectives, to discuss *where, when,* in what *way* and with what kind of *consequences,* her literary characters negotiate, possess, re-shape, and abandon their temporary positions.

References

Primary Sources

Fagerholm, Monika 1990: *Patricia. Berättelser.* [Patricia. Stories] Söderströms, Helsingfors.
Fagerholm, Monika 1994: *Underbara kvinnor vid vatten. En roman om syskon.* Femte tryckningen. Albert Bonniers förlag, Stockholm.
Fagerholm, Monika 1997: *Wonderful Women by the Sea.* Translated by Joan Tate. New Press, New York.
Fagerholm, Monika 1998: *Diva. En uppväxts egna alfabet med docklaboratorium (en bonusberättelse ur framtiden)* [DIVA. The Alphabet of Adolescence with a Laboratory of Dolls (A Bonus Tale from the Future)]. Söderströms, Helsingfors.
Fagerholm, Monika 2010: *The Glitter Scene. A Novel* [2009]. Translated by Katarina E. Tucker. Other Press, New York.

---

29 Cpr. with Judith Halberstam and Ira Livingston (1995: 10).

Secondary Sources

Adams, Carol J. (Ed.) 1993: *Ecofeminism and the Sacred*. Continuum, New York.

Barad, Karen 2008: Posthumanist Performativity. Toward an Understanding of How Matter Comes to Matter [2003]. In *Material Feminisms*. Eds. Stacy Alaimo and Susan Hekman. Indiana University Press, Bloomington, Indianapolis, 120–154.

Braidotti, Rosi 2002: *Metamorphoses. Towards a Materialist Theory of Becoming*. Polity Press, Cambridge, Malden.

Butler, Judith 1993: *Bodies That Matter. On the Discursive Limits of 'Sex'*. Routledge, New York, London.

Butler, Judith 1990: *Gender Trouble. Feminism and the Subversion of Identity*. Routledge, New York, London.

Davidson, Arnold I. 1987: Sex and the Emergence of Sexuality. – *Critical Inquiry* 14, 1/1987, 16–48.

Davidson, H. R. Ellis 1978: Shape-Shifting in the Old Norse Sagas. In *Animals in Folklore*. Eds. J.R. Porter and W.M.S. Russell. D.S. Brewer Ltd., Cambridge, 126–142.

Deleuze, Gilles and Guattari, Félix 1987: *Kafka. Toward a Minor Literature*. Transl. Dana Polan. University of Minnesota Press, Minneapolis, London.

Edelfeldt, Inger 1986: *Kamalas bok*. [Kamala's Book] AWE/Geber, Stockholm.

Fagerholms nya kretsar kring brott och myter. [Fagerholm's New One Circles around Crimes and Myths] – *Dagens Nyheter* 19.9.2009. http://www.dn.se/dnbok/fagerholms-nya-kretsar-kring-brott-och-myter/ (Accessed 12.12.2013)

Fass Leavy, Barbara 1994: *In Search of the Swan Maiden. A Narrative on Folklore and Gender*. New York University Press, New York, London.

Favorite Folktales from around the World 1986: Ed. Jane Yolen. Pantheon Books, New York.

Ferzoco, George and Gill, Miriam 2005: Introduction. *De Hereditate Protei*: Ways of Metamorphoses. In *Proteus. The Language of Metamorphosis*. Eds. Carla Dente, George Ferzoco, Miriam Gill and Marina Spunta. Ashgate, Hants, Burlington.

Fuss, Diana 1996: Introduction. Human, All Too Human. In *Human, All Too Human*. Ed. Diana Fuss. Routledge, New York, London.

Gaard, Greta (Ed.) 1993: *Ecofeminism. Women, Animals, Nature*. Temple University Press, Philadelphia.

Halberstam, Judith and Livingston, Ira 1995: Introduction. Posthuman Bodies. In *Posthuman Bodies*. Eds. Judith Halberstam and Ira Livingston. Indiana University Press, Bloomington, Indianapolis.

Hammershaimb, V. U. 2007: *The Seal-Woman*. Transl. A.E. Petersen. Postverk Føroya, Frímerkjadeildin, Torshavn Faroe Islands.

hooks, bell 1990: *Yearning. Race, Gender, and Cultural Politics*. South End Press, Boston, Massachusetts.

Icelandic Folktales and Legends 1972: Ed. Jacqueline Simpson. University of California Press, Berkeley.

Johansson, Sofia Rapp 2005: *Silverfisken*. [Silverfish] Bonniers, Stockholm.

Kalevala. The Land of the Heroes 1985: Transl. W.F. Kirby. The Athlone Press, London, Dover, New Hampshire.

Katz, Jonathan N. 1995: *The Invention of Heterosexuality*. Dutton, New York.

Kristeva, Julia 1980: *Desire in Language. A Semiotic Approach to Literature and Art* [1977]. Ed. Leon S. Roudiez, transl. Thomas Gora, Alice Jardine and Leon S. Roudiez. Columbia University Press, New York.

Laqueur, Thomas 1990: *Making Sex. Body and Gender from the Greeks to Freud*. Harvard University Press, Cambridge, London.

Lykke, Nina 2010: *Feminist Studies. A Guide to Intersectional Theory, Methodology and Writing*. Routledge, New York, London.

Lönngren, Ann-Sofie 2011: Mellan metafor och litterär materialisering – heteronormer och djurblivande i Monika Fagerholms novell 'Patricia Kanin'. [Between Metaphor and Literary Materialization – Heteronormativity and Becoming Animal in Monika Fagerholm's Short Story 'Patricia Rabbit' (1990)] – *lambda nordica* 16 (4) 2011, 53–84.

Lönngren, Ann-Sofie 2015: *Following the Animal. Power, Agency, and Human-Animal Transformations in Modern, Northern-European Literature.* Cambridge Scholars Publishing, New Castle upon Tyne.

Nenola, Aili 1993: Folklore and the Genderized World. Or Twelve Points from a Feminist Perspective. In *Nordic Frontiers. Recent Issues in the Study of Modern Traditional Culture in the Nordic Countries.* Eds. Pertti J. Anttonen and Reimund Kvideland. Nordic Institute of Folklore, Turku, 49–62.

Rich, Adrienne 1993: Compulsory Heterosexuality and Lesbian Existence [1980]. In *The Lesbian and Gay Studies Reader.* Eds. Henry Abelove, Michèle Aina Barale & David M. Halperin. Routledge, New York, London, 227–254.

Roudiez, Leon, S. 1980: Introduction. In Julia Kristeva, *Desire in Language. A Semiotic Approach to Literature and Art* [1977]. Ed. Leon S. Roudiez, trans. by Thomas Gora, Alice Jardine, and Leon S. Roudiez. Columbia University Press, New York.

Russell, W.M.S. and Russell, Claire 1978: The Social Biology of Werewolves. In *Animals in Folklore.* Ed. J.R. Porter and W.M.S. Russell. D. S. Brewer Ltd., Cambridge, 143–182.

Sandin, Maria 1991: Det ofärdiga jagets förvandlingar. Samtal med Monika Fagerholm. [Transformations of the Uncompleted Self. Conversation with Monika Fagerholm] – *Horisont* 5–6/1991, 2–10.

Soper, Kate 2000: Naturalized Woman and Feminized Nature. In *The Green Studies Reader. From Romanticism to Ecocriticism.* Ed. Laurence Coupe. Routledge, New York.

Stenwall, Åsa 2001: *Portföljen i skogen. Kvinnor och modernitet i det sena 1900-talets finlandssvenska litteratur.* [Briefcase in the Woods. Women and Modernity in Late 20th Century Finland-Swedish Literature] Schildts, Helsingfors.

The Poetic Edda 1996: Transl. with an introduction and notes by Carolyne Larrington. Oxford University Press, Oxford.

Trotzig, Birgitta 1975: *I kejsarens tid. Sagor.* [In the Time of the Emperor: Fairy Tales] Bonniers, Stockholm.

Warner, Marina 1994: *From the Beast to the Blonde. On Fairy Tales and Their Tellers.* Vintage, London.

Wolfe, Cary 2009: *What is Posthumanism?* University of Minnesota Press, Minneapolis.

Wolfe, Cary 2003: *Animal Rites. American Culture, the Discourses of Species, and Posthumanist Theory.* University of Chicago Press, Chicago.

Österholm, Maria Margareta 2012: *Ett flicklaboratorium i valda bitar. Skeva flickor i svenskspråkig prosa från 1980 till 2005.* [A Girl Laboratory in Chosen Parts. Queer Girls in Swedish and Finland-Swedish Literature from 1980 to 2005] Rosenlarv förlag, Stockholm.

Mia Österlund

'A Work You Cannot Explain, Only Experience'

The Struggle with Readability in the Reception of Monika Fagerholm's Novel *Lola uppochner*

Monika Fagerholm's genre pastiche *Lola uppochner* [Lola Upsidedown] (2012) is a deeply puzzling, mocking, repetitive, strange and visionary novel. It is an assemblage[1] where the process – the becoming – is the art work itself. To underline the structure of an assemblage Fagerholm uses metafictional devices[2] and consequently the novel is full of passages that can be interpreted as comments on how the novel should be read.[3] The aim of this article is to discuss the struggle with readability in the reception of Monika Fagerholm's novel *Lola uppochner* by exploring a selection of Swedish and Finnish reviews. The key question asked will be how Fagerholm's assemblage style is perceived in the reception and how the critics address the issue of readability. The first part will discuss *Lola uppochner* from the point of view of readability and reading. Then girlhood is commented on as an important site of interpretation that generates meaning in the readings, whereas the following part will discuss critics' comments on genre, form, content, context and emotional response in the context of readability. Finally, a conclusion on how readability is framed in the reception of the novel is presented.

The background for my discussion of the reception of *Lola uppochner* is the use of metafiction. One example of an episode that can be understood as a metafictive comment is the one depicting Anita Bäck. She is an enigmatic 19-year-old girl crippled by an aggressive muscle disease. Isolated in her room at the top of the Mill in the small town of Flatnäs, she occupies herself with a giant jigsaw-puzzle:

1 For the complex concept *assemblage*, see Deleuze and Guattari (2005: 4). In short, it means a combination of segments, territorial movements and viscosity that appears in a literary work. According to Rosi Braidotti assemblages constitute an escape from phallogocentrism, as a process of unsettling binarism, linearity and other 'sedimented unitary habits', thus creating transformation (Braidotti 2002: 94).
2 See Kaisa Kurikka (2008) and Pauliina Haasjoki (2012) for a discussion of Fagerholm's use of metafiction in *DIVA*.
3 Here, however, I only note metafiction as a background for the discussion of the reception of the novel. See Kurikka and Lahdenperä in this volume for a discussion of metafiction.

Anita, who sat in a wheelchair in a room high up in the Mill, on the floor among the pieces of the jigsaw puzzle she laid, laid, laid – enormous that puzzle, over – no exaggeration – twenty thousand pieces. (*Lola uppochner* 2012: 23)[4]

Up in the Mill Anita Bäck is sorting some books alphabetically according to title onto the bookshelf. Or just across the floor, on the jigsaw-puzzle, the pieces of the jigsaw-puzzle, or on some other free surface. Books, books in high heaps. Sorting books is a hobby, a pastime. (*Lola uppochner* 2012: 83)

Descriptions of Anita, busy sorting books or laying a giant puzzle recur in the novel. These passages can be read as a key scene that provides clues to possible ways of reading the whole novel. One would assume that Anita is a reader since she surrounds herself with a multitude of books but she is not. She merely collects and organizes her books and mumbles the titles out loud. These titles typically comment on different aspects of girlhood, which is the main motif of the novel. Anita's ambiguous, enigmatic speech also resembles the style in which Fagerholm writes, which is a speech act and a style that consist of cultural references in disorder, repetition and a rhizomatic structure.

The metafictional dimension of this scene has been emphasized in reviews. The Swedish newspaper *Upsala Nya Tidning* published a review of *Lola uppochner* already on 4 November 2012 when the novel had been published in Finland, but not yet in Sweden.[5] Finnish novels written in Swedish, especially those by authors with a large Nordic readership are often published simultaneously in a Swedish edition. However, due to circumstances in marketing, *Lola uppochner* was published in Sweden later (Schottenius 2012), which resulted in headlines in many Swedish newspapers, all evidence of the high interest in Fagerholm's work in Sweden. In his review, Sebastian Johans (2012) called the novel a billowing collective novel and identified the puzzle of 20, 000 pieces in Anita Bäck's room as a recurring metafictive episode in the novel. According to him, the reader has to solve a similar complex 'puzzle' piecing together themes such as loyalty, class, guilt, shame and sorrow. As a result, the reader is faced with constant rearrangements, abundant intertextuality, and a constellation of girls in the epicentre of the narration, which merge in a complex assemblage.[6]

Metafiction, metafictionality and metaliterature are concepts that point in the direction of a narrative self-reflexivity (Hägg et al. 2008: 11). According to scholars such as Linda Hutcheon (1985: 1) metafiction is fiction

---

4   Anita som satt i rullstolen i ett rum högst uppe i Kvarnen, på golvet bland pusselbitarna i pusslet som hon pusslade, pusslade, pusslade – Hade varit enormt det där pusslet, över – ingen överdrift – tjugotusen bitar. (*Lola uppochner* 2012: 23) All translations of *Lola uppochner* are my own.

    Uppe i Kvarnen sorterar Anita Bäck vissa böcker i bokhyllan alfabetiskt, enligt titel. Eller över golvet bara, på pusslet, pusselbitar, eller på någon annan ledig yta. Böcker böcker i högar staplar. Att sortera böcker är en hobby, ett tidsfördriv. (*Lola uppochner* 2012: 83)

5   The day of first reviews was 21.9.2012 in Finland (Ekman, Lindberg) and 1.2.2013 in Sweden (Björk, Dahlman, Lingebrandt, Lokko, Rabe and Svensson).

6   For a discussion on girlhood, see Kurikka (2005) and Österholm (2012).

about fiction, that is, fiction that includes commentary on its own narrative identity. In turn, Patricia Waugh (1984: 2) sees metafiction as fiction that systematically draws attention to the relationship between fiction and reality. Metafiction can be overt or hidden; it can thematise narration or it can be a result of reading as occurs when a reader interprets a passage in the novel that harmonizes with the interpretation in making. Thus, metafictive episodes are read as comments on the text as a whole or on its form and structure. Metafiction in Fagerholm's case consists of episodes that relate to or resemble reading, such as assembling different parts but – as in the example above – not being able to solve the whole puzzle.

Due to the assemblage technique employed in many of Monika Fagerholm's novels, her postmodern prose is quite demanding to read. In her book on women and modernity in Finland-Swedish literature, literary scholar Åsa Stenwall (2001) raises the question of readability in Fagerholm's oeuvre in connection to Fagerholm's iconic novel *DIVA* (1998). Stenwall contextualizes Fagerholm's novel within a trend of gloomy and self-centred Nordic women's literature that Fagerholm, according to her, writes against. Stenwall also shows how effective Fagerholm's experimental, utopian girl vision is in terms of both characterization and narrative structure. However, since the novel is radically new in form and content, it is not an easy read. According to Stenwall (2001: 235), *DIVA* mobilizes something even more than renewed reading strategies. Her polemic final point is: 'Diva does not demand a new reading strategy. Diva demands revolution' (Stenwall 2001: 241). By 'revolution' Stenwall refers to a shift in reading, criticism and discourses on femininity and women's writing. Novelties always meet resistance, she states, and this was exemplified in the early 20th century response to Finland-Swedish avant-garde pioneer, Edith Södergran whose poetry was questioned before she was canonised (Stenwall 2001: 236). Consequently, readers and critics have to ask themselves how far they are prepared to stretch literary conventions. Therein lies the revolutionary potential to which Stenwall refers.

Despite Stenwall's imperative for a revolution, the starting point in this article is the presumption that Fagerholm's award-winning, ground-breaking fiction demands new ways of reading. In the direction of a revolution, I consider a discussion of reading strategies as highly relevant. The main skill needed is the ability to let go of normal textual logic and form, such as chronology and coherence and perceive the text on an emotional level. Postmodern prose has for decades demanded renewed reading strategies that collide with more traditional text concepts such as coherence, linearity, or progression. Similarly, Fagerholm's novel produces vivid visions of an uncertain reality or rather of being and becoming. As Finland-Swedish literary scholar Pia Ahlbäck (2007) points out, the activity of reading is acknowledged as problematic, implying that reading always introduces ambivalence into the most stable of texts. The struggle with finding a new reading strategy when confronted with an unstable text is visible in comments on Fagerholm's earlier work. For example, literary critic Mervi Kantokorpi (2009) states in her review of *The Glitter Scene* (2009) in the major Finnish newspaper *Helsingin Sanomat* that the tremendous success of

Den amerikanska flickan (2004) in the Nordic countries in 2004–2005 was met with 'very varied response almost as if every reader had read a different book'.

New Ways of Reading and the Crisis in Criticism

To read a novel includes applying traditional genre conventions, to read through a theoretical lens or focus on different aspects of the reading act such as affective responses to conscious readings against the grain. Readings emerge on a spectrum consisting of possible positions, such as the different theoretical contexts of posthuman, feminist, queer and girlhood studies or generic and biographical contexts. Literary criticism is influenced by literary theory and therefore traces of new ways of reading also enter criticism. Some critics promote so called institutionally formed readings that mirror the work in question in relation to literary traditions. Oppositional readings are often tied to concrete literary theories and they tend to emerge from opposing fields such as feminism or girlhood studies as a way of reading in other ways but are in fact also institutional by adopting certain reading patterns themselves. After a while oppositional readings tend to be assimilated into institutional ones. Both practices offer contextualized and sometimes ideological, readings. Usually a review is a combination of institutional and oppositional readings, where the critic alternates between institutional and oppositional comments since few daily papers would print a more theoretical piece. Therefore, critics have to communicate their readings within the somewhat limited forum of a public review that is supposed to cover a wider range of both description and evaluation of a work. It is not an easy task to review a complex novel such as *Lola uppochner* under these conditions.

However, some help can be found in various resources. For example, in *Literary Theory. A Toolkit*, literary scholar Herman Rapaport (2011: 4) lists four common types of critical reading: close reading, contextual analysis, the application of a critical approach and social critique. Close reading is text-based and stresses the content of the literary text and any inferences. Contextual analysis establishes contexts for the literary work and suggests to which literary tradition the work belongs. Contextual analysis may take into account biographical knowledge about the author as well as social, political and cultural contexts likely to have a bearing on the work's meanings (Rapaport 2011: 5). With a critical approach a range of theoretical perspectives are referenced, while systematic interpretation according to a certain body of thought, that is a theory, is mapped onto a literary work (Rapaport 2011: 7). Finally, social criticism includes politically motivated interpretations of literary texts as responding to current societal phenomena and trends (Rapaport 2011: 10). These different approaches serve as a background for my discussion of the reception of Fagerholm's novel and have inspired the view on the struggle with readability presented here.

In her book *Theories of Reading* (2006), literary scholar Karin Littau supplements Rapaport's thoughts on reading strategies while she provides a historical overview of theories of reading and the bias connected to different reading strategies advocated at a certain historical moment and within different interpretation communities. Littau notes that intellectual repertoires and emotional responses tend to fluctuate and be given more or less validity from time to time. While Rapaport provides a differentiation between reading conventions, Littau contextualises these conventions as situated in history. Fagerholm's new kind of writing, which according to earlier criticism and to scholars like Stenwall (2001: 235), requires new ways of reading, simultaneously demands new ways of communicating these readings in the reception.

Altogether, there are around fifty reviews of *Lola uppochner*, of which thirty have been published in Sweden and twenty in Finland.[7] I have chosen to discuss a smaller selection of reviews, mainly the ones published in the major newspapers, but I have also included examples from local or evening press. Fagerholm is a very influential and widely read author in Sweden, which is mirrored in the fact that many Swedish local newspapers publish reviews of her work. The reviews presented here are chosen in order to exemplify how critics comment on readability and demonstrate their struggle in order to discover fruitful ways of reading.

The critical reception of *Lola uppochner* is clearly divided into two camps: one in which the novel is praised as part of Fagerholm's oeuvre and one in which the novel is considered to be a failure. All reviewers underline Fagerholm's greatness, but many note that it is difficult even for her to accomplish the expected 'Fagerholmian' prose. For example, in *Upsala Nya Tidning* the reviewer Sebastian Johans (2012) claims that the author's literary reputation has resulted in 'astronomic expectations' and demands.[8]

Lola uppochner was also used in a debate initiated by the major Swedish newspaper *Dagens Nyheter*'s young critic Lyra Ekström Lindbäck (2012), who paints a picture of literary criticism as an outdated and prolonged arm of publishing houses. She accuses reviewers of merely repeating marketing slogans and uses the phrase, 'a creepy story about unusual people' from the marketing of Fagerholm's novel to illustrate her point. Stina Otterberg (2014), also a literary critic at *Dagens Nyheter*, responded to this debate article by mentioning seven Swedish and Finnish reviews that show a great variation in the reception 'from overwhelmingly positive to disclaiming and negative' opinions. Ekström Lindbäck has chosen to use the quote from the marketing of *Lola uppochner* because it is a striking example of how a conventional description of the novel according to genre conventions no longer fits. Fagerholm's prose has actualised a need for new conventions that match this new kind of literary text better. Thus, Fagerholm's novel

---

7   The material for this article consists of reviews collected from the following databases: the Swedish Mediearkivet for Swedish press material, the Finnish media archives Arto and Akseli for Finnish press material and the Finland-Swedish archive Brages Pressarkiv for Finland-Swedish material. Identical reviews under modified titles are mentioned in the references.

8   'Och eftersom det står Monika Fagerholms namn på romanens omslag så är förväntningarna på de cirka 450 sidorna av gungfly mellan berättelsens inledning och slut snudd på astronomiska'.

not only attracted a wide range of reviews, it was also part of a debate on how contemporary criticism has developed in the digital era to meet the demands on a renewed form of criticism.

Small Town Girls and the Thriller-Genre – Towards a New Aesthetics of Girlhood

What critics are confronted with in Monika Fagerholm's novel *Lola uppochner* is a narration of girlhood framed by a murder mystery, yet the novel mocks the genre and is written in playful opposition to the ongoing fad for Nordic crime fiction. Therefore, it is no surprise that no single review neglects the thriller element. Fagerholm deconstructs the crime story already in her diptych *The End of the Glitter Scene* (2004–2009) and in *Lola uppochner* she returns to her familiar setting of the small town scenario and uses crime fiction devices and props in order to expose undercurrents in the text. According to Amanda Svensson (2013) in the major Swedish evening paper *Expressen*, 'no one flirts as actively with the crime novel as Fagerholm'.[9] In Svensson's mind the need to deconstruct the crime story derives from the popularity of Nordic Noir. Nordic Noir is a label coined by Anglo-American publishers to promote and capture the specificity of Nordic crime fiction. Non-glamorous, realistic, gloomy, dark and wintery are some of the traits of these bestselling books, which are accompanied by popular TV series (see Arvas and Nestingen 2011). Svensson reminds the reader of the diptych *The End of the Glitter Scene*, which combines elements from thrillers, fairy tales and poetry as a background for its eclectic aesthetics. Kaisa Kurikka (2013) in *Turun Sanomat*, a local Finnish newspaper, also finds the genre label 'thriller' on the blurb only one of many choices the reader can make and notes Fagerholm's (mis)use of the conventions from this genre. However, as many critics note, crime is only a generic frame Fagerholm uses as her canvas; reviewers comment on a range of other contexts at work in the novel *Lola uppochner* such as girlhood, small town life or themes such as love and friendship or revenge and guilt.

In fact, the context of girlhood is used as a cure to the dilemma with readability by offering solutions to traits in the novel that might otherwise be perceived as unstable. Fagerholm rewrites the map of Nordic literature. Her new coordinates are the suburb in *DIVA*, the District in *The Glitter Scene*, and small town life in *Lola uppochner*. These geographical settings are not new, but making girls and girlhood the focal point of these settings is innovative. In *Lola uppochner* Fagerholm elaborates on fixed preconceptions of girlhood and writes a suggestive story with many intertwining voices and themes. The gallery of characters presented as a preface is long: a catalogue lists thirty-three names.[10]

---

9 'På svenska bedriver dock ingen en så aktiv flört med deckargenren som Fagerholm'.
10 Not surprisingly Fagerholm has been called the protector of minor characters (Kjersén Edman 2013).

The novel consists of two plots. The first takes place in 2011 when one of the protagonists, Jana Marton is invited to a reunion in her old home town Flatnäs and experiences that she still fits in as badly as she did before. During this plot-line, the unsolved murder of the young man Flemming Petterson, whom Jana found dead years ago, is finally solved. As a distant backdrop, the retrospective plot of the novel is set in 1994, at the same time as the Estonia catastrophe, when a ferry named *Estonia* travelling between Estonia and Sweden sank and several hundred died. The tragedy is important in connection to ideas of the Nordic welfare state since it shook the belief that the Nordic countries were safe havens spared from disasters of this kind.

The aesthetics of girlhood is remarkable in Fagerholm's novel and it is connected to a feminist tradition of revisioning femininity. Make up, for example, is used in a revolutionary way. The girl characters in the novel use cosmetics and clothes in an exaggerated manner when performing their situated girlhoods and thus these girls bodies allude to certain scripts of girlhood. The girls Anna Svanberg and Anita Bäck's sister Ca Bäck both experiment with female insignia: 'Anna Svanberg applies more colour, and more and more – smudges a tremendously messy-edged giant mouth in fuchsia – "What are you doing?" Ca giggles, grabbing the lipstick from her and dropping it into the sink' (*Lola uppochner* 2012: 290).[11] As Österholm has shown in her study of gurlesque aesthetics in Fagerholm's work, girlhood consists of visions, desire, creativity, materiality, lived experience, memory, language and emotions.[12] The girls form an intrinsic network of small-town relations and embody power relations that promote change.

Fagerholm's novel belongs to a tradition of small town depictions. As Lisbeth Larsson (2013) underlines in her review in the major Swedish newspaper *Göteborgsposten*, the small town motif is a recognizable Fagerholmian specialty. Fagerholm sketches her story in the small town of Ekenäs in southern Finland, where she worked as a writer in residence in the 1990s, but she twists the town's name into 'Flatnäs' ('Flatness') thereby underlining a characteristic of the small town inhabitants.[13] Local colour is added in puzzling details such as vaguely identifiable persons such as a local female writer and cultural events, which create a feeling of an uncanny unfamiliar familiarity for local readers, not for outsiders, although these could be stereotypes of any small town.

In connection to the motif of girlhood in a small town setting it is interesting to compare *Lola uppochner* to another Nordic narrative on girlhood that marks a shift in how girlhood is depicted, as well as received. Lukas Moodysson's film *Show Me Love/Fucking Åmål* (1998) about two

---

11 Anna Svanberg brer på mera färg, och mera, mera – kladdar på sig en oerhörd slarvkantad jättemun i fuchsia – 'Vad gör du?' Ca fnissar, river läppstiftet från henne och fäller det i lavoaren (*Lola uppochner* 2012: 290).

12 See Österholm (2012) and her essay in this volume for a presentation of gurlesque aesthetics in Fagerholm's work.

13 In interviews, Fagerholm reveals her feelings of being looked upon as 'that crazy lady', see Lindqvist (2012).

teenage girls in a small town coming out as lesbians is central to this category.[14] Feminist literary scholar Tiina Rosenberg (2002: 103–115) has studied the reception of Moodysson's film and shows that film critics have been unable to interpret *Show Me Love* as a story about girlhood and sexuality. Instead, the girl's film – to use film and media scholar Heta Mulari's (2015) expression – has been received as a story of small town anxiety.[15] The reception of Moodysson's film shows that the motif of girlhood was still marginalized in the 1990s since it was so hard for the critics to admit that girlhood matters in the narrative. Contrary to reviewers of Moodysson's film, all reviewers of *Lola uppochner* focus on girlhood. Something has apparently happened during the last decade concerning how girlhood is perceived; most probably the consolidation of the field of Girlhood Studies has helped to push the boundaries in this direction (Österlund 2013: 12).

In *Lola uppochner* Fagerholm uses girlhood as a central trope. The novel builds on parallel visions of girls. There is, for example, the innocent-looking little girl Missne, who kills her hamster with a hammer and Anita who plays her twisted games using her Skeleton army of anorectic and gloomy girls that obey her commands including performing odd rituals at the new graveyard.

Girlhood is a manifold concept in Fagerholm's writing. The girls are more than simply girls, they are human beings, no less, no more, but they are still girls that embrace the insignia of girlness. This combination of the universal and the girlish marks a shift from the cultural repression of girlhood as 'marginal' (see Österlund et al. 2013). Fagerholm is a well-known portrayer of girlhood. In many interviews she underlines that girls and girlhood are not to be interpreted as marginalized and narrow and in the Fagerholmian universe girlhood is indeed portrayed as nothing less than universal. Girlhood also becomes a bifurcation point in the struggle with readability. The appreciation of the novel even depends on what view of girlhood the critic embraces.

'Girls, girls, these girls everywhere,'[16] Susanne Sterner (2013) exclaims in her review in the local Swedish newspaper *Corren* and lists the most important girl characters alongside the sisters Anita and Ca Bäck: 'Jana Marton, Minnie Backlund, Anna Svanberg, Lila in the lilac hat, Missne with her sick hamster'.[17] According to Sterner, Fagerholm investigates the world of girls, which is inhabited by headstrong, imaginative, goodhearted and mean girls. Sterner finds this devotion to girlhood to go hand in hand with Fagerholm's aesthetics of 'cram-full bubbling poetic language that winds like

---

14 See Mulari (2014) for a discussion of girlhood in Swedish film.
15 Rosenberg (2002: 106). Söderling (2012) in *Ny Tid* also makes intertextual connections to how the small town is treated by Gustave Flaubert in *Madame Bovary* and by Anton Chekhov in *Three Sisters* thus positioning Fagerholm in a tradition.
16 'Flickor, flickor, dessa flickor överallt'.
17 'Jana Marton, Minne Backlund, Anna Svanberg. Lila i den lila hatten, Missne med sin sjuka hamster'. Kangasniemi (2012) also circles around the Fagerholmian girl type, a sexually free little bird, a mentally broken wanderer or/and a wild forest animal. For example Ca Bäck running in the woods is compared to Almqvist's enigmatic Tintomara-figure.

brooks, sometimes rivers, through a landscape, a Fagerholmian landscape'.[18] This landscape mentioned by the reviewer refers to the conceptualization of spatiality in Fagerholm's novels; the odd districts, suburbs, or seemingly glamourous surroundings that turn out to be both uncanny and shabby. For her, the description of girlhood is the most rewarding entrance to the textual universe of Fagerholm's prose since it offers a poetics of girlhood that also corresponds with the transformative form of the text. Sterner offers a reading where 'the power games with their strange dominance, loyalty and bizarre undercurrents' are in focus. In her opinion, the relations between the girls are the most intriguing aspect of the novel *Lola uppochner*; thus, she locates her interpretation in a wider context of examining how girlhood is used in art and literature. This contextual reading brings a new order of girlhood to the reading. As a result, the reading is less messy since there is a pattern behind the motif of girlhood that one can relate to where the shattered form of the novel becomes logical. Stenwall (2001: 210) discusses this aesthetic in relation to *DIVA* when she notes Fagerholm's connection to feminist writing in the spirit of Hélène Cixous and Julia Kristeva's views on language.

However, not every critic is intrigued by girlhood. Dan Sjögren (2013), in the local Swedish newspaper *Norrländska Socialdemokraten*, voices a personal comment based on identification: 'I find it harder to get through the parts that depict the girls because the young seldom have anything really interesting to communicate to me'.[19] Therefore, a reading that is not open to the motif of youth in the form of girlhood loses one of the central opportunities for a reader to grasp the novel. The focus on girlhood in the novel is commented on in some of the reviews as constituting a shift in focus that puts girls in the middle of the narrative and lets them be narrators. This focus has consequences for how readable the novel is presented as, whereas girlhood offers a frame for interpretation. Some critics have a problem with this shift, while others are thrilled and find girlhood a productive way to grasp the novel when struggling with readability.

A Form in Flux

Many critics in my material focus on form and transformation in the reception of *Lola uppochner*. If a novel is difficult to read, the solution is, according to those who consider the novel a failure, connected to Fagerholm's use of form and her constant transformation of literary conventions and style. Many critics comment on the title *Lola uppochner*. In the Swedish evening paper *Aftonbladet*, Claes Wahlin (2013) stresses the effect of the word upside-down. According to him, Fagerholm's choice of title suggests a distorted point of departure, a *mundus inversus*, where nothing is as it

---

18 'Det vindlar och hoppar och bucklar ihop sig och slingrar fram likt bäckar, och ibland älvar, genom ett landskap, det Fagerholmska landskapet'.

19 'Jag har också svårare att ta mig igenom de partier som handlar om flickorna eftersom de unga så sällan har något riktigt intressant att meddela mej'.

seems to be. Wahlin mentions the plasticity of the mindscape/landscape that Fagerholm inhabits in her novels and reads her work as picturing and examining different decades, from the 1960s in *Wonderful Women by the Sea* (1994) to the 1990s in *DIVA* 'where protagonists either hold outsider positions or are totally absorbed by contemporary trends, almost unaware of the forces that shape their wishes'.[20] According to Wahlin, 'Places beyond the radar of media and modernity are satirised whereas long time lines are contrasted to shorter ones where Fagerholm's language and style is the glue'.[21] It is evident that Fagerholm's renewal of style and form marks a radical shift in Nordic prose and many critics willingly comprehend her writing as more of a landscape to stroll in than a traditionally structured text. Herein lies a large part of the struggle with meaning-making and it is evident that critics tend to produce some kind of imagery for how they consider the dynamics of the novel.

What makes the novel difficult to read then? Does it have to do with how Fagerholm alters literary conventions? One of the first to review *Lola uppochner* was one of Finland's leading Swedish-speaking critics, Michel Ekman (2012). His review covers an entire spread in the major Finland-Swedish newspaper *Hufvudstadsbladet*. Ekman is among those who consider the novel a failure. Nonetheless, he begins his review by adding to the aura around Fagerholm, stating that she does not tell stories but conjures up worlds and that her magic touch transforms and gives life to the elements she touches.[22] Ekman states that while Marcel Proust wrote about eccentric people, Fagerholm writes about common people and therefore she does not make it easy for herself. According to Ekman, the trivial is depicted as archetypal and supernatural in her novels. This succeeds best in her masterpiece *DIVA* where one is 'radiantly happy when reading'[23] he concludes.

Ekman's reading focuses on language and structure, as well as on what the novel *does*. His institutional reading mirrors the novel in a literary tradition of archetypal patterns, focuses on tragedy and underlines the discrepancy between form and content in the novel. His verdict is that 'still *Lola uppochner* is not a good novel'.[24] He finds tremendous flaws in both structure and language, which should be Fagerholm's bravura: 'One

20 '[...] placerar sina fiktiva figurer i antingen ett slags outsiderposition, eller som helt upptagna av tidens trender, närmast omedvetna om vilka krafter som formar deras önskningar'.
21 'Platserna de lever på ligger utanför mediernas radar, modernitetssträvanden uppifrån skildras gärna med en satirisk udd och ett slags långa tidslinjer ställs mot de kortare, trendbestämda. Det är språket hos Fagerholm som håller ihop berättelsens alla fragment'.
22 'Monika Fagerholm berättar inte historier utan frammanar världar. Fastän det händer mycket och myllrar av gestalter i hennes romaner är det språket som är huvudsaken, det och författarens hand som förvandlar och gjuter liv i de element hon vidrör'.
23 'Av att läsa Diva blir man [...] upprymd'.
24 'Ändå är *Lola uppochner* ingen bra roman'.

can get the feeling that this is only half ready'.²⁵ On the whole Ekman finds the novel shattered and lacking 'inner necessity'.²⁶ According to him, Fagerholm is unclear about her relation to the thriller genre and the threefold closure does not correspond practically or psychologically with her use of tragedy. Therefore, by not living up to the literary conventions, the novel fails. Ekman is by no means alone in thinking that the ending is extreme. Sebastian Johans (2012), among many others, also comments on the ending of the novel: 'All bridges fall down and the solution explodes like an unruly rocket on New Year's Eve or a *deus ex machina* motif'.²⁷ He interprets it as Fagerholm playing with the readers, as well as her own, underlying need for linear narration, also hinting that this is excessive. In the journal *Swedish Book Review*, Darcy Hurford (2013) sees exaggeration as Fagerholm's main device. Fagerholm's impact is huge as she has 'practically created a genre of her own', that is 'Fagerholmism', characterized by female narrative voices, melancholy, an eye for detail and peripheral settings. As an example of the exaggeration, Hurford mentions the denouement scenes that consist of unexpected confessions, gatherings and violent confrontations, all familiar from the thriller genre, yet used in an unconventional manner that could imply failure depending on the way in which the novel is read. Her comments show that the use and transformation of generic conventions can be seen either as narrative method or as generic collapse.

In the paperback version of *Lola uppochner*, Fagerholm offers a rewritten ending apparently triggered by Michel Ekman's comments, since she especially rewrites the denouement scenes. The rewritten version makes a whole range of clarifications, most often by more lengthy descriptions and sometimes by rearrangements. Some metafictive parts are also added, such as yet another episode that returns to Anita Bäck's jigsaw-puzzle:

> Dirty feet across pieces of a jigsaw puzzle in a room, wheel-chair wheels across a huge pathetic sky, in just blue blue blue. Pathetic, that is. For what did it mean? What had it meant, ever? Correct answer: nothing. Because it never was that kind of story: a join-together-the-pieces-in-the-right-way-and-the-right-pattern-will-appear-kind-of-story. Of course it would have been easier if that had been the case, because then she [Jana] could have been believable at the end in the role as the clever one who, after keeping a low profile, suddenly could point the gun at the guilty one. (*Lola uppochner* 2013: 483–484)²⁸

---

25 '[...] att man kan få känslan av att den helt enkelt är halvfärdig'.
26 'Helheten är hackig och saknar inre nödvändighet'.
27 '[...] rämnar alla broar och lösningen exploderar som en ostyrig nyårsraket eller ett deus ex machina-motiv'.
28 'Smutsiga fötter över pusselbitar i ett rum, rullstolshjul över en väldig patetisk himmel, i bara blått blått blått. Patetiskt, alltså. För vad betydde det? Vad hade det betytt, nånsin? Rätt svar: ingenting. För det var ju aldrig en sådan historia: en pussla-bitarna-rätt-så framträder-det-rätta-mönstret-historia. Förstås hade det ju varit enklare om det varit det för då hade hon [Jana] på slutet verkligen kunnat vara trovärdig i rollen som den klipske som efter att ha hållit låg profil plötsligt kunde rikta pistolen mot den skyldiga'.

As the quote shows, Fagerholm is very clear about how she treats genre conventions and how she relates to readability. Fagerholm's extensively rewritten closure of *Lola uppochner* will not be further discussed here, but it is a strong response to the reception of the novel that would be interesting to examine further.

Andres Lokko's (2013) review in the local paper *Kristianstadsbladet* goes a step further than Michel Ekman in his rejection of the novel by bluntly spelling out in the headline that *Lola uppochner* is 'Fagerholmian, but boring'. According to Lokko, the novel 'lacks suspense and is too messy'.²⁹ He admits having had to struggle while reading the novel: 'Yes, I really struggle with this novel. Still, I read it with a growing admiration for the handicraft and the ambition'.³⁰ He considers the novel unique but claims that it suffers from its 'burning indifference'.³¹ Lokko also comments on the devoted readership's craving for 'the new Fagerholm',³² implying that since the author's popularity and readers' interest in her new book are so established, she need not even write a good novel for there to be interest in her work.

It is clear from the reception reflected in the reviews that many critics are troubled by Fagerholm's experiment with the novel. They think that the novel is overloaded. Therefore, some call it a failure, but as an extenuating circumstance all state that the author's ambition is enormous. Some, like Ekman, offer a fruitful discussion about the possible limitations of the novel, others like Lokko are more provocative. A critic who admits to being bored by the work he reviews is rather unusual and might be a sign of an influence from social media where quick and emotional responses are the rule. Critics who consider *Lola uppochner* a failure typically bear witness, as Lokko does, to how they have had to struggle with reading the novel.

In the major Swedish newspaper *Svenska Dagbladet*, Annina Rabe (2013) describes Fagerholm's novel as simultaneously paradoxically 'demanding and inviting'.³³ She expresses her struggle with readability as a major concern and calls the novel difficult to unravel. What signifies Fagerholm, according to Rabe, is that her novels communicate 'so much effort, in every sentence. It is not supposed to be easy, neither for the author, nor for the reader'.³⁴ According to Rabe, this focus on effort increases with every new novel Fagerholm writes. Rabe describes Fagerholm's authorship as 'a landscape or world of novels that grows, ramifies/forms bifurcating points and comprises tighter and more complicated vegetation as more fiction is written'.³⁵ Thus, Rabe compares Fagerholm's writing to something organic, an assemblage

---

29 '[...] historien är ospännande och alltför rörig'.
30 'Ja, jag tampas verkligen med den här romanen. [...] Samtidigt så läser jag den ändå med en ökande beundran över själva hantverket och ambitionsnivån'.
31 'Nu följer jag den istället med ett brinnande ointresse'.
32 '*Lola uppochner*' är "nya Fagerholm". Det räcker nog så'.
33 '[...] svår och lättillgänglig på en gång'.
34 '[...] den enorma ansträngning som hela verket tycks utgöra. Det känns i varje mening; det ska inte vara lätt, vare sig för författaren eller läsaren'.
35 'För varje bok är det som om hennes romanvärld växer, förgrenar sig, bildar en allt tätare och snårigare växtlighet'.

in motion, where every new text adds to the whole. Despite all this effort, Fagerholm is not a difficult writer in Rabe's eyes since '[t]he reader who appreciates Fagerholm willingly and effortlessly agrees to be drawn into this complexity'.[36] Rabe points to inherent paradoxes in reading: for the reader, reading a complicated work always includes feeling lost and struggling with meaning-making, but it is usually possible to overcome one's confusion and even read without effort if agreeing to the reading contract Fagerholm offers via her metafictive comments. What attracts and stimulates the Fagerholmian reader is, according to Rabe, the author's highly personal language: 'Mastery, maybe the only contemporary author who really investigates the relationship between surface and depth, between emptiness and content'.[37] Herein lies the key to readability. There might be a content, or there might not. There might be content presented in an unfamiliar form so that the reader has to create new ways to read. The way Rabe puts it, the purpose of the text is to make the reader undergo a transformation and struggle to learn to read again. Rabe also mentions Fagerholm as trendsetting, yet unsurpassed. Syntax and poetic language are the touchstones in her reception. Furthermore, she also notes the aesthetics of the soiled and shabby and comments on national specificity, such as the Finland-Swedish language that differs in vocabulary and syntax from standard Swedish. Therefore, she is an example of a critic who makes the struggle with meaning-making significant.

Yet another way to handle the struggle with readability is to turn to either a biographical context or to go directly to Fagerholm's own statements on how to read the novel. In many cases the reviews of *Lola upp ochner* are accompanied by interviews in which Fagerholm answers questions about readability, or biographical passages that are inserted into the reviews. In some cases her own life and statements find their way into the reception of her novel. For example, Thomas Löthman (2013) in the Finland-Swedish literary journal *Horisont* turns to a biographical reading. He mentions Fagerholm's upbringing in an ultra-academic family in Helsinki and calls her a literary scholar in exile since she has also had an academic career. Moreover, he mentions her alcoholism and addiction to writing, and the real-life, small town environment as a backdrop for the novel. Löthman also refers to Fagerholm's own view of the novel as being 'hypothetical in its approach, a sketch for a possible course of events'.[38] He quotes her extensively as a form of authority on her own text.[39] Here the author functions as a guide to her own work. Making the novel readable in this case requires the author as a co-reader.

---

36 'Den som uppskattar Fagerholm låter sig villigt dras in i de där snåren och känner inte ens motståndet'.
37 'Som vanligt är Fagerholm en mästare, kanske den enda samtida skönlitterära författare jag vet som verkligen på riktigt utforskar förhållandet mellan yta och djup, mellan tomhet och innehåll'.
38 '[...] men mera av ett utkast till ett tänkbart förlopp, hypotesartat och till vissa delar fullt av luckor och motstridigheter och frågetecken'.
39 '[...] som hon själv sagt'.

Another example of biographical context is found in Kristin Nord's (2013) interview with Fagerholm which is called 'Murder mystery where the pieces don't fit' in the local Swedish newspaper *Sydsvenskan*. Here Fagerholm's biography is presented in an interview that is followed by a list of information where the author offers some reading instructions: 'There are keys in the text, but you do get the most important ones a couple of times. So just relax, just enter the text. If you miss something it doesn't matter.'[40] Here Fagerholm shows how aware she is of the struggle with readability and she tells readers to simply let go thereby underlining the affective aspects of reading. In the struggle to grasp Fagerholm's prose, readers may find that the author's comments on reading function as guidelines for how to read what many critics call challenging 'Fagerholmian' prose.

A Text Producing Affective and Intermedial Readings

When struggling with the readability of an unstable text like *Lola uppochner*, readers might take Monica Fagerholm's advice to let go and simply enter the text. This choice points in the direction of affective reading. Karin Littau (2006: 9) traces the historical tradition of affective reading and affective criticism when discussing reading. According to her, contemporary literary theory of reading systematically marginalizes, excludes, or ignores the reader's physical and emotional reactions to the text (Littau 2006: 11). Littau (2006: 1) stresses the materiality of reading strategies, or what she calls 'the anatomy of reading'. The paradigm of excluding emotional responses has also been true for reviewers, although the neoliberal era that has seen recent changes in the structures in the literary field, the media landscape and public service due to an application of an individualistic and market-orientated discourse has invested more in personal aspects such as memories or feelings in reception. Littau (2006: 12) notes that exclusions from the literary canon have been made by systematic hierarchies that privilege reason over passion. However, although Fagerholm operates with emotions and passions, as Helle shows in her article in this volume, she is by no means excluded from the literary canon; on the contrary she represents a shift towards a more affective writing.[41]

The reception of *Lola uppochner* is full of comments on affect and emotion. For example, Nina Björk (2013) in the major Swedish newspaper *Dagens Nyheter* confesses to enjoying being invaded, widened, and contaminated by 'Fagerholmian language'[42]: 'It's like champagne, rising joy, it's like intoxication.'[43] Björk's reading pinpoints the essence of great literature, which is to touch the reader not only intellectually but also emotionally and

---

40 'Läsanvisning till hennes romaner. Det finns nycklar i texten, men de viktigaste får du ett antal gånger. Slappna därför av, gå bara in i texten. Om du missar något är det inte hela världen'.
41 See Fjelkestam (2013) for a discussion on the affective turn.
42 'Njuter av att invaderas av det Fagerholmska språket.'
43 'Som bubblande champagne, uppåtstigande glädje.'

she, like many other reviewers, uses strong metaphors to communicate her reading experience.

Another critic whose response expresses the same kind of affective reading is Sebastian Johans (2012) in *Upsala Nya Tidning* who experiences the story as on the edge of being overloaded and thinks he has lost a grip on the reading.[44] Still, when feeling this way he finds himself totally absorbed by the novel and 'back in Flatnäs' as if his reading actually places him among the fictional characters in the fictional small town.[45]

Taking a broader view, Kaisa Kurikka (Kurikka 2012) in *Turun Sanomat* prefers a reception that is open to multiple readings and stresses affective responses as a crucial part of the reading process. She considers the novel yet another variation on themes familiar from Fagerholm's earlier works, but does not think it is as impressive. She does note that the author's rebellious language comes of age. Commenting on readability Kurikka, concludes that the novel is 'not to be explained, but to be experienced'.[46] However, what happens to literary criticism and the presentation of public readings if there really is nothing to explain about the novel? Does reading not always include experiencing? Is *Lola uppochner* really so different that it cannot be explained, not even through a range of different readings? I think the answer is to be found in the multiple ways to read the novel, including affective response, presented here. Texts, especially texts that challenge readability, must be discussed. This is the only way literary conventions and reading are kept alive and engaging.

The struggle with readability also makes the critics seek answers in other art forms. This comes as no surprise since Fagerholm herself uses many references to other art forms when she borrows structures from music, dance and visual art (painting, film, TV series and comics) in her narration. The comparison to other art forms such as dance or music constitutes an intermedial reading. Many reviewers comment on Fagerholm's use of music; Wahlin (2013) in *Aftonbladet* summarizes Fagerholm's poetics as musical. He appreciates the work the reader has to do in order to crack the Fagerholmian code. According to Wahlin, Fagerholm's metafictive poetics make the reader part of the meaning-making process. The other option for the reader, he suggests, is to let go of meaning-making and instead follow a stream of language and images presented in the novel, similar to listening to music. Comments such as these suggest an intermedial reading strategy where analytical tools from other art fields are used in the interpretation of the novel.

In many reviews critics comment upon the transformation they undergo while reading. For example, Anna Paju's (2012) review in the local Finnish paper *Kansan Uutiset* is entitled: 'In my head a chorus sings, where horror

---

44 'Ibland blir Monika Fagerholms berättelse på gränsen till överladdad, och jag tror att jag har tappat grep [sic!] om läsningen'.
45 'Trots att *Lola uppochner* då och då förlorar fokus lyckas Monika Fagerholm tränga sig in under huden och stanna kvar som ett knappt märkbart [sic!] men ändå högst påtaglig mask som inte ger sig förrän jag skymtar den in utkanten av mitt eget öga'.
46 '*Lola ylösalaisin* on jälleen teos, jota ei voi selittää vaan joka täytyy kokea'.

meets beauty'. She labels Fagerholm's style as hypnotic, similar to a piece of music, where themes are varied. According to Paju, the novel is visual and paints scenarios that are both beautiful and disconsolate. Paju also mentions her surprise, since she considers herself a reader who is a friend of order and truth-seeking and thus most likely to be bothered by Fagerholm's novel, which from time to time is so hard to interpret. Paju is stunned that she loves Fagerholm's 'merry-go-round of words' and is thus an example of a critic who thinks Fagerholm succeeds in writing a novel that goes beyond the reviewer's preferred genre expectations. Paju accepts the novel as different and states that movement and soundtrack are her keywords when describing her reading experience, thus pointing to the affective layers in the reading. Paju's discussion testifies to a struggle with readability that produces a surprising transformation the critic herself had not expected.

In her review in the major Finnish paper *Helsingin Sanomat*, Sanna Kangasniemi (2012) labels Fagerholm's style kaleidoscopic, implying that the visions and episodes presented in the text are in constant flux and that therefore traditional meaning-making is fruitless. The genre label thriller is not to be trusted, according to her, since the Fagerholmian mindscape consists of feelings, events and narration that are one.[47] She compares Flatnäs to a scene in Shakespeare's *A Midsummer Night's Dream*, although in Fagerholm's version the characters make their moves in an autumn landscape. Kangasniemi also compares the structure of the novel to a metafictive episode in the novel, that is, a description of a garden of statues, where Fagerholm highlights different parts of the garden, bit by bit. Many critics, like Kangasniemi, cling to key scenes, epigrams or intertextual references that point to a variety of possible interpretations. The reception of *Lola uppochner* shows that in their struggle critics' turn to both affective and intermedial reading models. It is as if they are lost and need to both express emotions and cling to metafiction in order to interpret the novel at all.

Beyond Readability? Really?

From my discussion of the reception of *Lola uppochner*, it is evident that the struggle with readability in the reception of *DIVA* (Stenwall 2001: 235) continues fourteen years later in the reception of *Lola uppochner*. This means that Fagerholm's writing still is very avant-garde and that a more theoretical approach such as a posthuman reading, a girlhood studies or a queer reading has not yet fully reached the reception. Most critics are puzzled by *Lola uppochner* and whereas some accept the difficulties of reading outside of cemented conventions, others consider the struggle too much and the (mis)use of generic conventions unconvincing and thus consider the novel a failure.

The same kind of oscillation between reading Fagerholm according to the literary conventions or not is obvious in the reception of *Lola*

---

47 '[…] fagerholmilaiseen (mielen) maisemaan, jossa tunteet, tapahtumat ja kerronnan kieli ovat erottamattomasti yhtä'.

uppochner, as in Fagerholm's earlier work such as *DIVA* and *The End of the Glitter Scene* diptych. For example Camilla Lindberg's headline in the local Finland-Swedish paper *Västra Nyland* contains the words 'a challenge to read' (Lindberg 2012) and she confesses that the text repeatedly forced her to question whether she accepted the premises or not. She 'hesitates, surrenders, hesitates again'.[48] The recognition of a 'Fagerholmian' poetics does not exclude that there appears to be a limit to how far a novel can stretch its transformative traits.

Amanda Svensson (2013) in the major Swedish evening paper *Expressen* summarises that *Lola uppochner* is 'Fagerholm's most demanding novel so far, but not the most rewarding. Her peculiar, dreamy language [...] is here unbearably woolly and sloppy'.[49] Svensson also overtly comments on a supposed professional reading: 'As a literary scholar one could have revelled for months in all visions, references and curiosa – as a reader one might have to swallow that you cannot understand it all'.[50] Thus, Svensson distinguishes between the professional reader and a common reader, stating that a trained, sophisticated reader, supposedly with the help of literary theory, might perform an intertextual reading that would be rewarding, but that this style of writing leaves the unsophisticated reader behind, without a possibility to fully understand the novel.

As I have shown, critics are divided into two camps, those who embrace Fagerholm as a thought-provoking trendsetter who writes fiction that alludes to the gurlesque, queer, posthumanist or produces new discourses and those who are disturbed by the uneasy ways of reading that Fagerholm's novels apparently demand. Herman Rapaport (2011: 9) pleads for unpredictable readings; that is he would like to see readings that not only apply theory to a text but also let the text generate theory: 'The theory should illuminate a work, and a work should illuminate theory'. Fagerholm's novel generates theory, but the unpredictable nature of the text seems to puzzle critics.[51] Overall, Fagerholm's novels demand a reader who challenges automatized reading strategies, such as seeking coherence and chronology. The readers' presupposed longing for mimesis and an underlying urge for order is reflected in the comments on the unreliability of the novel's style.

The reception of Monika Fagerholm's novel *Lola uppochner* exposes a variety of different readings. I have discussed the effect of the struggle with readability in a selection of Swedish and Finnish reviews. Most critics testify to having had to struggle with meaning-making and readability. Critics have been shown to combine generic elements such as thriller and tragedy

---

48 'Ibland tvekar jag. Faller till föga. Tvekar'.
49 '*Lola uppochner* är kanske Fagerholms mest krävande roman hittills, men inte den mest belönande. [...] Också Fagerholms säregna, drömska språk – som brukar vara den stora behållningen med att läsa henne – är i *Lola uppochner* ibland plågsamt luddigt, ja slappt'.
50 'Som litteraturvetare hade man kunnat gotta sig i månader åt alla bilder, referenser och kuriositeter – som läsare får man kanske helt enkelt svälja att man inte kan ta in allt'.
51 See Lahdenperä in this volume for a discussion of text as theory.

or girlhood tropes and to comment on the Fagerholmian style and form. Many have also found metafictive devices used in the novel and applied them as guidelines for interpretation. Others admit that reading this type of billowing narration demands a more affective reading, which includes both intellectual and emotional responses. Some critics present an intermedial reading and compare their reading act to dancing, looking at paintings, or listening to music.

From my material it is clear that Fagerholm's narrative transformations also invite transformations of reading. The most striking trait in the reception of *Lola uppochner* is that critics respond to this transformation. They comment on their emotions, excitement, and confusion and they are eager to unravel literary contexts. Emotions also emerge as a considerable part of the reading experience. Fiction has visual, auditory and tactile dimensions that colour the reading experience and admitting to this also means that affective or intermedial readings are activated. Thus, reading involves imagination, intellect and emotions equally, only in the reception of Fagerholm's work these elements are elaborated on in a way that leaves the reader with no escape and definitely places the reader and the critic outside of their comfort zones. These difficulties are apparently embraced by some, while others are too struck by Fagerholm's de-familiarization of ordinary literary conventions to be able to enjoy it. As Inger Dahlman (2013) exclaims in her review in the local paper *Moratidning/Borlänge tidning*: 'Soon it feels like you have ended up with Fagerholm's characters in a bottle that is constantly shaken'.[52]

The reception of Fagerholm's novel *Lola uppochner* reveals an ongoing negotiation of readability that literary critics communicate to readers when they report on their encounter with the text. All critics referred to in this article describe Fagerholm's oeuvre as unique and outstanding; they say that she almost performs the impossible. Therefore, it is no surprise that reading Fagerholm requires modified reading strategies. A struggle with being forced to transform one's ways of reading and the need to develop new ways of reading are at the core of the reception of *Lola uppochner*.

References

Primary Sources

Fagerholm, Monika 2012: *Lola uppochner*. Schildts & Söderströms, Helsingfors.
Fagerholm, Monika 2013: *Lola uppochner*. Bonniers/Månpocket, Stockholm. [Revised version].

---

52 'Snart känns det som om man hamnat med Fagerholms personer inuti en flaska som oavbrutet skakas häftigt'.

Björk, Nina 2013: Monika Fagerholm har gjort det igen. Pur glädje över stor konst. [Monika Fagerholm Did It Again. Pure Joy over Great Art] – *Dagens Nyheter* 1.2.2013.

Ekman, Michel 2012: En splittrad genreparodi. [A Shattered Genre Parody] –*Hufvudstadsbladet* 21.9.2012.

Ekström Lindbäck, Lyra 2012: På spaning efter den kritiker som inte flyr framtiden. [Looking for the Critic Who Does Not Flee the Future] – *Dagens Nyheter* 23.3.2012.

Dahlman, Inger: Bitvis lysande. [Partly Brilliant] – *Mora tidning* 4.2.2013, Bitvis lysande av Fagerholm. [Partly Brilliant by Fagerholm] – *Borlänge tidning* 1.2.2013.

Hurford, Darcy 2013: Monika Fagerholm *Lola uppochner* (*Lola Upside-down*). – *Swedish Book Review* 2013.

Johans, Sebastian 2012: Otrohet, mord och svågerpolitik. [Infidelity, Murder and Nepotism] – *Upsala Nya tidning* 4.11.2012.

Kangasniemi, Sanna 2012: Kohdevalaistu ihmistarha. Monika Fagerholm vei kaleidoskooppi-kerrontansa Estonian uppoamisen aikaan. [Spotlighted Garden of Humanity. Monika Fagerholm Took her Kaleidoscopic Narration to the Time of Estonia's Sinking] – *Helsingin Sanomat* 21.9.2012.

Kantokorpi, Mervi 2009: On neidille punapanta. Monika Fagerholmin odotettu romaani on huimaava spektaakkeli tunteiden pyörönäyttämöllä. [A Red Ribbon for the Maid. Monika Fagerholm's Much Longed for Novel is a Breath-Taking Spectacle on the Revolving Stage of Feelings] – *Helsingin Sanomat* 11.10.2009.

Kjersén Edman, Lena 2013: Att bli alla fåglar. [To Become All Birds] – *Västerbottenskuriren* 4.2.2013.

Kurikka, Kaisa 2013: Thrillerissä soi Ravelin Bolero. [In the Thriller Ravel's Bolero Plays] –*Turun Sanomat* 15.1.2013.

Larsson, Lisbeth 2013: Fagerholm lägger solkigt pussel. [Fagerholm Lays a Shabby Puzzle] – *Göteborgsposten* 31.1.2013.

Lindberg, Camilla 2012: Fagerholms nya thriller är utmanande läsning. [Fagerholm's New Thriller Is a Challenge to Read] – *Västra Nyland* 21.9.2012.

Lindqvist, Marit 2012: Monika Fagerholm. Lola uppochner. – *Svenska YLE* 21. 9.2012.

Lingebrandt, Ann 2013: Fagerholm uppochner. [Fagerholm Upsidedown] – *Helsingborgs dagblad/ Landskronaposten* 1.2.2013, Förtrollning och fantasier utan magi. [Enchantment and Fantasies Without Magic] – *Norrköpings tidningar* 1.2.2013.

Lokko, Andres 2013: Thriller utan spänning. [Thriller without Suspence] – *Borås tidning*, Fagerholm, men trist. [Fagerholm, But Boring] – *Kristianstadsbladet /Ystads Allehanda*, Fagerholm skriver thriller utan spanning. [Fagerholm Writes Thriller without Suspence] – *Blekinge Länstidning*, Rörigt försök till spänning. [Messy Try for Suspence] – *Oskarhamnstidningen* 1.2.2013.

Löthman, Thomas 2013: Burlesk grundton tar över. [A Burlesque Tone Takes Over] – *Horisont* 60/2013, 61–63.

Löthman, Thomas 2013: Inte mycket sfinxiskt leende hos litteraturvetaren i akademisk exil. [Not Much of a Sphinx's Smile for the Academic in Exile] – *Tidningen Kulturen* 13. 2.2013.

Nord, Kristin 2013: Mordgåta där bitarna inte passar. [Murder Mystery Where the Pieces Do Not Fit] – *Sydsvenskan* 10.2.2013.

Otterberg, Stina 2013: De okritiska upprepningarna finns på nätet snarare än på kultursidorna. [The Uncritical Repetitions Are Found on the Web, Rather Than on the Culture Pages] – *Dagens Nyheter* 12.4.2013.

Paju, Anna 2012: Kauhean kaunista kauhua à la Fagerholm. [The Beauty of Horror in Fagerholm] – *Kansan Uutiset* 7.11.2012.

Rabe, Annina 2013: Svårnystad thrillergåta av Fagerholm. [A Thriller Mystery Hard to Wind by Fagerholm] – *Svenska Dagbladet* 1.2.2013.

Schottenius, Maria 2012: Varför får vi vänta på Monika Fagerholm? [Why Do We Have to Wait for Fagerholm?] – *Dagens Nyheter* 6.10.2012.

Sjögren, Dan 2013: Fagerholm avslutar – rafflande i överkant. [Fagerholm Stops – Too Thrilling] – *Norrländska Socialdemokraten* 4.2.2013.

Sterner, Susanne 2013: Monika Fagerholm rör sig häftigt i flickornas värld. [Monika Fagerholm Moves Brilliantly in the Girl's World] – *Östgöta Correspondenten* 5.2.2013.

Svensson, Amanda 2013: Deckarflörten. [Flirting with the Crime Story] – *Expressen/ Göteborgs Tidning* 1.2.2013.

Söderling, Trygve 2012: Moralens tillstånd i Flatnäs. [The State of Morality in Flatnäs] – *Ny Tid* 19.11.2012.

Wahlin, Claes 2013: En felvänd värld utmanar läsaren. [An Inverted World Challenges the Reader] – *Aftonbladet* 2.2.2013.

Österlund, Mia 2012: På återbesök i docklaboratoriet (en småstads egna alfabet om flatheten, en bonusberättelse om dåtiden.) [Revisiting the Doll's Laboratory (a Small Town's Own Alphabet on Flatness, a Bonus Story from the Past] – *Lysmasken* 12.10.2012.

Secondary Sources

Ahlbäck, Pia 2007: The Reader! The Reader! The Mimetic Challenge of Addressivity and Response in Historical Writing. – *Storia della Storiografia* 52/2007, 34–48.

Arvas, Paula and Nestingen, Andrew (Eds.) 2011: *Scandinavian Crime Fiction*. Wales University Press, Cardiff.

Braidotti, Rosi 2002: *Metamorphoses. Towards a Materialist Theory of Becoming*. Polity Press, Cambridge.

Deleuze, Gilles and Guattari, Félix 2005: *A Thousand Plateaus, Capitalism and Schizophrenia*. Minnesota University Press, Minneapolis & London.

Fjelkestam, Kristina 2013: The Turn of the Screwd. Teoretiska vändningar då och (mest) nu. [The Turn of the Screwed. Theoretical Turns Then and (Mostly) Now] In *Fält i förvandling*. [A Field in Transformation.] Eds. Eva Heggestad et al. Gidlunds, Örlinge, 103–114.

Haasjoki, Pauliina 2012: *Häilyvyyden liittolaiset. Kerronnan ja seksuaalisuuden ambivalenssit*. [Allies in Wavering. The Ambivalences of Narrative and Sexuality] Turun yliopiston julkaisuja, Annales Universitatis Turkuensis Sarja – Ser. C Osa – Tom. 343, Scripta lingua Fennica edita. Turun yliopisto, Turku.

Hutcheon, Linda 1980/1985: *Narcissistic Narrative. The Metafictional Paradox*. Methuen, New York and London.

Hägg, Samuli et al. (Eds.) 2008: *Metaliterary Layers in Finnish Literature*. Studia Fennica Litteraria 3. Finnish Literature Society, Helsinki.

Kurikka, Kaisa 2005: Tytöksi tulemisen-tilat. Monika Fagerholmin *Diva* utopistisena tekstinä. [The Spaces of Becoming-Girl. Monika Fagerholm's *Diva* as a Utopian Text] *PoMon tila. Kirjoituksia kirjallisuuden postmodernismista*. [The Space of PoMo. Texts on Postmodern Literature] Eds. Anna Helle and Katariina Kajannes. Jyväskylän ylioppilaskunnan julkaisusarja numero 74. Kampus kustannus, Jyväskylä, 56–72.

Kurikka, Kaisa 2008: To Use and Abuse, to Write and Rewrite. Metafictional Trends in Contemporary Finnish Prose. In *Metaliterary Layers in Finnish Literature*. Eds. Samuli Hägg, Erkki Sevänen and Risto Turunen. Studia Fennica Litteraria 3. Finnish Literature Society, Helsinki, 48–63.

Littau, Karin 2006: *Theories of Reading. Books, Bodies and Bibliomania*. Cambridge University Press, Cambridge.

Mulari, Heta: *New Feminisms, Gender Equality and Neoliberalism in Swedish Girl Films, 1995–2006*. Turku University Press, Turku.

Rapaport, Herman 2011: *Literary Theory. A Toolkit.* Whiley-Blackwell, Chichester.
Rosenberg, Tiina 2002: *Queerfeministisk agenda.* [A Queer Feminist Agenda] Atlas, Stockholm.
Samuelsson, Lina 2013: *Kritikens ordning. Svenska bokrecensioner 1906, 1956, 2006.* [The Order of Critique. Swedish Literary Reviews] Bild, Text & Form, Karlstad.
Stenwall, Åsa 2001: *Portföljen i skogen. Kvinnor och modernitet i det sena 1900-talets finlandssvenska litteratur.* [Briefcase in the Woods. Women and Modernity in Late 20th Century Finland-Swedish Literature] Schildts, Helsingfors.
Waugh, Patricia 1984: *The Theory and Practice of Self-Conscious Fiction.* Methuen, London and New York.
Österholm, Maria Margareta 2012: *Ett flicklaboratorium i valda bitar. Skeva flickor i svenskspråkig prosa från 1980 till 2005.* [A Girl Laboratory in Chosen Parts. Queer Girls in Swedish and Finland-Swedish Literature from 1980 to 2005] Rosenlarv förlag, Stockholm.
Österlund, Mia and al. 2013: Litteratur och konst som flickforskningens teoretiska språngbräda. [Literature and Art as the Theoretical Footbridge for Girlhood Studies] In *Flicktion. Perspektiv på flickan i fiktionen.* [Fliction. Perspectives on Girlhood in Fiction] Eds. Eva Söderberg, Mia Österlund, Bodil Formark. Universus Academic Press, Malmö, 11–28.

List of Authors

ANNA HELLE, Ph.D. is Senior Researcher in Literature at the University of Jyväskylä, Finland. Helle is co-editor of an anthology of essays on Finnish literature and affects (forthcoming, 2016). She has published several articles on contemporary Finnish literature.

KAISA KURIKKA, Ph.D. is Adjunct Professor in Finnish Literature at the University of Turku, Finland. Kurikka has published articles on contemporary Finnish prose; she is the editor of volumes on authorship studies, literary spaces and new materialism. She has also published a book on Algot Untola, an early 20th-century Finnish avant-garde writer known for his polyonomous authorship. Recently, Kurikka has focused on adaptation studies and experimental literature.

LENA KÅRELAND, Ph.D. is Professor in Literature at Uppsala University, Sweden. She has published several books and articles about children's literature authors, for instance Lennart Hellsing and Tove Jansson. She has also studied the modernism movement in children's literature and written about literature in school from a gender perspective.

HANNA LAHDENPERÄ is a doctoral student at the Department of Finnish, Finno-Ugrian and Scandinavian Studies at the University of Helsinki, Finland. Her dissertation on Monika Fagerholm's novel *DIVA* (1998) discusses queer theory and sexual difference theory through subjectivity, liminality and materiality. Lahdenperä's research interests include gender, literature and philosophy, and postmodernism.

ANN-SOFIE LÖNNGREN, Ph.D. is Associate Professor in Literature at Uppsala University, Sweden. Her interest in Monika Fagerholm stems from a larger project, published as a monograph in 2015, about human-animal transformations in modern literature from Europe's northernmost sphere. Apart from this, she has co-edited several anthologies and published articles and essays regarding modern, Nordic literature, intersectionality, human-animal studies, and queer- and transgender theory.

KRISTINA MALMIO, Ph.D. is Adjunct Professor in Nordic Literature at University of Helsinki, Finland. Her research interests include modern and latemodern Finland-Swedish literature, literary theory and sociology of literature. Malmio's latest publication is an anthology, *Values of Literature* (together with Hanna Meretoja, Pirjo Lyytikäinen, and Saija Isomaa, Brill/Rodopi 2015). She has published extensively on Finland-Swedish fiction and edited several scholarly anthologies. Malmio is the leader of a research project, *Late Modern Spatiality in Finland-Swedish Prose 1990–2010* (2014–2017) supported by The Society of Swedish Literature in Finland.

MARIA MARGARETA ÖSTERHOLM, Ph.D. teaches Gender Studies at Stockholm University and Uppsala University, Sweden. In her dissertation (2012) she wrote about girlhoods in Swedish and Finland-Swedish contemporary literature. She has published poetry and fiction, as well as articles about academic writing, girls and the gurlesque that have been inspired by queer theory.

MIA ÖSTERLUND, Docent, is Adjunct Professor in Comparative Literature at Åbo Akademi University, Turku, Finland. Her research interests are girlhood, gender studies and children's literature. Österlund has published a book on gender transgression in young adult fiction and has co-edited anthologies of literature studies. She has published extensively on gender in picture books and is editor of *Barnboken. Journal of Children's Literature Research*.

Abstract

Novel Districts
Critical Readings of Monika Fagerholm

Edited by Kristina Malmio and Mia Österlund

Finland-Swedish writer Monika Fagerholm is one of the most important contemporary Nordic authors. Her experimental, puzzling and daring novels, such as *Underbara kvinnor vid vatten* (1994) and *Den amerikanska flickan* (2004), have attracted much critical attention. She has won several literary awards, including the Nordic prize from the Swedish Academy in 2016; her works have travelled across national and cultural borders as they have now been translated in USA, Europe, Eastern Europe and Russia. Fagerholm's wild and visionary depictions of girlhood have long had an impact on the Nordic literary landscape; currently, she has many literary followers among young female writers and readers in Finland and Sweden.

Novel Districts. Critical Readings of Monika Fagerholm is the first major study of Fagerholm's works. In this edited volume, literary scholars explore the central themes and features that permeate Fagerholm's works and introduce novel ways to understand and interpret her writings. The book begins with an introduction to her life, letters and the minority literature context of her writing and briefly describes the scholarship on Fagerholm's works. After that, Finnish and Swedish scholars and experts on Fagerholm scrutinize her oeuvre in the light of up-to-date literary theory. The insights, theories and concepts of gender, feminist and girlhood studies as well as narratology, poststructuralism, posthumanism and reception studies are tested in close readings of Fagerholm's works published between 1990 and 2012.

Thus, the volume enhances and deepens the understanding of Fagerholm's fiction and invites the attention of readers not yet familiar with her work. The articles demonstrate the multitude of ways in which literary and cultural conventions can be innovatively re-employed within 20th and 21th century literature to reveal new perspectives on contemporary Finnish and Nordic literature and ongoing cultural and social developments.

Index

Aarseth, Espen J. 69, 70, 72, 74, 78
Ahlbäck, Pia 136, 153
Ahmed, Sara 111, 115
Alanko, Outi 92, 98
Ambjörnsson, Fanny 104, 112, 115
Arvas, Paula 139, 153

Bakhtin, Mikhail 15, 25, 36
Barthes, Roland 5, 18, 53, 56-58, 63-64, 70
Beckman, Åsa 67, 78
Berg, Hubert van den 75, 78
Björk, Nina 54, 64, 135, 147, 152
Bogue, Ronald 43, 51
Bourassa, Alan 92, 98
Boutang, Pierre-André 48, 52
Braidotti, Rosi 100, 123, 131-132, 134, 153
Bronfen, Elisabeth 87, 90, 92-93, 96-98
Brooks, Peter 84-86, 89-90, 98
Brushwood Rose, Chloë 102, 115
Butler, Judith 120, 124, 132

Camilleri, Anna 102, 115
Castells, Manuel 73, 76-78
Cixous, Hélène 26, 36, 142
Colebrook, Claire 38, 40, 47-48, 51
Connell, Liam 77, 78
Critchley, Simon 92, 98

Dahl, Alva 15-16, 19
Dahl, Ulrika 101-102, 115
Dahlman, Inger 135, 151-152
Davidson, Arnold I. 120, 132
Davidson, H. R. Ellis 119, 132
Deleuze, Gilles 17, 39-41, 43-45, 47-52, 71, 98, 100, 120, 123-124, 132, 134, 153
Doxtater, Amanda 15, 19

Ekman, Michel 9-10, 14, 19-20, 37, 135, 143-145, 152
Ekström Lindbäck, Lyra 138, 152

Eskelinen, Markku 70, 74, 78
Espmark, Kjell 25, 36

Fagerholm, Monika 3, 5-20, 25-32, 34-41, 44, 47-48, 50-55, 59, 64, 66-69, 71, 73, 75-76, 78-79, 83-87, 89, 92, 96-101, 103-106, 108-109, 115, 119-121, 123- 126, 131-155, 157
Fass Leavy, Barbara 127-130, 132
Ferzoco, George 119, 132
Flaxman, Gregory 43, 44, 51
Franck, Mia 28, 36
Frih, Anna-Karin 29, 36

Gere, Charlie 69, 71-74, 78
Gilbert, Sandra 102, 116
Gill, Miriam 119, 132
Glenum, Lara 18, 113, 116
Greenberg, Arielle 18, 100-104, 116
Guattari, Félix 17, 40-41, 43-45, 47, 49, 50-51, 71, 100, 120, 123-124, 132, 134, 153
Gubar, Susan 102, 116

Haasjoki, Pauliina 15, 20, 39, 44, 46, 51, 54, 63-64, 67, 70, 73, 78, 134, 153
Halberstam, Judith/Jack 32, 36, 109-111, 116, 131, 132
Hammershaimb, V. U. 129, 132
Hedman, Kaj 67, 78
Heiskala, Risto 77-78
Helle, Anna 5, 14, 18, 20, 51, 62, 64, 79, 83, 85, 87, 98, 132, 147, 153, 155
hooks, bell 125, 132
Hurford, Darcy 144, 152
Hutcheon, Linda 97, 135, 153

Ingström, Pia 9, 13-14, 20, 28, 37
Ingvarsson, Jonas 67-68, 71-72, 75, 77-78

Jameson, Fredric 18, 67-68, 74-75, 79
Jansson, Bo G. 16, 20
Johans, Sebastian 135, 138, 144, 148, 152

Kangasniemi, Sanna 141, 149, 152
Kantokorpi, Mervi 136, 152
Korsström, Tuva 9, 11, 20
Koskimaa, Raine 70, 72, 74, 79
Kristeva, Julia 17, 25-27, 37, 120, 132-133, 142
Kurikka, Kaisa 5, 14, 17-18, 20, 38-39, 44, 46, 51, 57, 63-64, 66, 68, 70-71, 73, 76, 79, 83, 98, 134-135, 139, 148, 152-153, 155
Kåreland, Lena 5, 14, 17, 20, 25, 30, 37, 57, 64, 66, 68, 79, 155

Lahdenperä, Hanna 5, 18, 53, 70, 134, 150, 155
Lambert, Gregg 44, 51
Larsson, Lisbeth 140, 152
Lauretis, Teresa de 18, 53, 55-56, 58, 63-64, 100, 108-109, 115-116
Lindberg, Camilla 135, 150, 152
Lindblom, Tomi 73, 79
Lindgren, Astrid 30-31, 37
Littau, Karin 137-138, 147, 153
Lokko, Andres 135, 145, 152
Lönngren, Ann-Sofie 6, 15, 18-20, 119, 121, 123, 133, 155
Löthman, Thomas 146, 152

Malmio, Kristina 5, 7-8, 14, 18, 20, 29, 37, 43, 46, 51, 57, 64, 66-67, 79, 83, 98, 156-157
Marsh, Nicky 77, 78
Martin, Royston 73, 78
Mazzarella, Merete 14, 20
McHale, Brian 74
Mercer, John 85, 98
Miettinen, Niina 83, 98
Miller, Hillis J. 39, 52
Moriarty, Michael 56-58, 63-64
Mulari, Heta 141, 153
Möller, Anna-Lena 67, 79

Neale, Steve 85, 98
Nemesvari, Richard 85, 98
Nenola, Aili 120, 133
Nestingen, Andrew 139, 153
Ngai, Sianne 113, 116
Nord, Kristin 147, 152

Ojajärvi, Jussi 16, 21, 59, 64, 66, 73-74, 79
Otterberg, Stina 138, 152

Paju, Anna 148-149, 152
Page, Ruth 70, 79
Parnet, Claire 39, 48, 51-52
Peterson, Marie 25, 37, 67, 79

Rabe, Annina 135, 145-146, 152
Rapaport, Herman 137-138, 150, 154
Rich, Adrienne 35, 37, 93, 98, 123, 133
Russell, Claire 120, 133
Russell, W.M.S. 120, 132-133
Russo, Mary 113, 116
Rosenberg, Tiina 30, 37, 141, 154
Ryan, Marie-Laure 70, 79

Sandin, Maria 26-27, 37, 119, 123, 133
Schottenius, Maria 135, 152
Sevänen, Erkki 51, 66, 77, 79, 153
Shingler, Martin 85, 98
Singer, Ben 85-86, 98
Sjögren, Dan 142, 153
Solomin, Nina 54, 65
Stenwall, Åsa 13, 21, 54, 57, 65-68, 73-74, 80, 121, 133, 136, 138, 142, 149, 154
Sterner, Susanne 141-142, 153
Sundström, Charlotte 67, 80
Svedjedal, Johan 69-70, 73-74, 80
Svensson, Amanda 135, 139, 150, 153
Söderberg, Eva 29, 36, 154

Tani, Stefano 88, 98
Theander, Birgitta 25, 37
Thomas, Bronwen 70, 79
Tidigs, Julia 10, 21
Toijer-Nilsson, Ying 28, 37
Trites, Roberta Seelinger 28, 37

Wahlin, Claes 142-143, 148, 153
Warner, Marina 123, 126, 133
Waugh, Patricia 136, 154
Werkelid, Carl Otto 66, 80
Westin, Boel 28, 37
Widegren, Kajsa 104, 116
Wolfe, Cary 119-120, 133

Zarzosa, Agustin 85, 98

Österholm, Maria Margareta 5, 11, 14, 18, 21, 29, 31, 37, 39, 52, 54-55, 65, 71, 73, 80, 84, 94, 98-100, 116, 121, 126, 133, 135, 140, 154, 156
Österlund, Mia 5-8, 19, 28, 34, 37, 54, 57, 65, 74, 102, 116, 134, 141, 153-154, 156

Studia Fennica Ethnologica

Memories of My Town
The Identities of Town Dwellers and Their Places in Three Finnish Towns
Edited by Anna-Maria Åström, Pirjo Korkiakangas & Pia Olsson
Studia Fennica Ethnologica 8
2004

Passages Westward
Edited by Maria Lähteenmäki & Hanna Snellman
Studia Fennica Ethnologica 9
2006

Defining Self
Essays on emergent identities in Russia Seventeenth to Nineteenth Centuries
Edited by Michael Branch
Studia Fennica Ethnologica 10
2009

Touching Things
Ethnological Aspects of Modern Material Culture
Edited by Pirjo Korkiakangas, Tiina-Riitta Lappi & Heli Niskanen
Studia Fennica Ethnologica 11
2008

Gendered Rural Spaces
Edited by Pia Olsson & Helena Ruotsala
Studia Fennica Ethnologica 12
2009

Laura Stark
The Limits of Patriarchy
How Female Networks of Pilfering and Gossip Sparked the First Debates on Rural Gender Rights in the 19th-century Finnish-Language Press
Studia Fennica Ethnologica 13
2011

Where is the Field?
The Experience of Migration Viewed through the Prism of Ethnographic Fieldwork
Edited by Laura Hirvi & Hanna Snellman
Studia Fennica Ethnologica 14
2012

Laura Hirvi
Identities in Practice
A Trans-Atlantic Ethnography of Sikh Immigrants in Finland and in California
Studia Fennica Ethnologica 15
2013

Eerika Koskinen-Koivisto
Her Own Worth
Negotiations of Subjectivity in the Life Narrative of a Female Labourer
Studia Fennica Ethnologica 16
2014

Studia Fennica Folkloristica

Pertti J. Anttonen
Tradition through Modernity
Postmodernism and the Nation-State in Folklore Scholarship
Studia Fennica Folkloristica 15
2005

Narrating, Doing, Experiencing
Nordic Folkloristic Perspectives
Edited by Annikki Kaivola-Bregenhøj, Barbro Klein & Ulf Palmenfelt
Studia Fennica Folkloristica 16
2006

Mícheál Briody
The Irish Folklore Commission 1935–1970
History, ideology, methodology
Studia Fennica Folkloristica 17
2008

Venla Sykäri
Words as Events
Cretan Mantinádes in Performance and Composition
Studia Fennica Folkloristica 18
2011

Hidden Rituals and Public Performances
Traditions and Belonging among the Post-Soviet Khanty, Komi and Udmurts
Edited by Anna-Leena Siikala & Oleg Ulyashev
Studia Fennica Folkloristica 19
2011

Mythic Discourses
Studies in Uralic Traditions
Edited by Frog, Anna-Leena Siikala & Eila Stepanova
Studia Fennica Folkloristica 20
2012

Cornelius Hasselblatt
Kalevipoeg Studies
The Creation and Reception of an Epic
Studia Fennica Folkloristica 21
2016

Studia Fennica Historica

Medieval History Writing and Crusading Ideology
Edited by Tuomas M. S. Lehtonen & Kurt Villads Jensen with Janne Malkki and Katja Ritari
Studia Fennica Historica 9
2005

Moving in the USSR
Western anomalies and Northern wilderness
Edited by Pekka Hakamies
Studia Fennica Historica 10
2005

DEREK FEWSTER
Visions of Past Glory
Nationalism and the Construction of Early Finnish History
Studia Fennica Historica 11
2006

Modernisation in Russia since 1900
Edited by Markku Kangaspuro & Jeremy Smith
Studia Fennica Historica 12
2006

SEIJA-RIITTA LAAKSO
Across the Oceans
Development of Overseas Business Information Transmission 1815–1875
Studia Fennica Historica 13
2007

Industry and Modernism
Companies, Architecture and Identity in the Nordic and Baltic Countries during the High-Industrial Period
Edited by Anja Kervanto Nevanlinna
Studia Fennica Historica 14
2007

CHARLOTTA WOLFF
Noble conceptions of politics in eighteenth-century Sweden (ca 1740–1790)
Studia Fennica Historica 15
2008

Sport, Recreation and Green Space in the European City
Edited by Peter Clark, Marjaana Niemi & Jari Niemelä
Studia Fennica Historica 16
2009

Rhetorics of Nordic Democracy
Edited by Jussi Kurunmäki & Johan Strang
Studia Fennica Historica 17
2010

Fibula, Fabula, Fact
The Viking Age in Finland
Edited by Joonas Ahola & Frog with Clive Tolley
Studia Fennica Historica 18
2014

Novels, Histories, Novel Nations
Historical Fiction and Cultural Memory in Finland and Estonia
Edited by Linda Kaljundi, Eneken Laanes & Ilona Pikkanen
Studia Fennica Historica 19
2015

JUKKA GRONOW & SERGEY ZHURAVLEV
Fashion Meets Socialism
Fashion industry in the Soviet Union after the Second World War
Studia Fennica Historica 20
2015

SOFIA KOTILAINEN
Literacy Skills as Local Intangible Capital
The History of a Rural Lending Library c. 1860–1920
Studia Fennica Historica 21
2016

Studia Fennica Anthropologica

On Foreign Ground
Moving between Countries and Categories
Edited by Marie-Louise Karttunen & Minna Ruckenstein
Studia Fennica Anthropologica 1
2007

Beyond the Horizon
Essays on Myth, History, Travel and Society
Edited by Clifford Sather & Timo Kaartinen
Studia Fennica Anthropologica 2
2008

TIMO KALLINEN
Divine Rulers in a Secular State
Studia Fennica Anthropologica 3
2016

Studia Fennica Linguistica

Minimal reference
The use of pronouns in Finnish and Estonian discourse
Edited by Ritva Laury
Studia Fennica Linguistica 12
2005

Antti Leino
On Toponymic Constructions as an Alternative to Naming Patterns in Describing Finnish Lake Names
Studia Fennica Linguistica 13
2007

Talk in interaction
Comparative dimensions
Edited by Markku Haakana, Minna Laakso & Jan Lindström
Studia Fennica Linguistica 14
2009

Planning a new standard language
Finnic minority languages meet the new millennium
Edited by Helena Sulkala & Harri Mantila
Studia Fennica Linguistica 15
2010

Lotta Weckström
Representations of Finnishness in Sweden
Studia Fennica Linguistica 16
2011

Terhi Ainiala, Minna Saarelma & Paula Sjöblom
Names in Focus
An Introduction to Finnish Onomastics
Studia Fennica Linguistica 17
2012

Registers of Communication
Edited by Asif Agha & Frog
Studia Fennica Linguistica 18
2015

Kaisa Häkkinen
Spreading the Written Word
Mikael Agricola and the Birth of Literary Finnish
Studia Fennica Linguistica 19
2015

Studia Fennica Litteraria

Metaliterary Layers in Finnish Literature
Edited by Samuli Hägg, Erkki Sevänen & Risto Turunen
Studia Fennica Litteraria 3
2008

Aino Kallas
Negotiations with Modernity
Edited by Leena Kurvet-Käosaar & Lea Rojola
Studia Fennica Litteraria 4
2011

The Emergence of Finnish Book and Reading Culture in the 1700s
Edited by Cecilia af Forselles & Tuija Laine
Studia Fennica Litteraria 5
2011

Nodes of Contemporary Finnish Literature
Edited by Leena Kirstinä
Studia Fennica Litteraria 6
2012

White Field, Black Seeds
Nordic Literacy Practices in the Long Nineteenth Century
Edited by Anna Kuismin & M. J. Driscoll
Studia Fennica Litteraria 7
2013

Lieven Ameel
Helsinki in Early Twentieth-Century Literature
Urban Experiences in Finnish Prose Fiction 1890–1940
Studia Fennica Litteraria 8
2014

Novel Districts
Critical Readings of Monika Fagerholm
Edited by Kristina Malmio & Mia Österlund
Studia Fennica Litteraria 9
2016